CAZENOVIA CO
Cazenovia, Ne
D0287782

EVERYMAN, I will go with thee,

and be thy guide,

In thy most need to go by thy side

DEMOSTHENES

Born at Athens in 384 B.C. Entered political life *c.* 355 and spent most of his career in an attempt to awaken his fellow countrymen to the danger of Macedonian expansion. Died on the island of Calauria 322 B.C.

Demosthenes' Public Orations

TRANSLATED AND INTRODUCED BY

A. W. PICKARD-CAMBRIDGE, M.A.

Fellow of Balliol College, Oxford

DENT: LONDON

EVERYMAN'S LIBRARY

DUTTON: NEW YORK

Printed in Great Britain
by
Latimer, Trend & Co. Ltd · Whitstable · Kent
for
J. M. DENT & SONS LTD
Aldine House · Bedford Street · London
First published in Everyman's Library 1906
Reissued in the Pickard-Cambridge translation
by arrangement with Clarendon Press 1963

NO. 546

CONTENTS

SELECT BIBLIOGRAPHY

WORKS. Greek text: Editio princeps, Aldus, Venice, 1504; I. Bekker (*Oratores Attici*), 1854–5; Vömel, 1843, 1845; W. Dindorf, 9 vols., 1846–51, 3rd ed., 3 vols., 1859–61; edited by F. Blass, 3 vols., 1885–9; S. H. Butcher and W. Rennie (Oxford Classical Texts), 1903–31; C. Fuhr and J. Sykutris, 1914–27; A. T. Murray, C. A. Vince and J. H. Vince (Loeb Classical Library, with translation), 1926– (unfinished).

Greek text with English notes and commentaries: *Select Private Orations*, C. T. Penrose, 1843; *Olynthiac Orations*, D. B. Hickie, 1844; R. Whiston (Bibliotheca Classica), 1851, etc., 1859–68; *Philippics*, T. K. Arnold, 1851; E. Abbott and P. E. Matheson, 4th ed., 1897; *Philippics, Olynthiacs* and *Embassy*, G. H. Heslop (Catena Classicorum), 1868–72, 1880; *Select Private Orations*, F. A. Paley and J. E. Sandys, 1874–5, 4th ed., 1910; *On the Crown* and *Philippics*, T. H. L. Leary, 1879; *Against Androtion* and *Timocrates*, W. Wayte, 1882, 2nd ed., 1893; *Against Canon* and *Callicles*, F. D. Swift, 1895; *Olynthiacs* and *First Philippic*, 1897; and *Second and Third Philippic*, *On the Peace* and *Chersonese*, J. H. Sandys (Macmillan's Classical Series), 1900; *First and Second Olynthiac*, P. E. Whelan, 1904.

ENGLISH TRANSLATIONS. *Olynthiacs* and *Philippics* (with life), Th. Wylson, 1570; *Orations*, by several hands, under the direction of Lord Somers, 1702, 1744; *Orations of Demosthenes and Aeschines*, P. Francis,

1757–8; *Philippics*, T. Leland, 1756; *Select Speeches*, C. R. Kennedy, 1841. *Works*, C. R. Kennedy (Bohn's Classical Library); *Olynthiacs* and *Philippics*, O. Holland, 1901.

SEPARATE WORKS:

Adversus Leptinem: J. E. Sandys, 1890; English translation by a graduate of Cambridge, 1879, 1885.

De Corona: Greek text with notes: B. Drake, 1851, 6th ed. (T. Gwatkin), 1880; T. K. Arnold, 1851; G. A. and W. H. Simcox (with *Aeschines Against Ctesiphon*), 1866; A. Holmes (Catena Classicorum), 1871, 1881; M. L. d'Ooge, 1875; E. Abbot and P. E. Matheson, 1899; W. W. Goodwin, 1901. Greek text with English translation: Henry, Lord Brougham, 1840; revised edition (Lubbock's Hundred Best Books), 1893. English translations: H. Owgan, 1852; W. Brandt, 1870; Sir R. Collier, 1875; J. Biddle, 1881; C. R. Kennedy (Bohn's Shilling Series) 1888.

Midias: Greek text and notes: C. A. M. Fennell, 1883; W. W. Goodwin, 1906. English translation: C. A. M. Fennell, 1882.

Olynthiacs: Greek text with notes: T. K. Arnold, 1849; H. M. Wilkins, 1860; Oxford Pocket Classics, 1870; T. R. Glover (Pitt Press Series), 1897; H. Sharpley (Blackwood's Classical Texts), 1900.

Philippics: Greek text with notes: J. A. Davies (Pitt Press Series), 1907. English translation (literal): Oxford translation of Classics, 1885.

BIOGRAPHY AND CRITICISM. Lucian, *Demosthenis Encomium* (English translation, T. Franklin, 1781); Dionysius of Halicarnassus, *History*; Plutarch, *Life of Demosthenes* (English translation, Everyman's Library, No. 409, pp. 163–86); S. H. Butcher, *Demosthenes*, 1881; A. Schäfer, *Demosthenes und seine Zeit*, 2nd ed., 1885–7; F. Blass, *Die Attische Beredskamkeit*, vol. iii, 2nd ed., 1898; A. W. Pickard-Cambridge, *Demosthenes and the Last Days of Greek Freedom*, 1914; C. D. Adams, *Demosthenes and his Influence*, 1927; W. Jaeger, *Demosthenes, the Origin and Growth of his Policy*, 1938.

INTRODUCTION

Demosthenes, the son of Demosthenes of Paeania in Attica, a rich and highly respected factory-owner, was born in or about the year 384 B.C. He was early left an orphan; his guardians mismanaged his property for their own advantage; and although, soon after coming of age in 366, he took proceedings against them and was victorious in the law-courts, he appears to have recovered comparatively little from them. In preparing for these proceedings he had the assistance of Isaeus, a teacher and writer of speeches who was remarkable for his knowledge of law, his complete mastery of all the aspects of any case with which he had to do, and his skill in dealing with questions of ownership and inheritance. Demosthenes' speeches against his guardians show plainly the influence of Isaeus, and the teacher may have developed in his pupil the thoroughness and the ingenuity in handling legal arguments which afterwards became characteristic of his work.

Apart from this litigation with his guardians, we know little of Demosthenes' youth and early manhood. Various stories have come down to us (for the most part not on the best authority), of his having been inspired to aim at an orator's career by the eloquence and fame of Callistratus; of his having overcome serious physical defects by assiduous practice; of his having failed, nevertheless, owing to imperfections of delivery, in his early appearances before the people, and having been enabled to remedy these by the instruction of the celebrated actor Satyrus; and of his close study of the *History* of Thucydides. Upon the latter point the evidence of his early style leaves no room for doubt, and the same studies may have contributed to the skill and impressiveness with which, in nearly every oration, he appeals to the events of the past, and sums up the lessons of history. Whether he came personally under the influence either of Plato, the philosopher, or of Isocrates, the greatest rhetorical teacher of his time, and a political pamphleteer of high principles but little practical insight, is much more doubtful. The two men were almost as different in temperament and aims as it was possible to be, but Demosthenes' familiarity with the published speeches of Isocrates, and with the rhetorical principles which Isocrates taught and followed, can scarcely be questioned.

In the early years of his manhood, Demosthenes undertook the composition of speeches for others who were engaged in litigation. This task required not only a very thorough knowledge of law, but the power of assuming, as it were, the character of each separate client, and writing in a tone appropriate to it; and, not less, the ability to interest and to rouse the active sympathy of juries, with whom feeling was perhaps as influential as legal justification. This part, however, of Demosthenes' career only concerns us here in so far as it was an admirable training for his later work in the larger sphere of politics, in which the same qualities of adaptability and of power both to argue cogently and to appeal to the emotions effectively were required in an even higher degree.

At the time when Demosthenes' interest in public affairs was beginning to take an active form, Athens was suffering from the recent loss of some of her most powerful allies.

In the year 358 B.C. she had counted within the sphere of her influence not only the islands of Lemnos, Imbros, and Scyros (which had been guaranteed to her by the Peace of Antalcidas in 387), but also the chief cities of Euboea, the islands of Chios, Cos, Rhodes, and Samos, Mytilene in Lesbos, the towns of the Chersonese, Byzantium (a city of the greatest commercial importance), and a number of stations on the south coast of Thrace, as well as Pydna, Potidaea, Methone, and the greater part of the country bordering upon the Thermaic Gulf. But her failure to observe the terms of alliance, laid down when the new league was founded in 378, had led to a revolt, which ended in 355 or 354 in the loss to her of Chios, Cos, Rhodes, and Byzantium, and of some of the ablest of her own commanders, and left her treasury almost empty. About the same time Mytilene and Corcyra also took the opportunity to break with her. Moreover, her position in the Thermaic region was threatened first by Olynthus, at the head of the Chalcidic League, which included over thirty towns; and secondly by Philip, the newly-established King of Macedonia, who seemed likely to displace both Olynthus and Athens from their positions of commanding influence.[1]

Nevertheless, Athens, though unable to face a strong combination, was probably the most powerful single state in Greece. In her equipment and capacity for naval warfare she had no rival, and certainly no other state could vie with her in commercial activity and prosperity. The power of Sparta in the Peloponnese had declined greatly. The establishment of Megalopolis as the centre of a confederacy of Arcadian tribes, and of Messene as an independent city

[1] See Introduction to First Philippic.

commanding a region once entirely subject to Sparta, had seriously weakened her position; while at the same time her ambition to recover her supremacy kept alive a feeling of unrest throughout the Peloponnese. Of the other states of South Greece, Argos was hostile to Sparta, Elis to the Arcadians; Corinth and other less important cities were not definitely attached to any alliance, but were not powerful enough to carry out any serious movement alone. In North Greece, Thebes, though she lacked great leaders, was still a great power, whose authority throughout Boeotia had been strengthened by the complete or partial annihilation of Plataeae, Thespiae, Orchomenus,[1] and Coroneia. In Athens the ill feeling against Thebes was strong, owing to the occupation by the Thebans of Oropus,[1] a frontier town which Athens claimed, and their treatment of the towns just mentioned, towards which the Athenians were kindly disposed. The Phocians, who had until recently been unwilling allies of Thebes, were now hostile and not insignificant neighbours, and about this time entered into relations with both Sparta and Athens. The subject of contention was the possession or control of the Temple of Apollo at Delphi, which the Phocians had recently taken by force from the Delphians, who were supported by Thebes; and in the 'Sacred War' to which this act (which was considered to be sacrilege) gave rise in 355 B.C., the Thebans and Locrians fought against the Phocians in the name of the Amphictyonic Council, a body (composed of representatives of tribes and states of very unequal importance[2]) to which the control of the temple traditionally belonged. Thessaly appears

[1] See notes on Speech for the Megalopolitans.

[2] See note on Speech on the Crown, § 140.

to have been at this time more or less under Theban influence, but was immediately dominated by the tyrants of Pherae, though the several cities seem each to have possessed a nominally independent government. The Greek peoples were disunited in fact and unfitted for union by temperament. The twofold desire, felt by almost all the more advanced Greek peoples, for independence on the one hand, and for 'hegemony' or leadership among other peoples, on the other, rendered any effective combination impossible, and made the relations of states to one another uncertain and inconstant. While each people paid respect to the spirit of autonomy, when their own autonomy was in question, they were ready to violate it without scruple when they saw their way to securing a predominant position among their neighbours; and although the ideal of Panhellenic unity had been put before Greece by Gorgias and Isocrates, its realization did not go further than the formation of leagues of an unstable character, each subject, as a rule, to the more or less tyrannical domination of some one member.

Probably the power which was most generally feared in the Greek world was that of the King of Persia. Several times in recent years (and particularly in 387 and 367) he had been requested to make and enforce a general settlement of Hellenic affairs. The settlement of 387 (called the King's Peace, or the Peace of Antalcidas, after the Spartan officer who negotiated it) had ordained the independence of the Greek cities, small and great, with the exception of those in Asia Minor, which were to form part of the Persian Empire, and of Lemnos, Imbros, and Scyros, which were to belong to Athens as before. The attempt to give effect to the arrangement negotiated in 367 failed, and the terms of the Peace of Antalcidas, though it was still appealed to, when convenient, as a charter of liberty, also came to be disregarded. But there was always a sense of the possibility or the danger of provoking the great king to exert his strength, or at least to use his wealth, to the detriment of some or all of the Greek states; though at the moment of which we are speaking (about 355) the Persian Empire itself was suffering from recent disorders and revolutions, and the king had little leisure for interfering in the affairs of Greece.

It was to the department of foreign and inter-Hellenic affairs that Demosthenes principally devoted himself. His earliest political speeches, however, were composed and delivered in furtherance of prosecutions for the crime of proposing illegal legislation. These were the speeches against Androtion (spoken by Diodorus in 355) and against Leptines (in 354). Both these were written to denounce measures which Demosthenes regarded as dishonest or unworthy of Athenian traditions. In the former he displays that desire for clean-handed administration which is so prominent in some of his later speeches; and in the prosecution of Leptines he shows his anxiety that Athens should retain her reputation for good faith. Both speeches, like those of the year 352 against Timocrates (spoken by Diodorus), and against Aristocrates (spoken by Euthycles), are remarkable for thoroughness of argument and for the skill which is displayed in handling legal and political questions, though, like almost all Athenian forensic orations, they are sometimes sophistical in argument.

The first speech which is directly devoted to questions of external policy is that on the Naval Boards in 354; and this is followed within the next two years by speeches delivered in support of appeals made to Athens by the people of Megalopolis and by the exiled democratic party of Rhodes. From these speeches it appears that the general lines of Demosthenes' policy were already determined. He was in opposition to Eubulus, who, after the disastrous termination of the war with the allies, had become the leading statesman in Athens. The strength of Eubulus lay in his freedom from all illusion as to the position in which Athens stood, in his ability as a financier, and in his readiness to take any measures which would enable him to carry out his policy. He saw that the prime necessity of the moment was to recruit the financial and material strength of the city; that until this should be effected, she was quite incapable of carrying on war with any other power; and that she could only recover her strength through peace. In this policy he had the support of the well-to-do classes, who suffered heavily in time of war from taxation and the disturbance of trade. On the other hand, the sentiments of the masses were imperialistic and militant. We gather that there were plenty of orators who made a practice of appealing to the glorious traditions of the past and the claim always made by Athens to leadership among the Greek states. To buy off the opposition which his policy might be expected to encounter, Eubulus distributed funds freely to the people, in the shape of 'Festival-money', adopting the methods employed before him by demagogues, very different from himself, in order that he might override the real sentiments of the democracy; and in spite of the large amounts thus spent he did in fact succeed, in the course of a few years, in collecting a considerable sum without resorting to extraordinary taxation, in greatly increasing the navy and in enlarging the dockyards. For the success of this policy it was absolutely necessary to avoid all entanglement in war, except under the strongest compulsion. The appeals of the Megalopolitans and the Rhodians, to yield to which would probably have meant war with Sparta and with Persia, must be rejected. Even in dealing with Philip, who was making himself master of the Athenian allies on the Thermaic coast, the fact of the weakness of Athens must be recognized, and all idea of a great expedition against Philip must be abandoned for the present. At the same time, some necessary measures of precaution were not neglected. It was essential to secure the route to the Euxine, over which the Athenian corn-trade passed, if corn was not to be sold at famine prices. For this purpose, therefore, alliance was made with the Thracian prince, Cersobleptes; and when Philip threatened Heraeon Teichos on the Propontis, an expedition was prepared, and was only abandoned because Philip himself was forced to desist from his attempt by illness. Similarly, when Philip appeared likely to cross the Pass of Thermopylae in 352, an Athenian force was sent (on the proposal of Diophantus, a supporter of Eubulus) to prevent him. The failure of Eubulus and his party to give effective aid to Olynthus against Philip was due to the more pressing necessity of attempting to recover control of Euboea: it had clearly been their intention to save Olynthus, if possible. But when this had proved impossible, and the attempt to form a Hellenic league against Philip had also failed, facts had once more to be recognized; and, since Athens was now virtually isolated, peace must be made with Philip on the only terms which he would accept—that each side should keep what it *de facto* possessed at the time.

Demosthenes was generally in opposition to Eubulus and his party, of which Aeschines (once an actor and afterwards a clerk, but a man of education and great natural gifts) was one of the ablest members. Demosthenes was inspired by the traditions of the past, but had a much less vague conception of the moral to be drawn from them than had the multitude. Athens, for him as for them, was to be the first state in Hellas; she was above all to be the protectress of democracy everywhere, against both absolutism and oligarchy, and the leader of the Hellenes in resistance to foreign aggression. But, unlike the multitude, Demosthenes saw that this policy required the greatest personal effort and readiness for sacrifice on the part of every individual; and he devotes his utmost energies to the task of arousing his countrymen to the necessary pitch of enthusiasm, and of effecting such reforms in administration and finance as, in his opinion, would make the realization of his ideal for Athens possible. In the speeches for the Megalopolitans and the Rhodians, the nature of this ideal is already becoming clear both in its Athenian and in its Panhellenic aspects. But so soon as it appeared that Philip, at the head of the half-barbarian Macedonians, and not Athens, was likely to become the predominant power in the Hellenic world, it was against Philip that all his efforts were directed; and although in 346 he is practically at one with the party of Eubulus in his recognition of the necessity of peace, he is eager, when the opportunity seems once more to offer itself, to resume the conflict, and, when it is resumed, to carry it through to the end.

We have then before us the sharp antagonism of two types of statesmanship. The strength of the one lies in the recognition of actual facts, and the avoidance of all projects which seem likely, under existing circumstances, to fail. The other is of a more sanguine type, and believes in the power of enthusiasm and self-sacrifice to transform the existing facts into something better, and to win success against all odds. Statesmen of the former type are always attacked as unpatriotic and mean-spirited; those of the latter, as unpractical and reckless. There is truth and falsehood in both accusations: but since no statesman has ever combined all the elements of statesmanship in a perfect and just proportion, and since neither prudence and clear-sightedness, nor enthusiastic and generous sentiment, can ever be dispensed with in the conduct of affairs without loss, a larger view will attach little discredit to either type. While, therefore, we may view with regret some of the methods which both Demosthenes and Aeschines at times condescended to use in their conflicts with one another, and with no less regret the disastrous result of the policy which ultimately carried the day, we need not hesitate to give their due to both of the contending parties: nor, while we recognize that Eubulus and Phocion (his sturdiest supporter in the field and in counsel) took the truer view of the situation, and of the character of the Athenians as they were, need we (as it is now fashionable to do) denounce the orator who strove with unstinting personal effort and self-sacrifice to rouse the Athenians into a mood in which they could and would realize the ideal to which they, no less than he, professed their devotion.

But the difficulties in the way of such a realization were wellnigh insuperable. Neither the political nor the military system of Athens was adapted to such a policy. The Sovereign Assembly, though capable of sensible and energetic action at moments of special danger, was more likely to be moved by feeling and prejudice than by businesslike argument, particularly at a time when the tendency of the best educated and most intelligent men was to withdraw from participation in public life; and meeting, as the Assembly did (unless specially summoned), only at stated intervals, it was incapable of taking such rapid, well-timed, and decisive action as Philip could take, simply because he was a single man, sole master of his own policy, and personally in command of his own forces. The publicity which necessarily attached to the discussions of the Assembly was a disadvantage at a time when many plans would better have been kept secret; and rapid modifications of policy, to suit sudden changes in the situation, were almost impossible. Again, while no subjects are so unsuited under any circumstances for popular discussion as foreign and military affairs, the absence in Athens of a responsible ministry greatly increased the difficulties of her position. It is true that the Controller of the Festival Fund (whose office gradually became more and more important) was now appointed for four years at a time, while all other offices were annual; and that he and his friends, and their regular opponents, were generally ready to take the lead in making proposals to the Council or the Assembly. But if they chose to remain silent, they could do so;[1] no one was bound to make any proposal at all; and, on the other hand, any one might do so. With such a want of system, far too much was left to chance or to the designs of interested persons. Moreover, the Assembly felt itself under no obligation to follow for any length of time any lead which might be given to it, or to maintain any continuity or consistency between its own decrees. In modern times, a minister, brought into

[1] See Speech on the Crown, §§ 170 ff.

power by the will of the majority of the people, can reckon for a considerable period upon the more or less loyal support of the majority for himself and his official colleagues. In Athens the leader of the moment had to be perpetually adapting himself afresh to the mood of the Assembly, and even to deceive it, in order that he might lead at all, or carry out the policy which, in his opinion, his country's need required. It is therefore a remarkable thing that both Eubulus and Demosthenes succeeded for many years in maintaining a line of action as consistent as that taken by practical men can ever be.

The fact that the Council of Five Hundred, which acted as a standing committee of the people, and prepared business for the Assembly and was responsible for the details of measures passed by the Assembly in general form, was chosen by lot and changed annually, as did practically all the civil and the military officials (though the latter might be re-elected), was all against efficiency and continuity of policy.[1] After the system of election by lot, the most characteristic feature of the Athenian democracy was the responsibility of statesmen and generals to the law-courts.[2] Any citizen might accuse them upon charges nominally limited in scope, but often serving in reality to bring their whole career into question. Had it been certain that the courts would only punish incompetence or misconduct, and not failure as such, little harm would have resulted. But although

[1] See Zimmern, *The Greek Commonwealth*, pp. 159 ff., for an excellent short account of the constitution and functions of the Council. That the councillors themselves sat (for administrative purposes) in relays, changing ten times a year, was also against continuity.

[2] See Speech on Embassy, § 2 n.

there were very many acquittals in political trials, the uncertainty of the issue was so great, and the sentences inflicted upon the condemned so severe (commonly involving banishment at least), that the liability to trial as a criminal must often have deterred the statesman and the general from taking the most necessary risks; while the condemnation of the accused had usually the result of driving a really able man out of the country, and depriving his fellow countrymen of services which might be urgently required when they were no longer available.

The financial system was also ill adapted for the purposes of a people constantly liable to war. The funds required for the bare needs of a time of peace seem indeed to have been sufficiently provided from permanent sources of income (such as the silver mines, the rent of public lands, court fees and fines, and various indirect taxes): but those needed for war had to be met by a direct tax upon property, levied *ad hoc* whenever the necessity arose, and not collected without delays and difficulties. And although the equipment of ships for service was systematically managed under the trierarchic laws,[1] it was still subject to delays no less serious. There was no regular system of contribution to State funds, and no systematic accumulation of a reserve to meet military needs. The raising of money by means of loans at interest to the State was only adopted in Greece in a few isolated instances:[2] and the practice of annually distributing surplus funds to the people,[3] however necessary or excusable under the circumstances, was wholly contrary to sound finance.

[1] See Introduction to Speech on Naval Boards, and Philippic I, §§ 36, 37.
[2] See Zimmern, *The Greek Commonwealth*, p. 205.
[3] See Introduction to the Olynthiacs.

An even greater evil was the dependence of the city upon mercenary forces and generals, whose allegiance was often at the call of the highest bidder, and in consequence was seldom reliable. There is no demand which Demosthenes makes with greater insistence, than the demand that the citizens themselves shall serve with the army. At a moment of supreme danger, they might do so. But in fact Athens had become more and more an industrial state, and men were not willing to leave their business to take care of itself for considerable periods, in order to go out and fight, unless the danger was very urgent, or the interests at stake of vital importance; particularly now that the length of campaigns had become greater and the seasons exempted from military operations shorter. In many minds the spread of culture, and of the ideal of self-culture, had produced a type of individualism indifferent to public concerns, and contemptuous of political and military ambitions. Moreover, the methods of warfare had undergone great improvement; in most branches of the army the trained skill of the professional soldier was really necessary; and it was not possible to leave the olive-yard or the counting-house and become an efficient fighter without more ado. But the expensiveness of the mercenary forces; the violent methods by which they obtained supplies from friends and neutrals, as well as foes, if, as often happened, their pay was in arrear; and the dependence of the city upon the goodwill of generals and soldiers who could without much difficulty find employment under other masters, were evils which were bound to hamper any attempt to give effect to a well-planned and far-sighted scheme of action.

It also resulted from the Athenian system of government

that the general, while obviously better informed of the facts of the military situation than any one else could be, and at the same time always liable to be brought to trial in case of failure, had little influence upon policy, unless he could find an effective speaker to represent him. In the Assembly and in the law-courts (where the juries were large enough to be treated in the same manner as the Assembly itself) the orator who could win the people's ear was all powerful, and expert knowledge could only make itself felt through the medium of oratory.

A constitution which gave so much power to the orator had grave disadvantages. The temptation to work upon the feelings rather than to appeal to the reason of the audience was very strong, and no charge is more commonly made by one orator against another than that of deceiving or attempting to deceive the people. It is, indeed, very difficult to judge how far an Athenian Assembly was really taken in by sophistical or dishonest arguments: but it is quite certain that such arguments were continually addressed to it; and the main body of the citizens can scarcely have had that first-hand knowledge of facts, which would enable them to criticize the orator's statements. Again, the oration appealed to the people as a performance, no less than as a piece of reasoning. Ancient political oratory resembled the oratory of the pulpit at the present day, not only because it appealed perpetually to the moral sense, and was in fact a kind of preaching; but also because the main difficulty of the ancient orator and the modern preacher was the same: for the Athenians liked being preached at, as the modern congregation 'enjoys' a good sermon, and were, therefore, almost equally immune against conversion. The conflicts of rival orators were regarded mainly as an entertainment. The speaker who was most likely to carry the voting (except when a great crisis had roused the Assembly to seriousness) was the one who found specious and apparently moral reasons for doing what would give the audience least trouble; and consequently one who, like Demosthenes, desired to stir them up to action and personal sacrifices, had always an uphill fight: and if he also at times 'deceived the people' or employed sophistical arguments in order to secure results which he believed to be for their good, we must remember the difficulty (which, in spite of the wide circulation of authentic information, is at least equally great at the present day) of putting the true reasons for or against a policy, before those who, whether from want of education or from lack of training in the subordination of feeling to thought, are not likely to understand or to listen to them. Nor, if we grant the genuineness of Demosthenes' conviction as to the desirability of the end for which he contended, can many statesmen be pointed out, who have not been at least as guilty as he in their choice of means. That he did not solve the problem, how to lead a democracy by wholly honest means, is the less to his discredit, in that the problem still remains unsolved.

It should be added that with an audience like the Athenian, whose aesthetic sensitiveness was doubtless far greater than that of any modern assembly, delivery counted for much. Aeschines' fine voice was a real danger to Demosthenes, and Demosthenes himself spoke of delivery, or the skilled acting of his part, as the all-important condition of an orator's success. But it is clear that this can have been no advantage from the standpoint of the public interest.

In the law-courts the drawbacks to which the commanding influence of oratory was liable were intensified. In the Assembly a certain amount of reticence and self-restraint was imposed by custom : an opponent could not be attacked by name or on purely personal grounds ; and an appearance of impartiality was commonly assumed. But in the courts much greater play was allowed to feeling ; and the arguments were often much more disingenuous, not only because the personal interests at stake made the speaker more unscrupulous, but also, perhaps, because the juries ordinarily included a larger proportion of the poorer, the idler, and the less-educated citizens than the Assembly. The legal question was often that to which the jury were encouraged to pay least attention, and the condemnation or acquittal of the accused was demanded upon grounds quite extraneous to the indictment. (The two court-speeches contained in these volumes afford abundant illustrations of this.) Personalities were freely admitted, of a kind which it is difficult to excuse and impossible to justify. To attempt to blacken the personal character of an opponent by false stories about his parentage and his youth, and by the ascription to him and his relations of nameless immoralities, is a very different thing from the assignment of wrong motives for his political actions, though even in purely political controversy the ancients far exceeded the utmost limits of modern invective. And this both Demosthenes and Aeschines do freely. There is also reason to suspect that some of the tales which each tells of the other's conduct, both while serving as ambassadors and on other occasions, may be fabrications. The descriptive passages for which such falsehoods gave an opening had doubtless their dramatic value in the oratorical performance : possibly they were even expected by the listeners; but their presence in the speeches does not increase our admiration either for the speaker or for his audience.

All the force of Demosthenes' oratory was unable to defeat the great antagonist of his country. To Philip of Macedon failure was an inconceivable idea. Resident during three impressionable years of his youth at Thebes, he had there learned, from the example of Epaminondas, what a single man could do: and he proceeded to each of the three great tasks of his life—the welding of the rough Macedonians into one great engine of war, the unification of Greece under his own leadership, and the preparation for the conquest of the East by a united Greece and Macedonia—without either faltering in face of difficulties, or hesitating, out of any scrupulosity, to use the most effective means towards the end which he wished at the moment to achieve; though in fact the charges of bad faith made against him by Demosthenes are found to be exaggerated, when they are impartially examined. Philip intended to become master of Greece: Demosthenes realized this early, and, with all the Hellenic detestation of a master, resolved to oppose him to the end. Philip was, indeed, in spite of the barbarous traits which revealed themselves in him at times, not only gracious and courteous by nature, but a sincere admirer of Hellenic—in other words, of Athenian—culture; the relations between his house and the people of Athens had generally been friendly; and there was little reason to suppose that, if he conquered Athens, he would treat her less handsomely than in fact he did. Yet this could not justify one who regarded freedom as Demosthenes regarded it, in making any concession not extorted by the necessities of the situation: his duty and his country's duty, as he conceived it, was to defeat the enemy of Hellenic independence or to fall in the attempt. Nor was it for him to consider (as Isocrates might) whether or no Philip's plans had now developed into, or could be transformed into, a beneficent scheme for the conquest of the barbarian world by a united Hellas, if the union was to be achieved at the price of Athenian liberty. It is because, in spite of errors and of the questionable methods to which he sometimes stooped, Demosthenes devoted himself unflinchingly to the cause of freedom, for Athens and for the Hellenes as a whole, that he is entitled, not merely as an orator but as a politician, to the admiration which posterity has generally accorded him. It is, above all, by the second part of his career, when his policy of antagonism to Philip had been accepted by the people, and he was no longer in opposition but, as it were, in office, that Demosthenes himself claims to be justified; and Aeschines' attempt to invalidate the claim is for the most part unconvincing.

It is not easy to describe in a few paragraphs the characteristics of Demosthenes as an orator. That he stands on the highest eminence that an orator has ever reached is generally admitted. But this is not to say that he was wholly free from faults. His contemporaries, as well as later Greek critics, were conscious of a certain artificiality in his eloquence. It was, indeed, the general custom of Athenian orators to prepare their speeches with great care: the speakers who, like Aeschines and Demades, were able to produce a great effect without preparation, and the rhetoricians who, like Alcidamas, thought of the studied oration as but a poor imitation of true eloquence, were only a small minority; and in general, not only was the arrangement of topics carefully planned, but the greatest attention was paid to the sound and rhythm of the sentences, and to the appropriateness and order of the words. The orator had also his collections of passages on themes which were likely to recur constantly, and of arguments on either side of many questions; and from these he selected such passages as he required, and adapted them to his particular purpose. The rhetorical teachers appear to have supplied their pupils with such collections; we find a number of instances of the repetition of the same passage in different speeches, and an abundance of arguments formed exactly on the model of the precepts contained in rhetorical handbooks.[1] Yet with all this art nothing was more necessary than that a speech should appear to be spontaneous and innocent of guile. There was a general mistrust of the 'clever speaker', who by study or rhetorical training had learned the art of arguing to any point, and making the worse cause appear the better. To have studied his part too carefully—even to have worked up illustrations from history and poetry—might expose the orator to suspicion.[2] Demosthenes, in spite of his frequent attempts to deprecate such suspicion, did not succeed wholly in keeping on the safe side. Aeschines describes him as a wizard and a sophist, who enjoyed deceiving the people or the jury. Another of his opponents levelled at him the taunt that his speeches 'smelt of the lamp'. Dionysius of Halicarnassus, one of the best of the ancient critics, says that the artificiality of Demosthenes and his

[1] The 'Art' of Anaximenes is an interesting extant example of a fourth-century handbook for practical orators. The Rhetoric of Aristotle stands on a higher plane, but probably follows the lines laid down by custom in the rhetorical schools.

[2] See Speech on Embassy, § 246, and note.

master Isaeus was apt to excite suspicion, even when they had a good case. Nor can a modern reader altogether escape the same impression. Sometimes, especially in the earlier speeches to the Assembly, the argument seems unreal, the joints between the previously prepared commonplaces or illustrations and their application to the matter in hand are too visible, the language is artificially phrased, and wanting in spontaneity and ease. There are also parts of the court speeches in which the orator seems to have calculated out all the possible methods of meeting a particular case, and to be applying them in turn with more ingenuity than convincingness. An appearance of unreality also arises at times (again principally in the earlier speeches) from a certain want of imagination. He attributes feelings and motives to others, which they were really most unlikely to have entertained, and argues from them. Some of the sentiments which he expects Artaxerxes or Artemisia to feel (in the Speeches on the Naval Boards and for the Rhodians) were certainly not to be looked for in them. Similar misconceptions of the actual or possible sentiments of the Spartans appear in the Speech for the Megalopolitans, and of those of the Thebans in the Third Olynthiac (§ 15). The early orations against Philip also show some misunderstanding of his character. And if, in fact, Demosthenes lived his early years largely in solitary studiousness and was unsociable by disposition, this lack of a quick grasp of human nature and motives is quite intelligible. But this defect grew less conspicuous as his experience increased; and though even to the end there remained something of the sophist about him, as about all the disciples of the ancient rhetoric, the greatness of his best work is not seriously affected by this. For, in his greatest speeches, and in the greatest parts of nearly all his speeches, the orator is white-hot with genuine passion and earnestness; and all his study and preparation resulted, for the most part, not in an artificial product, but in the most convincing expression of his real feeling and belief; so that it was the man himself, and not the rhetorical practitioner that spoke.

The lighter virtues of the orator are not to be sought for in him. In gracefulness and humour he is deficient: his humour, indeed, generally takes the grim forms of irony and satire, or verges on personality and bad taste. Few of his sentences can be imagined to have been delivered with a smile; and something like ferocity is generally not far below the surface. Pathos is seldom in him unmixed with sterner qualities, and is usually lost in indignation. But of almost every other variety of tone he has a complete command. The essential parts of his reasoning (even when it is logically or morally defective) are couched, as a rule, in a forcible and cogent form;[1] and he has a striking power of close, sustained, and at the same time lucid argumentation. His matter is commonly disposed with such skill that each topic occurs where it will tell most powerfully; and while one portion of a speech affords relief to another (where relief is needed, and particularly in the longer orations) all alike bear on the main issue or strengthen the orator's position with his audience. Historical allusions are not (as they often are by Aeschines and Isocrates) enlarged out of proportion to their importance, but are limited to what is necessary, in

[1] He is especially fond of the dilemma, which is not indeed cogent in strict logic, but is peculiarly telling and effective in producing conviction in large audiences.

order to illustrate the orator's point or drive his lesson home. Add to these qualities his combination of political idealism with absolute mastery of minute detail; the intensity of his appeal to the moral sense and patriotism of his hearers; the impressiveness of his denunciation of political wrong; the vividness of his narrative, the rapid succession of his impassioned phrases, and some part of the secret of his power will be explained. For the rest, while there is in his writing every degree of fullness or brevity, there is no waste of words, no 'fine language' out of place. His language, indeed, is ordinarily simple—sometimes even colloquial; though in the arrangement of his words in their most telling order he shows consummate art, and his metaphors are often bold and sometimes even violent. In the use of the 'figures of speech' he excels; above all, in the use of antitheses (whether for the purpose of vivid contrast or of precise logical expression), and of the rhetorical question, used now in indignation, now in irony, now in triumphant conclusion of an argument: and at times there are master-strokes of genius, which defy all analysis, such as the great appeal to the men of Marathon in the Speech on the Crown.[1] He does not as a rule (and this is particularly true of the Speech on the Crown) cover the whole of the ground with the same adequacy; but so concentrates all his forces upon certain points as to be irresistible, and thus 'with thunder and lightning confounds'[2] the orators who oppose him. It is no wonder that some of the

[1] See [Longinus] 'On the Sublime', especially chap. xvi–xviii (English translation by A. O. Prickard in this series). This treatise should be read by all students of Demosthenes, especially chap. xii, xvi–xviii, xxxii, xxxiv, xxxix.

[2] 'On the Sublime', chap. xxxiv.

greatest of English orators, and notably of those of the eighteenth and early nineteenth centuries, borrow from him not only words and phrases, but inspiration and confidence in their cause, and look upon him as a model whom they may emulate, but cannot excel.

ON THE NAVAL BOARDS (OR. XIV)

[*Introduction.* The speech was delivered in 354 B.C. News had been brought to Athens that the Persian King Artaxerxes Ochus was making great military and naval preparations, and though these were, in fact, directed against his own rebellious subjects in Egypt, Phoenicia, and Cyprus, the Athenians had some ground for alarm : for, two years before this, Chares, in command of an Athenian fleet, had given assistance to Artabazus, Satrap of Ionia, who was in revolt against the king. The king had made a protest, and (late in 355) Athens had ordered Chares to withdraw his aid from Artabazus. A party in Athens now wished to declare war on Persia, and appealed strongly to Athenian traditions in favour of the proposal. Demosthenes opposes them, on the ground that it was not certain that the king was aiming at Athens at all, and that the disunion of the Hellenic peoples would render any such action unsafe : Athens had more dangerous enemies nearer home, and her finances were not in a condition for such a campaign. But he takes advantage of the interest aroused, to propose a reform of the trierarchic system, designed to secure a more efficient navy, and to remedy certain abuses in the existing method of equipping vessels for service.

In earlier times, the duty of equipping and commanding each trireme was laid upon single citizens of means, the hull and certain fittings being found by the state. When, early in the fourth century, the number of wealthy men had diminished, each ship might be shared by two citizens, who commanded in turn. In 357 a law was passed, on the proposal of Periander, transferring the responsibility from individuals to 'Symmories' or Boards. (The system had been instituted in a slightly different form for the collection of the war-tax in the archonship of Nausinicus, 378–7 B.C.)

The collection of the sums required became the work of twenty Boards, formed by the subdivision of the 1,200 richest citizens: each contributor, whatever his property, paid the same share. The richer men thus got off with the loss of a very small proportion of their income, as compared with the poorer members of the Boards,[1] and in managing the business of the Boards they sometimes contrived to exact the whole sum from their colleagues, and to escape payment themselves. At the same time the duties of the several Boards and their members were not allocated with sufficient precision to enable the responsibility to be brought home in case of default; and the nominal Twelve Hundred had fallen to a much smaller number, on whom the burden accordingly fell with undue weight. Demosthenes' proposal provided for the distribution of the responsibility of equipping the vessels and providing the funds, in the most detailed manner, with a view to preventing all evasion; but it was not carried. In fact, it was not until 340 that he succeeded in reforming the trierarchy, and he then made the burden vary strictly with property. The proposal, however, to declare war upon Persia went no further.

While, in this speech, Demosthenes is in accord with the policy of Eubulus, so far as concerns the avoidance of war with Persia, his proposals of financial reform would not be viewed with favour by the wealthy men who were Eubulus' firm supporters. Some of the themes which recur continually in later speeches are prominent in this—the futility of rhetorical appeals to past glories, without readiness for personal service, and the need of a thorough organization of the forces. While the speech shows rather too strongly the marks of careful preparation, and seldom rises to eloquence—the style, indeed, is often rather cramped and stiff, and the sentiments, especially at the beginning, artificially phrased—it is moderate and practical in tone, and shows a characteristic mastery of minute detail.]

[1] See Speech on Crown, §§ 102 ff. and notes.

THOSE who praise your forefathers,[n] men of Athens, desire, 1 no doubt, to gratify you by their speeches; and yet I do not think that they are acting in the interests of those whom they praise. For the subject on which they attempt to speak is one to which no words can do justice; and so, although they thus win for themselves the reputation of capable speakers, the impression which they convey to their hearers of the merit of our forefathers is not adequate to our conception of it. For my part I believe that their highest praise is constituted by Time: for the time that has passed has been long, and still no generation has arisen, whose achievements could be compared with advantage to theirs. As for myself, 2 I shall attempt to point out the way in which, in my opinion, you can best make your preparations. For the truth is, that if all of us who propose to address you were to succeed in proving to you our rhetorical skill, there would not be the slightest improvement in your condition—I am sure of it; but if a single speaker were to come forward, whoever he might be, who could instruct and convince you as to the nature of the preparations which would meet the city's need, as to their extent, and the resources upon which we can draw for them, your present fears would instantly be dissolved. This I will attempt to do—if indeed it is in my power. But first I must briefly express my views as to our relations with the king.

I hold the king to be the common enemy of all the Hellenes; 3 and yet I should not on that account urge you, alone and unsupported, to raise war against him. For I observe that there is no common or mutual friendship even among the Hellenes themselves: some have more faith in the king than in some other Hellenes. When such are the conditions, your interest requires you, I believe, to see to it that you only begin war from a fair and just cause, and to make all proper 4 preparations: this should be the basis of your policy. For I believe, men of Athens, that if it were made plain to the eyes and understandings of the Hellenes, that the king was making an attempt upon them, they would both fight in alliance with those who undertook the defence for them and with them, and would feel very grateful to them. But if we quarrel with him prematurely, while his intentions are still uncertain, I am afraid, men of Athens, that we may be forced to fight not only against the king, but also against those for whose benefit we are exercising such forethought. 5 For he will pause in the execution of his project, if indeed he has really resolved to attack the Hellenes, and will bribe some of them with money and offers of friendship; while they, desirous of bringing their private wars to a successful end, and animated only by such a spirit, will disregard the common safety of all. I urge you then, not to hurl the city needlessly into the midst of any such chaos of selfish passions. 6 Moreover, I see that the question of the policy to be adopted towards the king does not even stand on the same footing for the other Hellenes as for you. It is open, I think, to many of them to manage certain of their own interests as they please, and to disregard the rest of the Hellenes. But for you it is not honourable, even if you are the injured party, and are dealing with those who have injured you, to punish them so severely as to leave some of them to fall under the 7 domination of the foreigner: and this being so, we must take care, first, that we do not find ourselves involved in an unequal war, and secondly, that he, whom we believe to be plotting against the Hellenes, does not gain credit from the supposition that he is their friend. How then can this be achieved? It will be achieved if it is manifest to all that the forces of Athens have been overhauled and put in readiness, and if her intentions in regard to their use are plainly righteous. But to those who take a bold line, and urge you, 8 without any hesitation whatever, to go to war, my reply is this—that it is not difficult to win a reputation for bravery, when the occasion calls for deliberation; nor to prove yourself an accomplished orator, when danger is at the door: but to display your courage in the hour of danger, and, in debate, to have wiser advice to offer than others—that is the hard thing, and that is what is required of you. For my 9 part, men of Athens, I consider that the proposed war with the king would be a difficult undertaking for the city; while the decisive conflict in which the war would result would be an easier matter, and for this reason. Every war, I suppose, necessarily requires ships and money and the command of positions. All such advantages the king, I find, possesses more abundantly than we. But a conflict of forces requires nothing so much as brave men; and of these, I believe, the larger number is with us, and with those who share our danger. For this reason I exhort you not to be the first, in any way 10 whatever, to take up the war; but for the decisive struggle I think you ought to be ready and your preparations made. And further, if the forces with which foreigners and Hellenes could respectively be repelled were really different in kind, the fact that we were arraying our forces against the king would naturally, it may be, admit of no concealment. But 11 since all military preparations are of the same character, and the main points of a force must always be the same—the means to repel enemies, to help allies, and to retain existing

advantages—why, when we have our acknowledged foes, do we seek to procure others? Let us rather prepare ourselves to meet the enemies whom we have, and we shall then repel
12 the king also, if he takes the aggressive against us. Suppose that you yourselves summon the Hellenes to your side now. If, when the attitude of some of them towards you is so disagreeable, you do not fulfil their demands, how can you expect that any one will listen to you? 'Why,' you say, 'we shall tell them that the king is plotting against them.' Good Heavens! Do you imagine that they do not foresee this themselves? Of course they do. But their fear of this does not yet outweigh the quarrels which some of them have against you and against each other. And so the tour of your
13 envoys will end in nothing but their own rhapsodies. But if you wait, then, if the design which we now suspect is really on foot, there is not one of the Hellenes who stands so much upon his dignity that he will not come and beg for your aid, when he sees that you have a thousand cavalry, and infantry as many as any one can desire, and three hundred ships: for he will know that in these lies his surest hope of deliverance. Appeal to them now, and we shall be suppliants, and, if unsuccessful, rejected suppliants. Make your own preparations and wait, and then they will be the suppliants and we their deliverers; and we may rest assured that they will all come to us for help.

14 In thinking out these points and others like them, men of Athens, my object was not to devise a bold speech, prolonged to no purpose: but I took the greatest pains to discover the means by which our preparations could be most effectively and quickly made; and therefore, if my proposal meets with your approval, when you have heard it, you ought, I think,

to pass it. Now the first element in our preparation, men of Athens (and it is the most important), must be this: your minds must be so disposed, that every one of you will perform willingly and heartily any service that is required of him. For you see, men of Athens, that whenever you have unani- 15 mously desired any object, and the desire has been followed by a feeling on the part of every individual, that the practical steps towards it were for himself to take, the object has never yet slipped from your grasp: but whenever the wish has had no further result than that each man has looked to his neighbour, expecting his neighbour to act while he himself does nothing, the object has never yet been attained. But suppos- 16 ing you to be filled with the keenness that I have described, I am of opinion that we should make up the Twelve Hundred to their full number, and increase it to 2,000, by the addition of 800. For if you can display this total, then, when you have allowed for the unmarried heiresses and orphans, for property outside Attica, or held in partnership, and for any persons who may be unable to contribute, you will, I believe, actually have the full 1,200 persons available. These you must divide 17 into twenty boards, as at present, with sixty persons to each board; and each of these boards you must divide into five sections of twelve persons each, taking care in every case to associate with the richest man the poorest men, to maintain the balance. Such is the arrangement of persons which I recommend, and my reason you will know when you have heard the nature of the entire system. I pass to the distribu- 18 tion of the ships. You must provide a total complement of 300 ships, forming twenty divisions of fifteen ships apiece, and including in each division five of the first hundred vessels, five of the second hundred, and five of the third

hundred. Next, you must assign by lot to each board of persons its fifteen ships, and each board must assign three
19 ships to each of its sections. This done, in order that you may have the payments also systematically arranged, you must divide the 6,000 talents (for that is the taxable capital of the country) into 100 parts of sixty talents each. Five of each of these parts you must allot to each of the larger boards—the twenty—and each board must assign one of these sums of sixty talents to each of its sections;
20 in order that, if you need 100 ships, there may be sixty talents to be taxed for the expense of each ship, and twelve persons responsible for it; if 200, thirty talents will be taxed to make up the cost, and six persons will be responsible; if 300, then twenty talents must be taxed to defray the ex-
21 pense, and four persons will be responsible. In the same way, men of Athens, I bid you make a valuation according to the register of all those fittings of the ships which are in arrear, divide them into twenty parts, and allot to each of the large boards one-twentieth of the debtors: these must then be assigned by each board in equal numbers to each of its sections, and the twelve persons composing each section must call up their share of the arrears, and provide, ready-equipped,
22 the ships which fall to them. Such is the plan by which, in my opinion, the expense, the ships, the trierarchs, and the recovery of the fittings could best be provided for and put into working order. I proceed to describe a simple and easy scheme for the manning of the vessels. I recommend that the generals should divide the whole space of the dockyards into ten, taking care to have in each space thirty slips for single vessels close together. This done they should apportion to each space two of the boards and thirty ships; and should

then assign a tribe to each space by lot. Each captain should 23 divide into three parts the space which falls to his tribe, with the corresponding ships, and should allot these among the three wards of each tribe, in such a way that if each tribe has one division of the entire docks, each ward will have a third of one of these divisions; and you will know, in case of need, first the position assigned to the tribe; next, that of the ward; and then the names of the trierarchs and their ships; each tribe will be answerable for thirty, and each ward for ten ships. If this system is put in train, circumstances as they arise will provide for anything that I may have overlooked to-day (for perhaps it is difficult to think of everything), and there will be a single organization for the whole fleet and every part of it.

But what of funds? What resources have we immediately 24 at our command? The statement which I am about to make on this subject will no doubt be astonishing; but I will make it nevertheless; for I am convinced that upon a correct view of the facts, this statement alone will be proved true, and will be justified by the event. I say then, that this is not the time to discuss the financial question. We have large resources upon which, in case of necessity, we may honourably and rightly draw: but if we inquire for them now, we shall not believe that we can rely upon them even against the hour of need; so far shall we be from supplying them now. 'What then,' you will ask me, 'are these resources, which are non-existent now, but will be ours then? This is really like a riddle.' I will tell you. Men of Athens, 25 you see all this great city. In this city there is wealth which will compare, I had almost said, with the united wealth of all other cities. But such is the disposition of those who own it, that if all your orators were to raise the alarm that the king was coming—that he was at the doors—that there was no possible escape; and if with the orators an equal number of prophets foretold the same thing; even then, far from contributing funds, they would show no sign[1] [and make no 26 acknowledgement] of their possession of them. If, however, they were to see in course of actual realization all the terrors with which at present we are only threatened in speeches, not one of them is so blind that he would not both offer his contribution, and be among the first to pay the tax. For who will prefer to lose his life and property, rather than contribute a part of his substance to save himself and the remainder of it? Funds, then, we can command, I am certain, if there is a genuine need of them, and not before; and accordingly I urge you not even to look for them now. For all that you would provide now, if you decided upon a levy, 27 would be more ludicrous than nothing at all. Suppose that we are told to pay 1 per cent. now; that gives you sixty talents. Two per cent. then—double the amount; that makes 120 talents. And what is that to the 1,200 camels which (as these gentlemen tell us) are bringing the king's money for him? Or would you have me assume a payment of one-twelfth, 500 talents? Why, you would never submit to this; and if you paid the money down, it would not be 28 adequate to the war. You must, therefore, make all your other preparations, but allow your funds to remain for the present in the hands of their owners—they could nowhere be more safely kept for the use of the State; and then, if ever the threatened crisis arises, you will receive them as the voluntary gift of their possessors. This, men of Athens, is not only a possible course of action, but a dignified and a politic one.

[1] δείξαιεν, codd.

It is a course of action which is worthy to be reported to the ears of the king, and which would inspire him with no slight apprehension. For he well knows that by two hundred ships, 29 of which one hundred were Athenian, his ancestors were deprived of one thousand; and he will hear that Athens alone has now equipped three hundred; so that, however great his infatuation, he could certainly not imagine it a light thing to make this country his foe. But if it is his wealth that suggests proud thoughts to his mind, he will find that in this respect too his resources are weaker than ours. It is 30 true that he is said to be bringing a great quantity of gold with him. But if he distributes this, he must look for more: for just so it is the way of springs and wells to give out, if large quantities are drawn from them all at once; whereas we possess, as he will hear, in the taxable capital of the country, resources which we defend against attack in a way of which those ancestors of his who sleep at Marathon can best tell him: and so long as we are masters of the country there is no risk of our resources being exhausted.

Nor again can I see any grounds for the fear, which some 31 feel, lest his wealth should enable him to collect a large mercenary force. It may be that many of the Hellenes would be glad to serve under him against Egypt, against Orontas, or against certain other foreign powers—not from a wish that the king should conquer any such enemies, but because each desires individually to obtain some private means to relieve his present poverty. But I cannot believe that any Hellene would march against Hellas. Whither will he turn afterwards? Will he go to Phrygia and be a slave? For the 32 war with the foreigner is a war for no other stake than our country, our life, our habits, our freedom, and all that we value. Where is the wretch who would sacrifice self, parents, sepulchres, fatherland, for the sake of some short-lived gain? I do not believe that he exists. And indeed it is not even to the king's own interest to conquer the Hellenes with a mercenary force; for an army which has conquered us is, even more certainly, stronger than he; and his intention is not to destroy us only that he may fall into the power of others: he wishes to rule, if it may be, over all the world; but if not, at least over those who are already his slaves.

33 It may be supposed that the Thebans will be on the king's side. Now this subject is one upon which it is hard to address you. For such is your hatred of them, that you cannot hear a good word about them, however true, without displeasure. And yet those who have grave questions to consider must not on any pretext pass over any profitable line 34 of argument. I believe, then, that so far are the Thebans from being likely ever to march with him against the Hellenes, that they would give a great deal, if they had it to give, for an opportunity of cancelling their former sins against Hellas. But if any one does believe that the Thebans are so unhappily constituted, at least you are all aware, I presume, that if the Thebans take the part of the king, their enemies must necessarily take the part of the Hellenes.

35 My own belief is that our cause, the cause of justice, and its supporters, will prove stronger in every emergency than the traitor and the foreigner. And therefore I say that we need feel no excessive apprehension, and that we must not be led on into taking the first step towards war. Indeed, I cannot even see that any of the other Hellenes has reason 36 to dread this war. Are they not all aware, that so long as they thought of the king as their common foe, and were

at unity with one another, they were secure in their prosperity; but that ever since they imagined that they could count upon the king as their friend, and fell to quarrelling over their private interests, they have suffered such evils as no malediction could have devised for them? Must we then dread a man whose friendship, thanks to Fortune and Heaven, has proved so unprofitable, and his enmity so advantageous? By no means! Let us not, however, commit any aggression, in view of our own interests, and of the disturbed and mistrustful spirit which prevails among the rest of the Hellenes. Were 37 it possible, indeed, to join forces with them all, and with one accord to attack the king in his isolation, I should have counted it no wrong even were we to take the aggressive. But since this is impossible, we must be careful to give the king no pretext for trying to enforce the claims of the other Hellenes against us. If you keep the peace, any such step on his part would arouse suspicion; but if you are the first to begin war, his hostility to you would make his desire to befriend your rivals appear natural enough. Do not then lay bare the evil condition 38 of Hellas, by calling the powers together when they will not obey, or undertaking a war which you will be unable to carry on. Keep the peace; take courage, and make your preparations. Resolve that the news which the king hears of you shall certainly not be that all Hellas, and Athens with it, in distress or panic or confusion. Far from it! Let him rather know that 39 if falsehood and perjury were not as disgraceful in Hellenic eyes as they are honourable in his, you would long ago have been on the march against him: and that though, as it is, your regard for yourselves forbids you to act thus, you are praying to all the gods that the same madness may seize him as once seized his ancestors. And if it occurs to him

to reflect upon this, he will find that your deliberations are
40 not conducted in any careless spirit. He at least shares the knowledge that it was your wars with his own ancestors that raised Athens to the summit of prosperity and greatness; while the peaceful policy which she previously pursued never gave her such a superiority as she now enjoys over any single state in Hellas. Aye, and he sees that the Hellenes are in need of one who, whether intentionally or not, will reconcile them one to another; and he knows that if he were to stir up war, he himself would assume that character in relation to them; so that the news which he will hear of you will be intelligible and credible to him.

41 But I do not wish to trouble you, men of Athens, by unduly prolonging my speech. I will therefore recapitulate my advice and retire. I bid you prepare your forces with a view to the enemies whom you have. If the king or any other power attempts to do you injury, you must defend yourselves with these same forces. But you must not take the aggressive by word or deed; and you must take care that it is your deeds, and not your platform speeches, that are worthy of your forefathers. If you act thus, you will be consulting both your own interests and those of the speakers who are opposing me; since you will have no cause to be angry with them afterwards, because you have decided wrongly to-day.

FOR THE MEGALOPOLITANS (Or. XVI)

[*Introduction.* In 371 B.C. the Thebans under Epaminondas defeated the Spartans at Leuctra, and, assisted by Thebes, the Arcadians and Messenians threw off the Spartan yoke. The former founded Megalopolis as their common centre, the latter Messene. But after the death of Epaminondas in 362, Thebes was left without a leader; and when, in 355, she became involved in the 'Sacred War' with the Phocians, the new Peloponnesian states turned towards Athens, and Messene received a solemn promise of Athenian assistance, if ever she was attacked by Sparta. In 353 Thebes was suffering considerably from the Sacred War, and the Spartans made an ingenious attempt to recover their power, in the form of a proposal for the restoration of territory to its original owners. This meant that Athens would recover Oropus, which had been in the hands of Thebes since 366, and had previously been the subject of a long-standing dispute; that Orchomenus, Thespiae, and Plataeae, which had all been overthrown by Thebes, would be restored; and that Elis and Phlius would also recover certain lost possessions. All these states would then be morally bound (so the Spartans thought) to help Sparta to reconquer Arcadia and Messenia.

On the occasion of this speech (delivered in 353) the Megalopolitans had appealed to Athens, and an Arcadian and a Spartan embassy had each had an audience of the Assembly, and had each received strong support from Athenian speakers. The principal motives of the supporters of Sparta were their hostility to Thebes, and their desire not to break with the Spartans, whom Athens had assisted at Mantineia in 362 against the Thebans and Megalopolitans.

Demosthenes supports the Arcadians, and lays great stress on the desirability of maintaining a balance of power between Sparta and Thebes, so that neither might become too strong. To allow Sparta to reconquer Arcadia, and, as the next step, Messenia, would be to render her too formidable; and to reject the proposal of Sparta would not preclude Athens from recovering Oropus and demanding the restoration of the Boeotian towns. But the promise of assistance to the Arcadians should be accompanied by a request for the termination of their alliance with Thebes.

Demosthenes' advice was not followed. In fact Athens was hardly in a position to risk becoming entangled in a war with Sparta, particularly in view of the danger to her northern possessions from Philip. She therefore remained neutral, while the Thebans, relieved from the pressure of the Sacred War owing to the defeat of the Phocian leader Onomarchus by Philip, were able to send aid to Megalopolis. A truce between Sparta and Megalopolis was made about 350. It was, however, a result of the neutrality of Athens, that she was unable, a few years later, to secure the support of the Arcadians against Philip, whose allies they subsequently became.

Lord Brougham describes the oration as 'one of extraordinary subtlety and address in handling delicate topics'; and, after quoting the passage in which Demosthenes urges the necessity of maintaining a balance of power between rival states, adds that 'this is precisely the language of modern policy'. At the same time, the speech has in places a somewhat academic and theoretical air: it is much occupied with the weighing of hypothetical considerations and obligations against one another: and though it enunciates some plain and reasonable political principles, and makes an honest attempt to satisfy those who wished to help the Arcadians, but at the same time desired to regain ground against Thebes, it is not always convincing, and the tone is more frankly opportunist than is usually the case with Demosthenes.]

I THINK, men of Athens, that those who have spoken on the 1 Arcadian side and those who have spoken on the Spartan, are alike making a mistake. For their mutual accusations and their attacks upon one another would suggest that they are not, like yourselves, Athenians, receiving the two embassies, but actually delegates of the two states. Such attacks it was for the two deputations to make. The duty of those who claim to advise you here was to discuss the situation impartially, and to inquire, in an uncontentious spirit, what course is best in your interests. As it is, if one could alter the 2 fact that they are known to us, and that they speak the dialect of Attica, I believe that many would imagine that those on the one side actually were Arcadians, and those on the other, Spartans. For my part, I see plainly enough the difficulty of offering the best advice. For you, like them, are deluded, in your desire for one extreme or the other: and one who endeavours to propose an intermediate course, which you will not have the patience to understand, will satisfy neither side and will forfeit the confidence of both. But in spite of this, I shall prefer, for my own part, to risk 3 being regarded as an idle chatterer (if such is really to be my lot), rather than to abandon my conviction as to what is best for Athens, and leave you to the mercy of those who would deceive you. And while I shall deal with all other points later, by your leave, I shall take for my starting-point, in explaining the course which I believe to be best, those principles which are admitted by all.

There can be no possible question that it is to the interest 4 of the city that both the Spartans and these Thebans should be weak; and the present situation, if one may judge at all from what has constantly been asserted in your presence, is

such, that if Orchomenus, Thespiae, and Plataeae are re-established, Thebes becomes weak; and that if the Spartans can reduce Arcadia to subjection and destroy Megalo-
5 polis, Sparta will recover her former strength. We must, therefore, take care not to allow the Spartans to attain a formidable degree of strength, before the Thebans have become insignificant, lest there should take place, unobserved by us, such an increase in the power of Sparta as would be out of proportion to the decrease in the power of Thebes which our interests demand. For it is, of course, out of the question that we should desire merely to substitute the rivalry of Sparta for that of Thebes: that is not the object upon which we are bent. Our object is rather that neither people shall be capable of doing us any injury. That is what will best enable us to live in security.

6 But, granted that this is what ought to be, still, we are told, it is a scandalous thing to choose for our allies the men against whom we were arrayed at Mantineia, and further, to help them against those whose perils we shared that day. I agree; but I think that we need to insert the condition, 'provided that the two parties are willing to act rightly.'
7 For if all alike prove willing to keep the peace, we shall not go to the aid of the Megalopolitans, since there will be no need to do so; and so there will be no hostility whatever on our part towards our former comrades in battle. They are already our allies, as they tell us; and now the Arcadians will become our allies as well. What more could we desire?
8 But suppose they act wrongfully and think fit to make war. In that case, if the question before us is whether we are to abandon Megalopolis to Sparta or not, then I say that, wrong though it is, I will acquiesce in our permitting this, and

declining to oppose our former companions in danger. But if you all know that, after capturing Megalopolis, they will march against Messene, let me ask any of those who are now so harshly disposed towards Megalopolis to say what action he will *then* advise. No answer will be given. In fact 9 you all know that, whether they advise it or not, we *must* then go to the rescue, both because of the oath which we have sworn to the Messenians, and because our interests demand the continued existence of that city. Ask yourselves, then, on which occasion you can most honourably and generously interpose to check the aggressions of Sparta—in defence of Megalopolis, or in defence of Messene? On the present 10 occasion it will be understood that you are succouring the Arcadians, and are anxious that the Peace, which you fought for and risked your lives to win, may be secure. But if you wait, all the world will see plainly that it is not in the name of right that you desire the existence of Messene, but because you are afraid of Sparta. And while we should always seek and do the right, we should at the same time take good care that what is right shall also be advantageous.

Now an argument is used by speakers on the other side 11 to the effect that we ought to attempt to recover Oropus, and that if we make enemies of those who might come to our assistance against it we shall have no allies. I too say that we should try to recover Oropus. But the argument that the Spartans will be our enemies now, if we make alliance with those Arcadians who desire our friendship, is an argument which no one has less right even to mention, than those who induced you to help the Spartans when they were in danger. Such was not their argument, when all the Pelo- 12 ponnesians came to you, entreating you to support them in their campaign against Sparta, and they persuaded you to reject the entreaty, with the result that the Peloponnesians took the only remaining course and applied to Thebes—when they bade you contribute funds and imperil your lives for the deliverance of the Spartans. Nor, I presume, would you have been willing to protect them, had they warned you that you must expect no gratitude for their deliverance, unless, after saving them, you allowed them once more to

13 do as they pleased and commit fresh aggressions. And further, however antagonistic it may be to the designs of the Spartans, that we should make the Arcadians our allies, they are surely bound to feel a gratitude towards us for saving them when they were in the utmost extremity, which will outweigh their vexation at our preventing their present wrongdoing. Must they not then either assist us to recover Oropus, or else be regarded as the basest of mankind? For, by Heaven, I can see no other alternative.

14 I am astonished, also, to hear it argued that if we make the Arcadians our allies, and carry out my advice, it will seem as though Athens were changing her policy, and were utterly unreliable. I believe that the exact reverse of this is the case, men of Athens, and I will tell you why. I suppose that no one in the world can deny that when this city saved the Spartans, and before them the Thebans, and finally the Euboeans, and subsequently made them her allies, she

15 had one and the same end always in view. And what was this? It was to deliver the victims of aggression. And if this is so, it is not we that should be changing, but those who refuse to adhere to the right; and it will be manifest that, although circumstances change from time to time with the ambitious designs of others, Athens does not change.

I believe that the Spartans are playing a very unscrupulous 16 part. At present they tell us that the Eleans are to recover part of Triphylia, and the Phliasians, Tricaranum; other Arcadians are to recover their own possessions, and we ourselves are to recover Oropus—not that they have any desire to see every state enjoying its own—far from it!—such generosity on their part would be late indeed in showing itself. They wish rather to present the appearance of 17 co-operating with each separate state in the recovery of the territory that it claims, in order that when they themselves march against Messene, all may take the field with them, and give them their hearty assistance, on pain of seeming to act unfairly, in refusing to return an equivalent for the support which each of them received from Sparta in regard to their own several claims. My own view is that, even 18 without the tacit surrender of some of the Arcadians to Sparta, we can recover Oropus, aided not only by the Spartans, if they are ready to act honourably, but by all who disapprove of allowing Thebes to retain what is not her own. But even if it were made quite plain to us, that without allowing Sparta to subdue the Peloponnese, we should not be able to take Oropus, I should still think it preferable, if I may dare to say so, to let Oropus go, rather than sacrifice Messene and the Peloponnese to Sparta. For our quarrel with them would not, I believe, be confined to this; since—I will not say what occurs to me; but there are many risks which we should run.

But, to pass on, it is a monstrous thing to use the hostile 19 actions which, they say, the Megalopolitans committed against us, under the influence of Thebes, as a ground of accusation against them to-day; and, when they wish to be friends and so atone for their action by doing us good, to look askance at them, to seek for some way of avoiding their friendship, to refuse to recognize that in proportion to the zeal which my opponents can prove the Megalopolitans to have shown in supporting Thebes will be the resentment to which my opponents themselves will deservedly be exposed, for depriving the city of such allies as these, when they have 20 appealed to you before appealing to Thebes. Such a policy is surely the policy of men who wish to make the Arcadians for the second time the allies of others. And so far as one can forecast the future by calculation, I am sure, and I believe that most of you will agree with me, that if the Spartans take Megalopolis, Messene will be in peril; and if they take Messene also, then I predict that we shall find ourselves allies 21 of Thebes. It is a far more honourable, a far better, course that we should ourselves take over the Theban confederacy, refusing to leave the field open to the cupidity of the Spartans, than that we should be so afraid of protecting the allies of Thebes, as first to sacrifice them, and then to save Thebes itself; and, in addition, to be in a state of apprehension for 22 our own safety. For if the Spartans capture Megalopolis and become a great power once more, the prospect, as I conceive it, is not one which this city can view without alarm. For I can see that even now they are determining to go to war, not to prevent any evil which threatens them, but to recover their own ancient power: and what their aims were when they possessed that power, you, I think, know perhaps better than I, and with that knowledge may well be alarmed.

23 Now I should be glad if the speakers who profess their hatred for Thebes on the one side, or for Sparta on the other,

would tell me if their professed hatred is based on consideration for you and your interests, or whether the one party hates Thebes from an interest in Sparta, and the other Sparta from an interest in Thebes. If the latter is the case, you should not listen to either, but treat them as insane: but if the former, why this inordinate exaltation of one side or the other? For it is possible, perfectly possible, to humiliate 24 Thebes without rendering Sparta powerful. Indeed, it is by far the easier course; and I will try to tell you how it can be done. We all know that, however unwilling men may be to do what is right, yet up to a certain point they are ashamed not to do so, and that they withstand wrongdoers openly, particularly if there are any who receive damage through the wrong done: and we shall find that what ruins everything and is the source of all evil is the unwillingness to do what is right without reserve. Now in order that no such obstacle 25 may stand in the way of the humiliation of Thebes, let us demand the re-establishment of Thespiae, Orchomenus, and Plataeae, co-operating with their citizens ourselves, and requiring others to do so; for the principle of refusing to allow ancient cities to lie desolate is a right and honourable one. But let us at the same time decline to abandon Megalopolis and Messene to the aggressors, or to suffer the destruction of existing and inhabited cities, on the pretext of restoring Plataeae and Thespiae. Then, if our policy is 26 made plain to all, there is no one who will not wish to terminate the Thebans' occupation of territory not their own. But if it is not, not only will our designs be opposed by the Arcadians, in the belief that the restoration of these towns carries with it their own ruin, but we shall have troubles without end. For, honestly, where can we expect to reach an end, when we permit the annihilation of existing cities, and require the restoration of those that have been annihilated?

27 It is demanded by those whose speeches display the strongest appearance of fairness, that the Megalopolitans shall take down the pillars which commemorate their alliance with Thebes, if they are to be trustworthy allies of Athens. The Megalopolitans reply that for them it is not pillars, but interest, that creates friendship; and that it is those who help them, that they consider to be their allies. Well, that may be their attitude. Nevertheless, my own view is, roughly speaking, this:—I say that we should simultaneously require the Megalopolitans to take down the pillars, and the Spartans to keep the peace: and that in the event of either side refusing to fulfil our request, we should at once take the part of those

28 who are willing to fulfil it. For if the Megalopolitans obtain peace, and yet adhere to the Theban alliance, it will be clear to all that they prefer the grasping policy of Thebes to that which is right. If, on the other hand, Megalopolis makes alliance frankly with us, and the Spartans then refuse to keep the peace, it will surely be clear to all that what the Spartans desire so eagerly is not the re-establishment of Thespiae, but an opportunity of subduing the Peloponnese while the

29 Thebans are involved in the war. And I am surprised to find that there are some who are alarmed at the prospect of the enemies of Sparta becoming allies of Thebes, and yet see nothing to fear in the subjugation of these enemies by Sparta herself; whereas the experience of the past can teach us that the Thebans always use such allies against Sparta, while, when Sparta had them, she used to use them against us.

30 There is another point which I think you should consider.

Suppose that you reject the overtures of the Megalopolitans. If they are annihilated and dispersed, Sparta can recover her power at once. If they actually survive—for things have happened before now beyond all hope—they will quite rightly be the firm allies of Thebes. But suppose you receive them. Then the immediate result, so far as they are concerned, is that they are saved by you: and as to the future, let us now transfer our calculation of possible risks to the case of the Thebans and Spartans. If the Thebans are crushed, 31 as they ought to be, the Spartans will not be unduly powerful, for they will always have these Arcadians at their doors to hold them in check. But if the Thebans actually recover and survive the attack, they will at least be weaker; for the Arcadians will have become our allies, and will owe their preservation to us. Thus on every ground it is to our interest not to sacrifice the Arcadians, nor to let them think that their deliverance, if they are really saved, is due to themselves, or to any other people than you.

And now, men of Athens, I solemnly declare that what I 3 have said has been prompted by no personal feeling, friendly or hostile, towards either side. I have told you only what I believe to be expedient for you; and I exhort you not to sacrifice the people of Megalopolis, and to make it your rule, never to sacrifice a smaller power to a greater.

FOR THE FREEDOM OF THE RHODIANS (OR. XV)

[*Introduction.* Dionysius of Halicarnassus places the speech in 351 B.C. He is not always accurate, and the internal evidence has been thought by some to suggest a date perhaps two years earlier. The reasons, however, for this are not strong, and there has recently been a disposition to accept Dionysius' date.

As the result of the Social War, Chios, Cos, Rhodes, and Byzantium had made themselves independent of Athens. They had been assisted by Mausolus, King of Caria, a vassal of Persia. After the termination of the war, a Carian garrison occupied Cos and Rhodes; the democratic constitution of Rhodes was overthrown and the democratic party driven into banishment, as the result of an oligarchic plot, which Mausolus had fostered. In 353 Mausolus died, and was succeeded by Artemisia, his sister and wife. The exiles appealed to Athens for restoration, and for the liberation of Rhodes from the Carian domination. It is evident that the feeling in Athens against the Rhodians was very strong, owing to their part in the late war, for which the democratic party had been responsible; and there was some fear of the possible consequences of offending Artemisia and perhaps becoming involved in war with Persia. Demosthenes, nevertheless, urges the people to assist them, and to forget their misconduct. He appeals to the traditional policy of Athens, as the saviour of the oppressed and protectress of democracies, and warns them of the danger which would threaten Athens herself, if the conversion of free constitutions into oligarchies were allowed to go unchecked. He takes a different view from that of his opponents of the probable attitude of Artemisia, and utters an impressive warning against corrupt and unpatriotic statesmen, which foreshadows his more vehement attacks in the orations against Philip.

The appeal was unsuccessful, for in the speech on the Peace (§ 25) Demosthenes speaks of Cos and Rhodes as still subject to Caria.

The speech is more eloquent than the last, and more outspoken. Political principles and ideals are enunciated with some confidence, and illustrated by striking examples from history. But there also appears for the first time that sense of the difficulty of rousing the Athenians to action of any kind, which is so strongly expressed in later speeches.]

It is, I think, your duty, men of Athens, when you are 1 deliberating upon affairs of such importance, to grant freedom of speech to every one of your advisers. And for my part, I have never yet felt any difficulty in pointing out to you the best course; for I believe that, broadly speaking, you all know from the first what this is. My difficulty is to persuade you to act upon your knowledge. For when a measure is approved and passed by you, it is as far from execution as it was before you resolved upon it. Well, you have to 2 render thanks to Heaven for this, among other favours—that those who went to war with you not long ago, moved by their own insolent pride, now place their own hopes of preservation in you alone. Well may we rejoice at our present opportunity! For if your decision in regard to it is what it should be, you will find yourselves meeting the calumnies of those who are slandering this city with a practical and a glorious refutation. For the peoples of Chios, Byzan- 3 tium, and Rhodes accused us of entertaining designs against them; and on this ground they combined against us in the recent war. But now it will be seen that, while Mausolus, who under the pretence of friendship towards Rhodes, directed and instigated their efforts, in reality robbed the Rhodians of their freedom ; while their declared allies, Chios and Byzantium, never came to aid them in their misfortunes ; 4 you, of whom they were afraid, and you alone, have been the authors of their salvation. And because all the world will have seen this, you will cause the popular party in every city to consider your friendship a guarantee of their own safety ; nor could you reap any greater blessing than the goodwill which will thus be offered to you, spontaneously and without misgivings, upon every hand.

5 I notice, to my surprise, that those who urge us to oppose the king in the interest of the Egyptians, are the very persons who are so afraid of him when it is the interest of the popular party in Rhodes that is in question. And yet it is known to every one that the Rhodians are Hellenes, while the Egyptians have a place assigned them in the Persian 6 Empire. I expect that some of you remember that, when you were discussing our relations with the king, I came forward and was the first to advise you (though I had, I believe, no supporters, or one at the most), that you would show your good sense, in my opinion, if you did not make your hostility to the king the pretext of your preparations, but prepared yourselves against the enemies whom you already had ; though you would resist him also, if he attempted to do you any injury. Nor, when I spoke thus, did I fail to convince 7 you, but you also approved of this policy. What I have now to say is the sequel to my argument on that occasion. For if the king were to call me to his side and make me his counsellor, I should give him the same advice as I gave you—namely, that he should fight in defence of his own possessions, if he were opposed by any Hellenic power, but should

absolutely forego all claim to what in no way belongs to him. If, therefore, you have made a general resolve, men of 8 Athens, to retire from any place of which the king makes himself master, either by surprise or by the deception of some of the inhabitants, you have not resolved well, in my judgement: but if you are prepared, in defence of your rights, even to fight, if need be, and to endure anything that may be necessary, not only will the need for such a step be less, the more firmly your minds are made up, but you will also be regarded as showing the spirit which you ought to show.

To prove to you that I am not suggesting anything 9 unprecedented in bidding you liberate the Rhodians, and that you will not be acting without precedent, if you take my advice, I will remind you of one of those incidents in the past which have ended happily for you. You once sent out Timotheus, men of Athens, to assist Ariobarzanes, adding to your resolution the provision that he must not break our treaty with the king; and Timotheus, seeing that Ariobarzanes was now openly in revolt against the king, but that Samos was occupied by a garrison under Cyprothemis, who had been placed there by Tigranes, the king's viceroy, abandoned his intention of helping Ariobarzanes, but sat down before Samos, relieved it, and set it free. And to this 10 day no war has ever arisen to trouble you on account of this. For to enter upon a war for the purpose of aggrandizement is never the same thing as to do so in defence of one's own possessions. Every one fights his hardest to recover what he has lost; but when men endeavour to gain at the expense of others, it is not so. They desire to do this, if it is allowed them; but if they are prevented, they do not consider that their opponents have done them any wrong.

11 Now listen for a moment, and consider whether I am right or wrong, when I conclude that if Athens were actively at work, Artemisia herself would now not even oppose our action. If the king effects in Egypt all that he is bent upon, I believe that Artemisia would make every attempt to secure for him the continued possession of Rhodes—not from any goodwill towards him, but from the desire to be credited with a great service to him, while he is still in her neighbourhood, and so to win from him as friendly a reception as 12 possible. But if he is faring as we are told, if all his attempts have failed, she will consider, and rightly, that the island can be of no further use to the king, except as a fortified post to command her own dominions—a security against any movement on her part. Accordingly she would prefer, I believe, that you should have it, without her openly surrendering it to you, rather than that he should occupy it. I think, therefore, that she would not even make an attempt to save it; or that if she actually did so, it would be but weakly and in- 13 effectively. For although I cannot, of course, profess to know what the king will do, I must insist that it is high time that it should be made clear, in the interests of Athens, whether he intends to lay claim to Rhodes or not: for if he does so, we have then to take counsel, not for the Rhodians alone, but for ourselves and for the Hellenes as a whole.

14 At the same time, even if the Rhodians who are now in possession of the town held it by their own strength, I should never have urged you to take them for your allies, for all the promises in the world. For I observe that they took to their side some of their fellow citizens, to help them overthrow the democracy, and that, having done this, they turned and expelled them: and I do not think that men who failed to keep faith with either party would ever be trust-

worthy allies for yourselves. And further, I should never 15 have made my present proposal, had I been thinking only of the interests of the popular party in Rhodes. I am not their official patron, nor have I a single personal friend among them; and even if both these things were otherwise, I should not have made this proposal, had I not believed it to be for your advantage. For as for the Rhodians, if I may use such an expression when I am pleading with you to save them, I share your joy[1] at what has happened to them. For it is because they grudged you the recovery of your rights that they have lost their own freedom; and that, instead of the equal alliance which they might have had with Hellenes, better than themselves, they are in bondage to foreigners and slaves, whom they have admitted to their citadels. Indeed, if you resolve to go to their aid, I may almost say 16 that this calamity has been good for them; for, Rhodians as they are, I doubt if they would ever have come to their right mind in prosperity; whereas actual experience has now taught them that folly generally leads to manifold adversities; and perhaps they will be wiser for the future. This lesson, I feel sure, will be no small advantage to them. I say then that you should endeavour to save these men, and should bear no malice, remembering that you too have been greatly deceived by conspirators against you, and yet would not admit that you deserved yourselves to suffer for such mistakes.

Observe this also, men of Athens. You have waged many 17 wars both against democracies and against oligarchies; and of this no doubt you are as well aware as I. But I doubt whether any of you considers for what objects you are fighting in each case. What then are these objects? In fighting

[1] ὑμῖν συγχαίρω.

against a democracy, you are fighting either over some private quarrel, when the parties have failed to settle their disputes by the means publicly provided; or you are contending for a piece of territory, or about a boundary, or for a point of honour, or for paramountcy. But in fighting against an oligarchy, it is not for any such objects—it is your consti-
18 tution and your freedom that are at stake. And therefore I should not hesitate to say that I believe it would be better for you, that all the Hellenic peoples should be democracies, and be at war with you, than that they should be governed by oligarchies, and be your friends. For with a free people you would have no difficulty, I believe, in making peace whenever you desired: but with an oligarchical State friendship itself cannot be safe. For there can be no goodwill between Few and Many—between those who seek for mastery, and those who have chosen the life of political equality.

19 It surprises me also that though Chios and Mytilene are ruled by oligarchies, and though now the Rhodians and all mankind, I may almost say, are being brought into the same bondage, no one considers that any danger threatens our own constitution also, or reflects that if every State is organized upon an oligarchic basis, it is not possible that your own democracy should be suffered to remain. For they know that no people but you could ever bring them forth into a state of liberty again; and they will wish to put an end to so likely a source of trouble to
20 themselves. As a rule we may regard wrongdoers as enemies only to those whom they have wronged. But when men destroy free constitutions and convert them into oligarchies, I say that you must think of them as the common enemies

of all whose hearts are set on freedom. Again, men of Athens, **21** it is only right that you, a democracy yourselves, should show towards other democracies in distress the same spirit as you would expect them to show towards you, if any such calamity (which God forbid !) should happen to you. It may be said that the Rhodians are justly punished. If so, this is not the time to exult over them. When men are prosperous they should always be found taking thought how best to help the distressed; for the future is unknown to all men.

I have often heard it stated here in your presence, that **22** when our democracy had met with disaster, you were joined by certain others in your anxiety for its preservation. Of these I will only refer on the present occasion to the Argives, and that briefly. For I cannot desire that you, who enjoy the reputation of being always the saviours of the distressed, should prove inferior to the Argives in that work. These Argives, though their territory borders on that of the Spartans, whom they saw to be masters by land and sea, neither hesitated nor feared to display their goodwill towards you; but when envoys came from Sparta (so the story goes) to demand the persons of certain Athenian refugees, they even voted that unless the envoys departed before sunset, they should be adjudged public enemies. If then the democracy of Argos **23** in those days showed no fear of the might of the Spartan Empire, will it not be a disgrace if you, who are Athenians, are afraid of one who is a barbarian—aye, and a woman? The Argives, moreover, could point to many defeats sustained at the hands of Sparta, while you have often defeated the king, and have not once proved inferior either to his servants or to himself. For if ever the king has gained any success against Athens, it has been by bribing the basest of the

Hellenes to betray their countrymen; in no other way has 24 he ever succeeded. Indeed, even such success has done him no good. You will find that no sooner had he rendered Athens weak, by the help of the Spartans, than he had to fight for his own kingdom against Clearchus and Cyrus. His successes, therefore, have not been won in the open field, nor have his plots brought him any good. Now some of you, I notice, are in the habit of speaking contemptuously of Philip, as though he were not worth reckoning with; while you dread the king, as a powerful enemy to any whom he chooses to oppose. But if we are not to defend ourselves against Philip, because he is so mean a foe, and are to give way in everything to the king, because he is so formidable, who is there, men of Athens, against whom we shall ever take the field?

25 Men of Athens, you have among you those who are particularly skilful in pleading with you the rights of the rest of the world; and I should be glad to give them this single piece of advice—that they should seek to plead your rights with the rest of the world, and so set an example of duty. It is monstrous to instruct you about rights, without doing right oneself; and it is not right that a fellow citizen of yours should have studied all the arguments against you 26 and none of those in your favour. Ask yourselves, in God's name, why it is that there is no one in Byzantium to tell the Byzantines that they must not occupy Chalcedon, which belongs to the king and formerly belonged to you, but upon which they had no sort of claim; or that they must not make Selymbria, once your ally, a contributory portion of the Byzantine state; or include the territory of Selymbria within the Byzantine frontier, in defiance of the sworn

treaty which ordains the independence of the cities? Why 27 was there no one to tell Mausolus, while he lived, and Artemisia after his death, that they must not occupy Cos and Rhodes and other Hellenic cities as well, which the king their master ceded to the Hellenes by the treaty, and for the sake of which the Hellenes of those days faced many a peril and fought many a gallant fight? Even if there actually are such advisers in both cases, at least it is not likely that they will find listeners. For my part I believe 28 that it is right to restore the exiled democracy of Rhodes. But even if it were not right, I think it would be proper to urge you to do it, when I consider the course taken by such speakers as these; and for this reason. If all the world, men of Athens, were bent upon doing right, it would be a disgrace to us if we alone were unwilling to do so: but when all the world is preparing itself in order to be able to commit wrong, then for us alone to abstain from every enterprise, on the plea of right, is no righteousness, to my mind, but cowardice. For I observe that the extent to which rights are admitted is always in proportion to the claimant's power at the moment. I can illustrate this by an instance 29 familiar to all of you. There are two treaties between the Hellenes and the king. The first was made by our own city, and all men praise it; the second by the Spartans, and it is denounced by all. The rights defined in these two treaties are not the same. For whereas a common and equal share of private rights is given by law to weak and strong alike, in a settlement of international rights it is the stronger who legislate for the weaker.

Well, you already know what the right course is. It 30 remains to inquire how you can carry out your knowledge into action; and this will be possible, if you come to be regarded as public champions of universal liberty. But the great difficulty which you find in doing your duty is, to my mind, natural enough. All other men have only one conflict to face—the conflict with their declared foes; and when these are subdued, there is no further obstacle to their 31 secure enjoyment of their happiness. But for you there is a double conflict. In addition to that to which all men are liable, there is another which is harder, and which must be faced first: for you have to win the victory in your councils over those who are deliberately working in your midst against the interests of the city; and because, thanks to them, you can effect nothing that is demanded of you without a struggle, 32 it is natural that you should often miss your mark. The chief reason for the fearless adoption of such a course in public life by so many men is perhaps to be found in the benefits which they obtain from those who hire them. Yet at the same time, some of the blame may fairly be laid at your own doors. For you ought, men of Athens, to think of a man's post in public life as you think of his post in the army in the field. And how do you think of this? If a man leaves the post assigned to him by his general, you think that he deserves to be disfranchised and to lose all share in the 33 privileges of a citizen. And so when men desert the post of civil duty, committed to them by our forefathers, and follow an oligarchical policy, they should forfeit the privilege of acting as advisers to yourselves. As it is, while you believe that those of your allies are best disposed towards you, who have sworn to have the same friends and foes as yourselves, the politicians in whom you place most faith are those whom you well know to have chosen the side of the enemies of Athens.

It is easy enough, however, to find reasons for accusing them and reproaching all of you. But to find words or actions which will enable us to rectify what is now amiss with us, is a task indeed. Moreover, the present is not, perhaps, the time for entering into every point: but if only you can confirm the policy which you have chosen by some suitable action, it may be that other conditions will each in turn show some improvement. I think, therefore, that you ought to take this enterprise in hand with vigour, and to act worthily of your country. Remember with what delight you listen to the praises of your forefathers, the recital of their deeds, the enumeration of their trophies. Consider then that your forefathers dedicated these trophies, not that you might gaze at them in idle wonder, but that you might imitate the actions of those who placed them there.

THE FIRST PHILIPPIC (Or. IV)

[*Introduction*. Philip became King of Macedonia in 359 B.C. Being in great difficulties both from external enemies and from internal division, he made peace with the Athenians, who were supporting the pretensions of Argaeus to the throne, in the hope of recovering (by agreement with Argaeus) the colony of Amphipolis on the Strymon, which they had lost in 424. Philip acknowledged the title of Athens to Amphipolis, and sent home the Athenian prisoners, whom he had captured among the supporters of Argaeus, without ransom. The Athenians, however, neglected to garrison Amphipolis. In 358 (the year in which Athens temporarily recovered her hold over Euboea, by compelling the Thebans to evacuate the island), Philip carried on a successful campaign against the Paeonian and Illyrian tribes, who were standing enemies of Macedonia. For the next three years Athens was kept occupied by the war with her allies, and Philip saw his opportunity. He besieged Amphipolis: when the citizens sent Hierax and Stratocles to ask Athens for help, he dispatched a letter promising the Athenians that he would give them Amphipolis when he had taken it; and a secret understanding was arrived at between Philip and the Athenian envoys sent to him, that Athens should give him Pydna (once a Macedonian town, but now an ally of Athens) in exchange. Athens, therefore, listened neither to Amphipolis nor to Olynthus, which had also made overtures to her. The Olynthians in consequence made a treaty with Philip, who gave them Anthemus and promised to help them against their old rival Poteidaea, a town in alliance with Athens. The Olynthians on their part agreed not to make peace with Athens except in conjunction with him. But Philip, when he had captured Amphipolis by a combination of siege and intrigue, did not give it up to

Athens, and instead of waiting to receive Pydna from Athens, besieged and took it, aided once more by treachery from within. In 356 he took Poteidaea (in conjunction with the Olynthians, to whom he gave the town), the Athenians arriving too late to relieve it; and then pursued his conquests along the Thracian coast. Further inland he expelled the Thasians (allies of Athens) from Crenides and founded Philippi on the site, in the centre of the gold-mines of Mount Pangaeus, from which he henceforward derived a very large revenue; while the forests of the district provided him with timber for ship-building, of which he took full advantage: for in the next few years his ships made descents upon the Athenian islands of Lemnos and Imbros, plundered the Athenian corn-vessels off the coast of Euboea, and even landed a force at Marathon. In the latter part of 356 and in 355 he was occupied with the conquest of the Paeonians and Illyrians, with whom Athens had made an alliance in 356. At the end of 355 he laid siege to Methone, the last Athenian port on the Thermaic gulf, and captured it in 354. (Some place the siege and capture of Methone in 354–3, but an inscription, C.I.G. II. 70, makes it at least probable that the siege had begun by the last month of 355.) In 353 Philip made his way to the Thracian coast, and conquered Abdera and Maroneia. At Maroneia we find him in company with Pammenes (his former host at Thebes), who had been sent by the Thebans to assist Artabazus in his revolt against the Persian king; and at the same place he received Apollonides of Cardia, the envoy of the Thracian prince Cersobleptes. On his way home his ships escaped from Chares, off Neapolis, by a ruse. In the same year he interfered in the affairs of Thessaly, where the Aleuadae of Larissa had invited his assistance against Lycophron and Peitholaus of Pherae, who had invoked the aid of the Phocians. (In opposing the Phocians, the antagonists of the Thebans in the Sacred War, Philip was also helping the Thebans themselves, and gaining credit as the opponent of the plunderers of the temple of Apollo at Delphi.) Onomarchus, the Phocian leader, twice defeated Philip, but was overthrown and slain in 352. Philip took Pherae and Pagasae (its port), occupied Magnesia, and, by means of promises, obtained financial aid from the Thessalians. The expedition sent by Athens to relieve Pagasae arrived too late; but when Philip, after putting down the tyrants of Pherae and arranging matters in Thessaly, advanced towards the Pass of Thermopylae, an Athenian force, sent on the advice of Diophantus and Eubulus, appeared in time to oblige him to retire to Macedonia. Late in the autumn of 352 we find him once more in Thrace. It was probably now that he assisted the peoples of Byzantium and Perinthus, together with Amadocus, a rival of Cersobleptes, against the latter; with the result that Cersobleptes was obliged to give up his son to Philip as a hostage. Philip had also made alliance with Cardia, which, like Byzantium, was on bad terms with Athens. He now laid siege to Heraeon Teichos, a fortress on the Propontis, but illness obliged him to suspend operations, and the rumour of his death prevented the Athenians from sending against him the expedition which they had resolved upon. (The retention of her influence in this region was essential for Athens, if her corn-supply was to be secure.) In 351, on recovering from his illness, he entered the territory of Olynthus, which, contrary to the agreement with him, had made peace with Athens in the previous year, apart from himself: but he did not at present pursue the invasion further. In October 351 Athens sent Charidemus to the Hellespont with ten ships, but no soldiers and little money. If these are the ships alluded to in § 43 of the present Speech, the Speech must have been delivered after that date. Otherwise any date after Philip's incursion into the territory of Olynthus would suit the contents of the Speech, and many writers place it earlier in the year. The question of the relations of Athens with Philip had been brought forward; and Demosthenes, who had risen first to speak, proposes the creation of a large permanent fleet, and of a smaller force for immediate action, laying great stress on the necessity of sending Athenian citizens both to command and to form a substantial proportion of the troops, which had so far been mostly mercenaries. The scheme was worked out in detail, both in its military and in its financial aspects, and supported with an eloquence and an earnestness which are far in advance of those displayed in the earlier speeches.

The statement of Dionysius of Halicarnassus, that the Speech as we have it, is really a conflation of two speeches, of which the second (beginning at § 30) was delivered in 347, is generally (and rightly) discredited.]

1 If some new subject were being brought before us, men of Athens, I would have waited until most of your ordinary advisers had declared their opinion; and if anything that they said were satisfactory to me, I would have remained silent, and only if it were not so, would I have attempted to express my own view. But since we find ourselves once more considering a question upon which they have often spoken, I think I may reasonably be pardoned for rising first of all. For if their advice to you in the past had been what it ought to have been, you would have had no occasion for the present debate.

2 In the first place, then, men of Athens, we must not be downhearted at our present situation, however wretched it may seem to be. For in the worst feature of the past lies our best hope for the future—in the fact, that is, that we are in our present plight because you are not doing your duty in any respect; for if you were doing all that you should do, and we were still in this evil case, we could not then even hope for any improvement. 3 In the second place, you must bear in mind (what some of you have heard from others, and those who know can recollect for themselves), how powerful the Spartans were, not long ago, and yet how noble and patriotic your own conduct was, when instead of doing

anything unworthy of your country you faced the war with Sparta in defence of the right. Now why do I remind you of these things? It is because, men of Athens, I wish you to see and to realize, that so long as you are on your guard you have nothing to fear; but that if you are indifferent, nothing can be as you would wish: for this is exemplified for you both by the power of Sparta in those days, to which you rose superior because you gave your minds to your affairs; and by the insolence of Philip to-day, which troubles us because we care nothing for the things which should

4 concern us. If, however, any of you, men of Athens, when he considers the immense force now at Philip's command, and the city's loss of all her strongholds, thinks that Philip is a foe hard to conquer, I ask him (right though he is in his belief) to reflect also that there was a time when we possessed Pydna and Poteidaea and Methone; when all the surrounding country was our own, and many of the tribes which are now on his side were free and independent, and more inclined

5 to be friendly to us than to him. Now if in those days Philip had made up his mind that it was a hard thing to fight against the Athenians, with all their fortified outposts on his own frontiers, while he was destitute of allies, he would have achieved none of his recent successes, nor acquired this great power. But Philip saw quite clearly, men of Athens, that all these strongholds were prizes of war, displayed for competition. He saw that in the nature of things the property of the absent belongs to those who are on the spot, and that of the negligent to those who are ready for toil and danger.

6 It is, as you know, by acting upon this belief, that he has brought all those places under his power, and now holds them—some of them by right of capture in war, others in

virtue of alliances and friendly understandings; for every one is willing to grant alliance and to give attention to those whom they see to be prepared and ready to take action as is necessary. If then, men of Athens, you also will resolve 7 to adopt this principle to-day—the principle which you have never observed before—if each of you can henceforward be relied upon to throw aside all this pretence of incapacity, and to act where his duty bids him, and where his services can be of use to his country; if he who has money will contribute, and he who is of military age will join the campaign; if, in one plain word, you will resolve henceforth to depend absolutely on yourselves, each man no longer hoping that he will need to do nothing himself, and that his neighbour will do everything for him; then, God willing, you will recover your own; you will take back all that your indolence has lost, and you will have your revenge upon Philip. Do not imagine that his fortune is built to last for 8 ever, as if he were a God. He also has those who hate him and fear him, men of Athens, and envy him too, even among those who now seem to be his closest friends. All the feelings that exist in any other body of men must be supposed to exist in Philip's supporters. Now, however, all such feelings are cowed before him: your slothful apathy has taken away their only rallying point; and it is this apathy that I bid you put off to-day. Mark the situation, men of Athens: 9 mark the pitch which the man's outrageous insolence has reached, when he does not even give you a choice between action and inaction, but threatens you, and utters (as we are told) haughty language: for he is not the man to rest content in possession of his conquests: he is always casting his net wider; and while we procrastinate and sit idle, he is setting

10 his toils around us on every side. When, then, men of Athens, when, I say, will you take the action that is required? What are you waiting for? 'We are waiting,' you say, 'till it is necessary.' But what must we think of all that is happening at this present time? Surely the strongest necessity that a free people can experience is the shame which they must feel at their position! What? Do you want to go round asking one another, 'Is there any news?' Could there be any stranger news than that a man of Macedonia is defeating Athenians
11 in war, and ordering the affairs of the Hellenes? 'Is Philip dead?' 'No, but he is sick.' And what difference does it make to you? For if anything should happen to him, you will soon raise up for yourselves a second Philip, if it is thus that you attend to your interests. Indeed, Philip himself has not risen to this excessive height through his own strength, so much as through our neglect. I go even further.
12 If anything happened to Philip—if the operation of Fortune, who always cares for us better than we care for ourselves, were to effect this too for us—you know that if you were at hand, you could descend upon the general confusion and order everything as you wished; but in your present condition, even if circumstances offered you Amphipolis, you could not take it; for your forces and your minds alike are far away.

13 Well, I say no more of the obligation which rests upon you all to be willing and ready to do your duty; I will assume that you are resolved and convinced. But the nature of the armament which, I believe, will set you free from such troubles as these, the numbers of the force, the source from which we must obtain funds, and the best and quickest way, as it seems to me, of making all further preparations—

all this, men of Athens, I will at once endeavour to explain when I have made one request of you. Give your verdict 14 on my proposal when you have heard the whole of it; do not prejudge it before I have done; and if at first the force which I propose appears unprecedented, do not think that I am merely creating delays. It is not those whose cry is 'At once', 'To-day', whose proposals will meet our need; for what has already happened cannot be prevented by any expedition now. It is rather he who can show the nature, 15 the magnitude, and the financial possibility of a force which when provided will be able to continue in existence either until we are persuaded to break off the war, or until we have overcome the enemy; for thus only can we escape further calamity for the future. These things I believe I can show, though I would not stand in the way of any other speaker's professions. It is no less a promise than this that I make; the event will soon test its fulfilment, and you will be the judges of it.

First then, men of Athens, I say that fifty warships must 16 at once be got in readiness: and next, that you must be in such a frame of mind that, if any need arises, you will embark in person and sail. In addition, you must prepare transports for half our cavalry, and a sufficient number of boats. These, 17 I think, should be in readiness to meet those sudden sallies of his from his own country against Thermopylae, the Chersonese, Olynthus, and any other place which he may select. For we must make him realize that there is a possibility of your rousing yourselves out of your excessive indifference, just as when once you went to Euboea, and before that (as we are told) to Haliartus, and finally, only the other day, to Thermopylae. Such a possibility, even if you are 18 unlikely to make it a reality, as I think you ought

to do, is not one which he can treat lightly; and you may thus secure one of two objects. On the one hand, he may know that you are on the alert—he will in fact know it well enough: there are only too many persons, I assure you, in Athens itself, who report to him all that happens here: and in that case his apprehensions will ensure his inactivity. But if, on the other hand, he neglects the warning, he may be taken off his guard; for there will be nothing to hinder you from sailing to his country, if he gives you the
19 opportunity. These are the measures upon which I say you should all be resolved, and your preparations for them made. But before this, men of Athens, you must make ready a force which will fight without intermission, and do him damage. Do not speak to me of ten thousand or twenty thousand mercenaries. I will have none of your paper-armies. Give me an army which will be the army of Athens, and will obey and follow the general whom you elect, be there one general or more, be he one particular individual, or be he who he may.
20 You must also provide maintenance for this force. Now what is this force to be? how large is it to be? how is it to be maintained? how will it consent to act in this manner? I will answer these questions point by point. The number of mercenaries—but you must not repeat the mistake which has so often injured you, the mistake of, first, thinking any measures inadequate, and so voting for the largest proposal, and then, when the time for action comes, not even executing the smaller one; you must rather carry out and make provision for the smaller measure, and add to it, if it proves
21 too small—the total number of soldiers, I say, must be two thousand, and of these five hundred must be Athenians, beginning from whatever age you think good: they must

serve for a definite period—not a long one, but one to be fixed at your discretion—and in relays. The rest must be mercenaries. With these must be cavalry, two hundred in number, of whom at least fifty must be Athenians, as with the infantry; and the conditions of service must be the same. You must also find transports for these. And what next? 22 Ten swift ships of war. For as he has a fleet, we need swift-sailing warships too, to secure the safe passage of the army. And how is maintenance to be provided for these? This also I will state and demonstrate, as soon as I have given you my reasons for thinking that a force of this size is sufficient, and for insisting that those who serve in it shall be citizens.

The size of the force, men of Athens, is determined by the 23 fact that we cannot at present provide an army capable of meeting Philip in the open field; we must make plundering forays, and our warfare must at first be of a predatory nature. Consequently the force must not be over-big—we could then neither pay nor feed it—any more than it must be wholly insignificant. The presence of citizens in the force that sails 24 I require for the following reasons. I am told that Athens once maintained a mercenary force in Corinth, under the command of Polystratus, Iphicrates, Chabrias and others, and that you yourselves joined in the campaign with them; and I remember hearing that these mercenaries, when they took the field with you, and you with them, were victorious over the Spartans. But even since your mercenary forces have gone to war alone, it is your friends and allies that they conquer, while your enemies have grown more powerful than they should be. After a casual glance at the war to which Athens has sent them, they sail off to Artabazus, or anywhere rather than to the war; and the general follows them naturally enough, for his power over them is gone when 25 he can give them no pay. You ask what I bid you do. I bid you take away their excuses both from the general and the soldiers, by supplying pay and placing citizen-soldiers at their side as spectators of these mysteries of generalship; for our present methods are a mere mockery. Imagine the question to be put to you, men of Athens, whether you are at peace or no. 'At peace?' you would say; 'Of course 26 not! We are at war with Philip.' Now have you not all along been electing from among your own countrymen ten captains and generals, and cavalry-officers, and two masters-of-the-horse? and what are they doing? Except the one single individual whom you happen to send to the seat of war, they are all marshalling your processions for you with the commissioners of festivals. You are no better than men modelling puppets of clay. Your captains and your cavalry-officers are elected to be displayed in the streets, not to be sent 27 to the war. Surely, men of Athens, your captains should be elected from among yourselves, and your master-of-the-horse from among yourselves; your officers should be your own countrymen, if the force is to be really the army of Athens. As it is, the master-of-the-horse who is one of yourselves has to sail to Lemnos; while the master-of-the-horse with the army that is fighting to defend the possessions of Athens is Menelaus. I do not wish to disparage that gentleman; but whoever holds that office ought to have been elected by you.

28 Perhaps, however, while agreeing with all that I have said, you are mainly anxious to hear my financial proposals, which will tell you the amount and the sources of the funds required. I proceed, therefore, with these at once. First

for the sum. The cost of the bare rations for the crews, with such a force, will be 90 talents and a little over—40 talents for ten swift ships, and 20 minae a month for each ship; and for the soldiers as much again, each soldier to receive rations to the value of 10 drachmae a month; and for the cavalry (two hundred in number, each to receive 30 drachmae a month) twelve talents. It may be said that the supply 29 of bare rations to the members of the force is an insufficient initial provision; but this is a mistake. I am quite certain that, given so much, the army will provide everything else for itself from the proceeds of war, without injury to a single Hellene or ally of ours, and that the full pay will be made up by these means. I am ready to sail as a volunteer and to suffer the worst, if my words are untrue. The next question then is of ways and means, in so far as the funds are to come from yourselves. I will explain this at once.

[*A schedule of ways and means is read.*]

This, men of Athens, is what we have been able to devise; 30 and when you put our proposals to the vote, you will pass them, if you approve of them; that so your war with Philip may be a war, not of resolutions and dispatches, but of actions.

I believe that the value of your deliberations about the 31 war and the armament as a whole would be greatly enhanced, if you were to bear in mind the situation of the country against which you are fighting, remembering that most of Philip's plans are successfully carried out because he takes advantage of winds and seasons; for he waits for the Etesian winds or the winter-season, and only attacks when it would be impossible for us to effect a passage to the scene of action.

32 Bearing this in mind, we must not carry on the war by means of isolated expeditions; we shall always be too late. We must have a permanent force and armament. As our winter-stations for the army we have Lemnos, Thasos, Sciathos, and the islands in that region, which have harbours and corn, and are well supplied with all that an army needs. And as to the time of year, whenever it is easy to approach the shore and the winds are not dangerous, our force can without difficulty lie close to the Macedonian coast itself, and block the mouths of the ports.

33 How and when he will employ the force is a matter to be determined, when the time comes, by the commander whom you put in control of it. What must be provided from Athens is described in the scheme which I have drafted. If, men of Athens, you first supply the sum I have mentioned, and then, after making ready the rest of the armament—soldiers, ships, cavalry—bind the whole force in its entirety, by law, to remain at the seat of war; if you become your own pay-masters, your own commissioners of supply, but require your general to account for the actual operations; then there will be an end of these perpetual discussions of one and the

34 same theme, which end in nothing but discussion: and in addition to this, men of Athens, you will, in the first place, deprive him of his chief source of supply. For what is this? Why, he carries on the war at the cost of your own allies, harrying and plundering those who sail the seas! And what will you gain besides this? You will place yourselves out of reach of disaster. It will not be as it was in the past, when he descended upon Lemnos and Imbros, and went off, with your fellow-citizens as his prisoners of war, or when he seized the vessels off Geraestus, and levied

an enormous sum from them ; or when (last of all) he landed at Marathon, seized the sacred trireme, and carried it off from the country ; while all the time you can neither prevent these aggressions, nor yet send an expedition which will arrive when you intend it to arrive. But for what reason do 35 you think, men of Athens, do the festival of the Panathenaea and the festival of the Dionysia always take place at the proper time, whether those to whom the charge of either festival is allotted are specially qualified persons or not— festivals upon which you spend larger sums of money than upon any armament whatsoever, and which involve an amount of trouble and preparation, which are unique, so far as I know, in the whole world— ; and yet your armaments are always behind the time—at Methone, at Pagasae, at Potidaea ? It is because for the festivals all is arranged by 36 law. Each of you knows long beforehand who is to supply the chorus, and who is to be steward of the games, for his tribe : he knows what he is to receive, and when, and from whom, and what he is to do with it. No detail is here neglected, nothing is left indefinite. But in all that concerns war and our preparation for it, there is no organization, no revision, no definiteness. Consequently it is not until the news comes that we appoint our trierarchs and institute exchanges of property for them, and inquire into ways and means. When that is done, we first resolve that the resident aliens and the independent freedmen shall go on board ; then we change our minds and say that citizens shall embark ; then that we will send substitutes ; and while all these delays 37 are occurring, the object of the expedition is already lost. For we spend on preparation the time when we should be acting, and the opportunities which events afford will not wait for our slothful evasions; while as for the forces on which we think we can rely in the meantime, when the critical moment comes, they are tried and found wanting. And Philip's insolence has reached such a pitch, that he has sent such a letter as the following to the Euboeans.

[*The letter is read.*]

38 The greater part of the statements that have been read are true, men of Athens; and they ought not to be true! but I admit that they may possibly be unpleasant to hear; and if the course of future events would pass over all that a speaker passes over in his speech, to avoid giving pain, we should be right in speaking with a view to your pleasure. But if attractive words, spoken out of season, bring their punishment in actual reality, then it is disgraceful to blind our eyes to the truth, to put off everything that is unpleasant,
39 to refuse to understand even so much as this, that those who conduct war rightly must not follow in the wake of events, but must be beforehand with them: for just as a general may be expected to lead his army, so those who debate must lead the course of affairs, in order that what they resolve upon may be done, and that they may not be forced to
40 follow at the heels of events. You, men of Athens, have the greatest power in the world—warships, infantry, cavalry, revenue. But none of these elements of power have you used as you ought, down to this very day. The method of your warfare with Philip is just that of barbarians in a boxing-match. Hit one of them, and he hugs the place; hit him on the other side, and there go his hands; but as for guarding, or looking his opponent in the face, he neither
41 can nor will do it. It is the same with you. If you hear

that Philip is in the Chersonese, you resolve to make an expedition there; if he is at Thermopylae, you send one there; and wherever else he may be, you run up and down in his steps. It is he that leads your forces. You have never of yourselves come to any salutary decision in regard to the war. No single event do you ever discern before it occurs—before you have heard that something has happened or is happening. Perhaps there was room for this backwardness until now; but now we are at the very crisis, and such an attitude is possible no longer. Surely, men of Athens, it is one of the gods—one 42 who blushes for Athens, as he sees the course which events are taking—that has inspired Philip with this restless activity. If he were content to remain at peace, in possession of all that he has won by conquest or by forestalling us—if he had no further plans—even then, the record against us as a people, a record of shame and cowardice and all that is most dishonourable, would, I think, seem complete enough to some of you. But now he is always making some new attempt, always grasping after something more; and unless your spirit has utterly departed, his conduct will perhaps bring you out into the field. It amazes me, men of Athens, that not one of you remembers 43 with any indignation, that this war had its origin in our intention to punish Philip; and that now, at the end of it, the question is, how we are to escape disaster at his hands. But that he will not stay his progress until some one arrests it is plain enough. Are we then to wait for that? Do you think that all is right, when you dispatch nothing but empty ships and somebody's hopes? Shall we not embark? Shall we 44 not now, if never before, go forth ourselves, and provide at least some small proportion of Athenian soldiers? Shall we not sail to the enemy's country? But I heard the question, 'At what point on his coast are we to anchor?' The war itself, men of Athens, if you take it in hand, will discover his weak points: but if we sit at home listening to the mutual abuse and recriminations of our orators, you can never realize any of the results that you ought 45 to realize. I believe that whenever any portion of Athens is sent with the forces, even if the whole city does not go, the favour of Heaven and of Fortune fights on our side. But whenever you dispatch anywhere a general with an empty resolution and some platform-hopes to support him, then you achieve nothing that you ought to achieve, your enemies laugh at you, and your allies are in deadly 46 fear of all such armaments. It is impossible, utterly impossible, that any one man should be able to effect all that you wish for you. He can give undertakings and promises; he can accuse this man and that; and the result is that your fortunes are ruined. For when the general is at the head of wretched, unpaid mercenaries, and when there are those in Athens who lie to you light-heartedly about all that he does, and, on the strength of the tales that you hear, you pass decrees at random, what *must* you expect?

47 How then can this state of things be terminated? Only, men of Athens, when you expressly make the same men soldiers, witnesses of their general's actions, and judges at his examination when they return home; for then the issue of your fortunes will not be a tale which you hear, but a thing which you will be on the spot to see. So shameful is the pass which matters have now reached, that each of your generals is tried for his life before you two or three times, but does not dare to fight in mortal combat with the enemy even once. They prefer the death of kidnappers and brigands

to that of a general. For it is a felon's death, to die by sentence of the court: the death of a general is to fall in battle with the enemy. Some of us go about saying that 48 Philip is negotiating with Sparta for the overthrow of the Thebans and the breaking up of the free states; others, that he has sent ambassadors to the king; others, that he is fortifying cities in Illyria. We all go about inventing each 49 his own tale. I quite believe, men of Athens, that he is intoxicated with the greatness of his successes, and entertains many such visions in his mind; for he sees that there are none to hinder him, and he is elated at his achievements. But I do not believe that he has chosen to act in such a way that the most foolish persons in Athens can know what he intends to do; for no persons are so foolish as newsmongers. But if we dismiss all such tales, and attend only to the 50 certainty—that the man is our enemy, that he is robbing us of our own, that he has insulted us for a long time, that all that we ever expected any one to do for us has proved to be against us, that the future is in our own hands, that if we will not fight him now in his own country we shall perhaps be obliged to do so in ours—if, I say, we are assured of this, then we shall have made up our minds aright, and shall be quit of idle words. For you have not to speculate what the future may be: you have only to be assured that the future must be evil, unless you give heed and are ready to do your duty.

Well, I have never yet chosen to gratify you by saying 51 anything which I have not felt certain would be for your good; and to-day I have spoken freely and without concealment, just what I believe. I could wish to be as sure of the good that a speaker will gain by giving you the best advice as of that which you will gain by listening to him. I should then have been far happier than I am. As it is, I do not know what will happen to me, for what I have said: but I have chosen to speak in the sure conviction that if you carry out my proposals, it will be for your good; and may the victory rest with that policy which will be for the good of all!

THE OLYNTHIAC ORATIONS (Or. I–III)

[*Introduction.* It has already been noticed that when Philip took Amphipolis in 357 B.C., the Olynthians made overtures to the Athenians, with whom they had been at war for some years, and that, being rejected, they became allies of Philip, who gave them Anthemus and Poteidaea. In 352, alarmed at Philip's growing power, they once more applied to Athens. Peace was made, and negotiations began with regard to an alliance. In 351 Philip appeared in the territory of Olynthus. He did not, however, at once carry the invasion further, but took pains, during this year and the next, to foster a Macedonian party in the town. In 349 Philip virtually declared war on the Olynthians by demanding the surrender of his step-brother Arrhidaeus, who had taken refuge with them. The Olynthians again appealed to Athens; an alliance was made; Chares was sent with thirty ships and 2,000 mercenaries, but seems to have mismanaged the war by misfortune or by design. Probably he had been badly supplied with funds, and instead of helping Olynthus, resorted to acts of piracy to satisfy his men. The Macedonian troops proceeded to take Stageira and other towns of the Olynthian League, though Philip still professed to have no hostile intentions against Olynthus (see Phil. III, § 11). Chares was recalled and put on his trial; and, probably in response to a further message from Olynthus, Charidemus was transferred thither from the Hellespont. With a considerable mercenary force at his disposal, Charidemus overran Pallene and Bottiaea, and did some damage to Philip's territory, but afterwards gave himself up to dissipation in Olynthus. In the meantime, some of the Thessalians had become restless under Philip's supremacy (see Olynth. I, § 22, II, § 11), and he was obliged to undertake an expedition to suppress the revolt, and to put down Peitholaus (who had apparently become tyrant of Pherae once more, though he had been expelled in 352). But early in 348 he appeared in person in Chalcidice, and took one after another of the towns of the League, including Mecyberna the port of Olynthus, and Torone. He thrice defeated the Olynthians in battle, and at last obtained possession of Olynthus itself by the treachery of Euthycrates and Lasthenes, the commanders of the Olynthian cavalry.

Athens had probably been occupied during the early part of the year[1] with an expedition which she sent (against the advice of Demosthenes) to help Plutarchus of Eretria to repel attacks which were partly, at least, instigated by Philip; and in consequence she had done little for Olynthus, though on a request of the Olynthians for cavalry, she had ordered some of those which had been sent to Euboea to go to Olynthus, and these may have been the Athenians whom Philip captured in that city. The seventeen ships, 2,000 infantry, and 300 cavalry (all citizens), which Athens dispatched under Chares in response to a last urgent appeal from Olynthus, were delayed by storms and arrived too late. Philip entirely destroyed Olynthus and thirty-two other towns, sold their inhabitants into slavery, brought the whole of Chalcidice within the Macedonian Empire, and celebrated his conquests by a festival in honour of the Olympian Zeus at Dium.

The First Olynthiac Oration was delivered before Olynthus itself was attacked or any other towns actually taken (Olynth. I, § 17); and both the First and Second before the discontent with Philip in Thessaly had taken an active form (I, § 22, II, § 7). Both, that is, belong to the summer of 349, and the situation implied is very much the same in both. The First was perhaps spoken when the Olynthians first appealed to Athens in that year, before the mission of Chares; the Second,

[1] See notes to Speech on the Peace, § 5. Some date the Euboean expedition and the sending of the cavalry one or two years earlier, and the whole chronology is much disputed; but there are strong arguments for the date (348) given in the text.

to counteract the effect of something which had caused despondency in Athens (possibly the conduct of the Athenian generals, or the account given by other orators of Philip's power). In both Demosthenes urges the importance of resisting Philip while he is still far away, and of sending, not mercenaries, but a citizen-army; and while hinting at what he regards as the true solution of the financial difficulty, proposes a special war-tax. The solution which he thinks the right one is more explicitly described in the Third Olynthiac, spoken (probably[1]) in the autumn of the same year, and certainly at a time when the situation had become much more grave. The root of the financial difficulty lay in the existence of a law which prohibited (evidently under severe penalties, Olynth. III, § 12) any proposal to devote to military purposes that portion of the revenues which constituted the 'Festival-' or 'Theoric Fund', and was for the most part distributed to the citizens to enable them to take part in the public festivals, and so join in fulfilling what was no doubt a religious duty as well as a pleasure. This particular form of expenditure is stated to have been introduced by the demagogue Agyrrhius in 394, when it revived in an extended form a distribution of theatre money instituted late in the fifth century by Cleophon; but the special law in question appears to have been of recent date (Olynth. III, § 12), and was almost certainly the work of Eubulus and his party. Demosthenes himself proposes an extraordinary Legislative Commission, to repeal the mischievous laws and leave the way clear for financial reform. At the same time he attacks the whole policy of Eubulus, charging him with distributing doles without regard to public service, adding to the amenities of Athens instead of maintaining her honour in war, and enriching her politicians while degrading her people. The main object of the speech was unsuccessful; and just about this time (though whether before or after the speech is disputed) Apollodorus proposed that the people should decide whether the surplus revenues should go to

[1] See note on Olynth. III, § 4.

the Festival Fund, or be applied to military purposes, and was heavily fined for the illegality of the proposal.

The Three Olynthiacs rank high among the Orations of Demosthenes. Some passages, indeed, show that he had hardly as yet appreciated the genius of Philip, or the unlikelihood of his making a false move either through over-confidence or because he had come to the end of his resources. But the noble patriotism of the speaker, the lofty tone of his political reflections, the clearness of his diagnosis of the evils of his time, and the fearlessness of his appeal for loyal and united self-sacrifice, are nowhere more conspicuous.]

THE FIRST OLYNTHIAC

1 I BELIEVE, men of Athens, that you would give a great sum to know what policy, in reference to the matter which you are now considering, will best serve the interests of the city, and since that is so, you ought to be ready and eager to listen to those who desire to give you their advice. For not only can you hear and accept any useful proposals which a speaker may have thought out before he came here; but such, I conceive, is your fortune, that the right suggestion will often occur to some of those present on the spur of the moment; and out of all these suggestions it should be easy for you to choose the most advantageous course.

2 The present time, men of Athens, seems almost to cry aloud that you must take matters into your own hands yonder, if you have any interest in a successful termination of the crisis: and yet our attitude appears to be—I do not know what. My own opinion, at all events, is that you should at once resolve to send this assistance; that you should prepare for the departure of the expedition at the

first possible moment—you must not fall victims to the same error as before—and that you should dispatch an embassy to announce our intention, and to be present at the scene of action. For what we have most to fear is this—that he, 3 with his unscrupulous cleverness in taking advantage of circumstances—now, it may be, by making concessions ; now by uttering threats, which he may well seem likely to fulfil ; now by misrepresenting ourselves and our absence from the scene—may turn and wrest to his own advantage some of the vital elements of our power. And yet it may fairly be 4 said, men of Athens, that our best hope lies in that very circumstance which renders Philip's power so hard to grapple with. The fact that the entire control over everything, open or secret, is concentrated in the hands of a single man ; that he is at one and the same time general, master, and treasurer ; that he is always present in person with his army —all this is a great advantage, in so far as military operations must be prompt and well-timed. But as regards the compact which he would so gladly make with the Olynthians, the effect is just the reverse. For the Olynthians know well 5 that they are not fighting now for honour and glory, nor for a strip of territory, but to avert the devastation and enslavement of their country. They know how he treated those who betrayed to him their city at Amphipolis, and those who received him at Pydna ; and it is, I imagine, universally true that tyranny is a faithless friend to a free state, and that most of all, when they occupy adjoining territories. With 6 this knowledge, men of Athens, and with all the reflections that the occasion calls for in your minds, I say that now, if ever before, you must make your resolve, rouse all your energies, and give your minds to the war you must contribute gladly, you must go forth in person, you must leave nothing undone. There is no longer any reason or excuse remaining, which can justify you in refusing to do your 7 duty. For every one was but recently harping on the desirability of exciting Olynthus to war with Philip; and this has now come to pass of itself, and in the way which most completely suits your interests. Had they taken up the war because you had persuaded them to do so, their alliance might perhaps have been precarious, and their resolution might only have carried them a certain way. But now their detestation of Philip is based upon grievances which affect themselves; and we may suppose that a hostility which is occasioned by their own fears and sufferings will be a lasting 8 one. Since, therefore, men of Athens, such an opportunity has been thrown in your way, you must not let it go, nor fall victims to the mistake from which you have often suffered before. If, for instance, when we had returned from our expedition in aid of the Euboeans, and Hierax and Stratocles came from Amphipolis and stood upon this platform and urged us to sail and take over the city; if, I say, we had continued to display in our own interest the eagerness which we displayed in the deliverance of the Euboeans, you would have kept Amphipolis then, and we should have been free 9 from all the trouble that we have had since. And again, when news kept coming of the investment of Pydna, Poteidaea, Methone, Pagasae, and all the other places—I will not stay to enumerate them all—if we had acted at once, and had gone to the rescue of the first place attacked, with the energy which we ought to have shown, we should now have found Philip much less proud and difficult to deal with. As it is, we are always sacrificing the present, always fancying that the future will turn out well of itself; and so we have raised Philip to a position of such importance as no king of Macedonia has ever before attained. And now an opportunity 10 has come to Athens, in this crisis at Olynthus, as great as any of those former ones: and I believe, men of Athens, that one who was to draw up a true account of the blessings which have been given us by the gods, would, in spite of much that is not as it should be, find great cause for thankfulness to them; and naturally so. For our many losses in the war must in fairness be set down to our own indifference; but that we did not suffer such losses long ago, and that an alliance has presented itself to us, which, if we will only take advantage of it, will act as a counterpoise to them—all this I, for one, should set down as a favour due to their goodness towards us. But it is, I imagine, in politics, as it is in money-making. If 11 a man is able to keep all that he gets, he is abundantly grateful to Fortune; but if he loses it all before he is aware, he loses with it his memory of Fortune's kindness. So it is in politics. When men have not made a right use of their opportunities, they do not remember any good that heaven may actually have granted them: for it is by the ultimate issue that men estimate all that they have enjoyed before. Therefore, men of Athens, you must pay the very utmost heed to the future, that by the better use you make of it, you may wipe out the dishonour of the past. But if you sacrifice these men also, men of 12 Athens, and Philip in consequence reduces Olynthus to subjection, I ask any of you to tell me what is to prevent him from marching where he pleases. Is there a man among you, men of Athens, who considers or studies the steps by which Philip, weak enough at first, has become so strong? First he took Amphipolis, next Pydna, then again Poteidaea, and then Methone. Next he set foot in Thessaly. Then when 13

Pherae, Pagasae, Magnesia were secured for his purposes, just as it suited him, he departed to Thrace. In Thrace, after expelling one prince and setting up another, he fell ill. When he grew easier again, he showed no inclination to take things easily, but at once attacked the Olynthians —and I am passing over his campaigns against the Illyrians and the Paeonians, against Arybbas, and in every possible direction.

14 Why, I may be asked, do I mention these things at the present moment? I wish you to understand, men of Athens, and to realize these two points: first, the unprofitableness of perpetually sacrificing your interests one by one; and, secondly, the restless activity which is a part of Philip's very being, and which will not allow him to content himself with his achievements and remain at peace. For if it is to be his fixed resolve, that he must always be aiming at something greater than he has yet attained; and ours, that we will never set ourselves resolutely to work; ask yourselves what

15 you can expect to be the end of the matter. In God's name, is there one of you so innocent as not to know that the war will be transferred from Olynthus to Attica, if we pay no heed? But if that happens, men of Athens, I fear that we shall be like men who light-heartedly borrow at a high rate of interest, and after a brief period of affluence, lose even their original estate; that like them we shall find that our carelessness has cost us dear; that through making pleasure our standard in everything, we shall find ourselves driven to do many of those unpleasant things which we wished to avoid, and shall find our position even in our own country imperilled.

16 I may be told that it is easy to criticize—any one can do that; but that a political adviser is expected to offer some

practical proposal to meet the existing situation. Now I am well aware, men of Athens, that in the event of any disappointment, it is not upon those who are responsible that your anger falls, but upon those who have spoken last upon the subject in question. Yet I do not think that consideration for my own safety should lead me to conceal my conviction as to the course which your interests demand. I say then 17 that there are two things which you must do to save the situation. You must rescue these towns for the Olynthians, and send troops to accomplish this: and you must damage Philip's country with your ships and with a second body of troops. If you neglect either of these things, our cam- 18 paign, I greatly fear, will be in vain. For suppose that you inflict damage on his country, and that he allows you to do so, while he reduces Olynthus; he will have no difficulty in repelling you when he returns. Suppose, on the other hand, that you only go to the help of Olynthus; he will see that he has nothing to fear at home, and so he will sit down before the town and remain at his task, until time enables him to get the better of the besieged. The expedition, therefore, must be large, and it must be in two parts.

Such is my view with regard to the expedition. As to 19 the sources of supply, you have funds, men of Athens—funds larger than any one else in the world; but you appropriate these without scruple, just as you choose. Now if you will assign these to your troops, you need no further supplies: otherwise, not only do you need further supplies—you are destitute of supplies altogether. 'Well' (does someone say?), 'do you move that this money should form a war-fund?' I assure you that I make no such motion. For while I do 20 indeed believe that a force ought to be made ready [and that this money should form a war-fund], and that the receipt of money should be connected, as part of one and the same system, with the performance of duty ; you, on the contrary, think it right to take the money, after your present fashion, for your festivals, and spare yourselves trouble. And therefore, I suppose, our only resource is a general tax—larger or smaller, according to the amount required. In any case, we need funds, and without funds nothing can be done that we ought to do. Various other sources of supply are suggested by different persons. Choose whichever you think best of these, and get to work, while you have the opportunity.

21 It is worth while to remember and to take into account the nature of Philip's position at this moment. For neither are his affairs at present in such good order, or in so perfectly satisfactory a state, as might appear to any but a careful observer ; nor would he ever have commenced this present war, if he had thought that he would really have to fight. He hoped at first that by his mere advance he would carry all before him ; and he has since discovered his mistake. This disappointment, then, is the first thing which disturbs him and causes him great despondency : and next there is 22 the disposition of the Thessalians, naturally inconstant as we know it has always been found by all men ; and what it has always been, that, in the highest degree, Philip finds it now. For they have formally resolved to demand from him the restitution of Pagasae ; they have prevented him from fortifying Magnesia, and I myself heard it stated that they intend even to refuse him the enjoyment of their harbour and market dues for the future. These, they say, should go to maintain the public administration of Thessaly, instead of being taken by Philip. But if he is deprived of these funds,

the resources from which he must maintain his mercenaries will be reduced to the narrowest limits. Nay, more: we must 23 surely suppose that the chieftains of the Paeonians and Illyrians, and in fact all such personages—would prefer freedom to slavery; for they are not accustomed to obey orders, and the man, they say, is a bully. Heaven knows, there is nothing incredible in the statement. Unmerited success is to foolish minds a fountain-head of perversity, so that it is often harder for men to keep the good they have, than it was to obtain it. It is for you then, men of Athens, to regard his difficulty as your 24 opportunity, to take up your share of the burden with readiness, to send embassies to secure all that is required, to join the forces yourselves, and to stir up every one else to do so. Only consider what would happen, if Philip got such an opportunity to strike at us, and there was war on our frontier. Can you not imagine how readily he would march against us? Does it arouse no shame in you, that, when you have the opportunity, you should not dare to do to him even as much as you would have to suffer, were he able to inflict it?

There is a further point, men of Athens, which must not 25 escape you. I mean that you have now to choose whether you are to carry on war yonder, or whether he is to do so in your own country. If the resistance of Olynthus is maintained, you will fight there and will inflict damage on Philip's territory, while you remain secure in the enjoyment of this land of your own which you now possess. But if Philip captures Olynthus, who is to hinder him from marching to Athens? The Thebans? It seems, I fear, too bitter a thing to say; 26 but they will be glad to join him in the invasion. The Phocians? They cannot protect their own country, unless you go to their aid, or some other power. 'But, my good Sir,' you say, 'he will not want to march here.' And yet it would be one of the strangest things in the world, if, when he has the power, he does not carry out the threats, which he 27 now blurts out in spite of the folly that they show. But I suppose that I need not even point out how vast is the difference between war here and war in his country. For had you to camp outside the walls yourselves, for only thirty days, and to take from the country such things as men in camp must have—and I am assuming that there is no enemy in the country—I believe that the loss your farmers would suffer would exceed your whole expenditure on the war up to the present time. What then must we think will be the extent of our loss, if ever war comes to our doors? And besides the loss there is his insolence, and the shame of our position, which to right-minded men is as serious as any loss.

28 When you take a comprehensive view of these things you must all go to the rescue and stave the war off yonder; you who are well-to-do, in order that, with a small expense in defence of the great fortunes which you quite rightly enjoy, you may reap the benefit of the remainder without fear; you who are of military age, that you may gain your experience of war in Philip's country, and so become formidable guardians of a fatherland unspoiled; and your orators, that they may find it easy to render an account of their public life; for your judgement upon their conduct will itself depend upon the position in which you find yourselves. And may that be a happy one, on every ground!

THE SECOND OLYNTHIAC

MANY as are the occasions, men of Athens, on which we may discern the manifestation of the goodwill of Heaven towards this city, one of the most striking is to be seen in the circumstances of the present time. For that men should have been found to carry on war against Philip; men whose territory borders on his and who possess some power; men, above all, whose sentiments in regard to the war are such that they think of the proposed compact with him, not only as untrustworthy, but as the very ruin of their country—this seems to be certainly the work of a superhuman, a divine, beneficence. 1

And so, men of Athens, we must take care that we do not treat ourselves less well than circumstances have treated us. For it is a shameful thing—nay, it is the very depth of shame—to throw away openly, not only cities and places which were once in our power, but even the allies and the opportunities which have been provided for us by Fortune. 2

Now to describe at length the power of Philip, men of Athens, and to incite you to the performance of your duty by such a recital, is not, I think, a satisfactory proceeding; and for this reason—that while all that can be said on this subject tends to Philip's glory, it is a story of failure on our part. For the greater the extent to which his success surpasses his deserts, the greater is the admiration with which the world regards him; while, for your part, the more you have fallen short of the right use of your opportunities, the greater is the disgrace that you have incurred. I will therefore pass 3 4 over such considerations. For any honest inquirer must see that the causes of Philip's rise to greatness lie in Athens, and not in himself. Of the services for which he has to thank those whose policy is determined by his interest—services for which you ought to require their punishment—the present is not, I see, the moment to speak. But apart from these, there are things which may be said, and which it is better that you should all have heard—things which (if you will examine them aright) constitute a grave reproach against him; and these I will try to tell you.

5 If I called him perjured and faithless, without giving his actions in evidence, my words would be treated as idle abuse, and rightly: and it happens that to review all his actions up to the present time, and to prove the charge in every case, requires only a short speech. It is well, I think, that the story should be told, for it will serve two purposes; first, to make plain the real badness of the man's character; and secondly, to let those who are over-alarmed at Philip, as if he were invincible, see that he has come to the end of all those forms of deceit by which he rose to greatness, and that 6 his career is already drawing to its close. For I, too, men of Athens, should be regarding Philip with intense fear and admiration, if I saw that his rise was the result of a righteous policy. But when I study and consider the facts, I find that originally, when certain persons wished to drive from your presence the Olynthians who desired to address you from this place, Philip won over our innocent minds by saying that he would deliver up Amphipolis to us, and by inventing 7 the famous secret understanding; that he afterwards conciliated the Olynthians by seizing Poteidaea, which was yours, and injuring their former allies by handing it over to them-

selves; and that, last of all, he recently won over the Thessalians, by promising to give up Magnesia to them, and undertaking to carry on the war with the Phocians on their behalf. There is absolutely no one who has ever had dealings with him that he has not deluded; and it is by deceiving and winning over, one after another, those who in their blindness did not realize what he was, that he has risen as he has done. And therefore, just as it was by these deceptions that he 8 rose to greatness, in the days when each people fancied that he intended to do some service to themselves; so it is these same deceptions which should drag him down again, now that he stands convicted of acting for his own ends throughout. Such, then, is the crisis, men of Athens, to which Philip's fortunes have now come. If it is not so, let any one come forward and show me (or rather you) that what I say is untrue; or that those who have been deceived at the outset trust him as regards the future; or that those who have been brought into unmerited bondage would not gladly be free.

But if any of you, while agreeing with me so far, still 9 fancies that Philip will maintain his hold by force, because he has already occupied fortified posts and harbours and similar positions, he is mistaken. When power is cemented by goodwill, and the interest of all who join in a war is the same, then men are willing to share the labour, to endure the misfortunes, and to stand fast. But when a man has become strong, as Philip has done, by a grasping and wicked policy, the first excuse, the least stumble, throws him from his seat and dissolves the alliance. It is impossible, men of 10 Athens, utterly impossible, to acquire power that will last, by unrighteousness, by perjury, and by falsehood. Such power holds out for a moment, or for a brief hour; it blossoms brightly, perhaps, with fair hopes; but time detects the fraud, and the flower falls withered about its stem. In a house or a ship, or any other structure, it is the foundations that must be strongest; and no less, I believe, must the principles, which are the foundation of men's actions, be those of truth and righteousness. Such qualities are not to be seen to-day in the past acts of Philip.

11 I say, then, that we should help the Olynthians; and the best and quickest method which can be proposed is the method which I approve. Further, we should send an embassy to the Thessalians—to some, to inform them of our intention; to others, to spur them on; for even now they have resolved to demand the restitution of Pagasae, and to 12 make representations in regard to Magnesia. Take care, however, men of Athens, that our envoys may not only have words to speak, but also actions of yours to point to. Let it be seen that you have gone forth in a manner that is worthy of Athens, and are already in action. Words without the reality must always appear a vain and empty thing, and above all when they come from Athens; for the more we seem to excel in the glib use of such language, the more it is 13 distrusted by every one. The change, then, which is pointed out to them must be great, the conversion striking. They must see you paying your contributions, marching to war, doing everything with a will, if any of them is to listen to you. And if you resolve to accomplish all this in very deed, as it should be accomplished, not only will the feeble and untrustworthy nature of Philip's alliances be seen, but the weakness of his own empire and power will also be detected.

14 The power and empire of Macedonia is, indeed, to speak generally, an element which tells considerably as an addition to

any other power. You found it so when it helped you against the Olynthians in the days of Timotheus; the Olynthians in their turn found its help of some value, in combination with their own strength, against Poteidaea; and it has recently come to the aid of the Thessalians, in their disordered and disturbed condition, against the ruling dynasty: and wherever even a small addition is made to a force, it helps in every way. But in itself the Macedonian Empire is weak and 15 full of manifold evils. Philip has in fact rendered his own tenure of it even more precarious than it naturally was, by these very wars and campaigns which might be supposed to prove his power. For you must not imagine, men of Athens, that Philip and his subjects delight in the same things. Philip has a passion for glory—that is his ambition; and he has deliberately chosen to risk the consequences of a life of action and danger, preferring the glory of achieving more than any King of Macedonia before him to a life of security. But his 16 subjects have no share in the honour and glory. Constantly battered about by all these expeditions, up and down, they are vexed with incessant hardships: they are not suffered to pursue their occupations or attend to their own affairs: for the little that they produce, as best they can, they can find no market, the trading stations of the country being closed on account of the war. From these facts it is not 17 difficult to discover the attitude of the Macedonians in general towards Philip; and as for the mercenaries and Infantry of the Guard who surround him, though they have the reputation of being a fine body of well-drilled warriors, I am told by a man who has been in Macedonia, and who is incapable of falsehood, that they are no better than any other body of men. Granted that there may be 18

experienced campaigners and fighters among them; yet, he tells me, Philip is so jealous of honour, that he thrusts all such men away from him, in his anxiety to get the credit of every achievement for himself; for in addition to all his other qualities, his jealousy is insurpassable. On the other hand, any generally temperate or upright man, who cannot endure the dissolute life there, day by day, nor the drunkenness and the lewd revels, is thrust on one side and counts
19 for nothing. Thus he is left with brigands and flatterers, and men who, when in their cups, indulge in dances of a kind which I shrink from naming to you now. And it is evident that this report is true; for men whom every one tried to drive out of Athens, as far viler than even the very juggler in the street—Callias the public slave and men like him, players of farces, composers of indecent songs, written at the expense of their companions in the hope of raising a laugh—these
20 are the men he likes and keeps about him. You may think that these are trivial things, men of Athens: but they are weighty, in the judgement of every right-minded man, as illustrations of the temper with which Philip is cursed. At present, I suppose, these facts are overshadowed by his continual prosperity. Success has a wonderful power of throwing a veil over shameful things like these. But let him only stumble, and then all these features in his character will be displayed in their true light. And I believe, men of Athens, that the revelation is not far off, if Heaven be willing
21 and you desirous of it. So long as a man is in good health, he is unconscious of any weakness; but if any illness comes upon him, the disturbance affects every weak point, be it a rupture or a sprain or anything else that is unsound in his constitution. And as with the body, so it is with a city or

a tyrant. So long as they are at war abroad, the mischief is hidden from the world at large, but the close grapple of war on the frontier brings all to light.

Now if any of you, men of Athens, seeing Philip's good fortune, thinks that this makes him a formidable enemy to fight against, he reasons like a sensible man: for fortune weighs heavily in the scale—nay, fortune is everything, in all human affairs. And yet, if I were given the choice, it is the fortune of Athens that I should choose, rather than that of Philip, provided that you yourselves are willing to act even to a small extent as you should act. For I see that there are far more abundant grounds for expecting the goodwill of Heaven on your side than on his. But here, of course, we are sitting idle; and one who is a sluggard himself cannot require his friends to help him, much less the gods. It is not to be wondered at that Philip, who goes on campaigns and works hard himself, and is always at the scene of action, and lets no opportunity go, no season pass, should get the better of us who delay and pass resolutions and ask for news; nor do I wonder at it. It is the opposite that would have been wonderful—if we, who do nothing that those who are at war ought to do, were successful against one who leaves nothing undone. But this I do wonder at, that you who once raised your hand against Sparta, in defence of the rights of the Hellenes—you, who with opportunities often open to you for grasping large advantages for yourselves, would not take them, but to secure for others their rights spent your own fortunes in war-contributions, and always bore the brunt of the dangers of the campaign—that you, I say, are now shrinking from marching, and hesitating to make any contribution to save your own possessions; and that, though you have often saved the rest of the Hellenes, now all together and now each in their turn, you are sitting idle, when you 25 have lost what was your own. I wonder at this; and I wonder also, men of Athens, that none of you is able to reckon up the time during which you have been fighting with Philip, and to consider what you have been doing while all this time has been going by. Surely you must know that it is while we have been delaying, hoping that some one else would act, accusing one another, bringing one another to trial, hoping anew—in fact, doing practically what we are 26 doing now—that all the time has passed. And have you now so little sense, men of Athens, as to hope that the very same policy, which has made the position of the city a bad one instead of a good, will actually make it a good one instead of a bad? Why, it is contrary both to reason and to nature to think so! It is always much easier to retain than to acquire. But now, owing to the war, none of our old possessions is left for us to retain; and so we must needs 27 acquire. This, therefore, is our own personal and immediate duty; and accordingly I say that you must contribute funds, you must go on service in person with a good will, you must accuse no one before you have become masters of the situation; and then you must honour those who deserve praise, and punish the guilty, with a judgement based upon the actual facts. You must get rid of all excuses and all deficiencies on your own part; you cannot examine mercilessly the actions of others, unless you yourselves have 28 done all that your duty requires. For why is it, do you think, men of Athens, that all the generals whom you dispatch avoid this war, and discover private wars of their own—if a little of the truth must be told even about the generals?

It is because in this war the prizes for which the war is waged are yours, and if they are captured, you will take them immediately for your own; but the dangers are the personal privilege of your commanders, and no pay is forthcoming: while in those wars the dangers are less, and the profits—Lampsacus, Sigeum, and the ships which they plunder—go to the commanders and their men. Each force therefore takes the road that leads to its own advantage. For your part, 29 when you turn your attention to the serious condition of your affairs, you first bring the commanders to trial; and then, when you have given them a hearing, and have been told of the difficulties which I have described, you acquit them. The result, therefore, is that while you are quarrelling with one another and broken into factions—one party persuaded of this, another of that—the public interest suffers. You used, men of Athens, to pay taxes by Boards: to-day you conduct your politics by Boards. On either side there is an orator as leader, and a general under him; and for the Three Hundred, there are those who come to shout. The rest of you distribute yourselves between the two parties, some on either side. This system you must give up: you 30 must even now become your own masters; you must give to all alike their share in discussion, in speech and in action. If you assign to one body of men the function of issuing orders to you, like tyrants; to another, that of compulsory service as trierarchs or tax-payers or soldiers; and to another, only that of voting their condemnation, without taking any share in the labour, nothing that ought to be done will be done in time. For the injured section will always be in default, and you will only have the privilege of punishing them instead of the enemy. To sum up, all must contribute, 31 each according to his wealth, in a fair proportion: all must go on active service in turn, until you have all served: you must give a hearing to all who come forward, and choose the best course out of all that you hear—not the course proposed by this or that particular person. If you do this, you will not only commend the proposer of that course at the time, but you will commend yourselves hereafter, for the whole position of your affairs will be a better one.

THE THIRD OLYNTHIAC

VERY different reflections suggest themselves to my mind, 1 men of Athens, when I turn my eyes to our real situation, and when I think of the speeches that I hear. For I observe that the speeches are all concerned with the taking of vengeance upon Philip; whereas in reality matters have gone so far, that we have to take care that we are not ourselves the first to suffer: so that those who speak of vengeance are actually, as it seems to me, suggesting to you a false conception of the situation which you are discussing. That there was a time 2 when the city could both keep her own possessions in safety, and punish Philip, I am very well aware. For it was not long ago, but within my own lifetime, that both these things were so. But I am convinced that it is now quite enough for us as a first step to make sure of the preservation of our allies. If this is safely secured, we shall then be able to consider upon whom vengeance is to fall, and in what way. But until the first step is properly conceived, I consider it idle to say anything whatever about the last.

If ever the most anxious deliberation was required, it is 3 required in the present crisis; and my greatest difficulty is not to know what is the proper advice to give you in regard to the situation: I am at a loss rather to know, men of Athens, in what manner I should address you in giving it. For I am convinced by what I have heard with my own ears in this place that, for the most part, the objects of our policy have slipped from our grasp, not because we do not understand what our duty is, but because we will not do it; and I ask you to suffer me, if I speak without reserve, and to consider only whether I speak truly, and with this object in view—that the future may be better than the past. For you see that it is because certain speakers make your gratification the aim of their addresses, that things have gone on getting worse, till at last the extremity has been reached.

4 I think it necessary, first, to remind you of a few of the events which have taken place. You remember, men of Athens, that two or three years ago the news came that Philip was in Thrace, besieging Heraeon Teichos. That was in the month of November. Amidst all the discussion and commotion which took place in this Assembly, you passed a resolution that forty warships should be launched, that men under forty-five years of age should embark in person, and that we 5 should pay a war-tax of 60 talents. That year came to an end, and there followed July, August, September. In the latter month, after the Mysteries, and with reluctance, you dispatched Charidemus with ten ships, carrying no soldiers, and 5 talents of silver. For so soon as news had come that Philip was sick or dead—both reports were brought—you dismissed the armament, men of Athens, thinking that there was no longer any occasion for the expedition. But it was the very occasion; for had we then gone to the scene of action with the same enthusiasm which marked our resolution to do so, Philip would not have been preserved to trouble us 6 to-day. What was done then cannot be altered. But now a critical moment in another campaign has arrived; and it is in view of this, and to prevent you from falling into the same error, that I have recalled these facts. How then shall we use this opportunity, men of Athens? For unless you will

go to the rescue 'with might and main to the utmost of your power', mark how in every respect you will have served Philip's interest by your conduct of the war. At the outset the 7 Olynthians possessed considerable strength, and such was the position of affairs, that neither did Philip feel safe against them, nor they against Philip. We made peace with them, and they with us. It was as it were a stumbling-block in Philip's path, and an annoyance to him, that a great city which had made a compact with us should sit watching for any opportunity he might offer. We thought that we ought to excite them to war with him by every means; and now this much-talked-of event has come to pass—by what means, I need not relate. What course then is open to us, men of Athens, 8 but to go to their aid resolutely and eagerly? I can see none. Apart from the shame in which we should be involved, if we let anything be lost through our negligence, I can see, men of Athens, that the subsequent prospect would be alarming in no small degree, when the attitude of the Thebans towards us is what it is, when the funds of the Phocians are exhausted, and when there is no one to prevent Philip, so soon as he has made himself master of all that at present occupies him, from bringing his energies to bear upon the situation further south. But if any of you is putting off until then his deter- 9 mination to do his duty, he must be desirous of seeing the terrors of war close at hand, when he need only hear of them at a distance, and of seeking helpers for himself, when now he can give help to others. For that this is what it must come to, if we sacrifice the present opportunity, we must all, I think, be fairly well aware.

'But,' some one may say, 'we have all made up our minds 10 that we must go to their aid, and we will go. Only tell us how we are to do it.' Now do not be surprised, men of Athens, if I give an answer which will be astonishing to most of you. You must appoint a Legislative Commission. But when the commissioners meet, you must not enact a single law —you have laws enough—you must cancel the laws which, in

11 view of present circumstances, are injurious to you. I mean the laws which deal with the Festival Fund—to put it quite plainly—and some of those which deal with military service: for the former distribute your funds as festival-money to those who remain at home; while the latter give immunity to malingerers, and thereby also take the heart out of those who want to do their duty. When you have cancelled these laws, and made the path safe for one who would give the best advice, then you can look for some one to propose what you

12 all know to be expedient. But until you have done this, you must not expect to find a man who will be glad to advise you for the best, and be ruined by you for his pains; for you will find no one, particularly when the only result will be that some unjust punishment will be inflicted on the proposer or mover of such measures, and that instead of helping matters at all, he will only have made it even more dangerous in future than it is at present to give you the best advice. Aye, and you should require the repeal of these laws, men of Athens, from the very persons who proposed them.

13 It is not fair that those who originally proposed them should enjoy the popularity which was fraught with such mischief to the whole State, and that the unpopularity, which would lead to an improvement in the condition of us all, should be visited to his cost upon one who now advises you for the best. Until you have thus prepared the way, men of Athens, you must entertain no expectation whatever that any one will be influential

enough here to transgress these laws with impunity, or senseless enough to fling himself to certain ruin.

14 At the same time, men of Athens, you must not fail to realize this further point. No resolution is worth anything, without the willingness to perform at least what you have resolved, and that heartily. For if decrees by themselves could either compel you to do what you ought, or could realize their several objects unaided, you would not be decreeing many things and performing few—nay, none—of the things that you decree, nor would Philip have insulted you so long. 15 If decrees could have done it, he would have paid the penalty long ago. But it is not so. Actions come later than speeches and voting in order of procedure, but in effectiveness they are before either and stronger than either. It is action that is still needed; all else you already have. For you have those among you, men of Athens, who can tell you what your duty is; and no one is quicker than you are to understand the speaker's bidding. Aye, and you will be able to carry it out even now, if you act aright. 16 What time, what opportunity, do you look for, better than the present? When, if not now, will you do your duty? Has not the man seized every position from us already? If he becomes master of this country too, will not our fate be the most shameful in the world? And the men whom we promised to be ready to save, if they went to war—are they not now at war? 17 Is he not our enemy? Are not our possessions in his hands? Is he not a barbarian? Is he not anything that you choose to call him? In God's name, when we have let everything go, when we have all but put everything into his hands, shall we then inquire at large who is responsible for it all? That we shall never admit our own responsibility, I am perfectly sure.

Just so amid the perils of war, none of those who have run away accuses himself; he accuses his general, his neighbour—any one but himself; and yet, I suppose, all who have run away have helped to cause the defeat. He who now blames the rest might have stood fast; and if every one had done so, the

18 victory would have been theirs. And so now, if a particular speaker's advice is not the best, let another rise and make a proposal, instead of blaming him; and if some other has better advice to give, carry it out, and good fortune be with you. What? Is the advice disagreeable? That is no longer the speaker's fault—unless, of course, he leaves out the prayer that you expect of him. There is no difficulty in the prayer, men of Athens; a man need only compress all his desires into a short sentence. But to make his choice, when the question for discussion is one of practical policy, is by no means equally easy. *Then* a man is bound to choose what is best, instead

19 of what is pleasant, if both are not possible at once. But suppose that some one is able, without touching the Festival Fund, to suggest other sources of supply for military purposes—is not he the better adviser? Certainly, men of Athens—if such a thing *is* possible. But I should be surprised if it ever has happened or ever should happen to any one to find, after spending what he has upon wrong objects, that what he has *not* is wealth enough to enable him to effect right ones. Such arguments as these find, I think, their great support in each man's personal desire, and, for that reason, nothing is easier than to deceive oneself;

20 what a man desires, he actually fancies to be true. But the reality often follows no such principle. Consider the matter, therefore, men of Athens, after this fashion; consider in what way our objects can be realized under the circumstances,

and in what way you will be able to make the expedition and to receive your pay. Surely it is not like sober or high-minded men to submit light-heartedly to the reproach which must follow upon any shortcomings in the operations of the war through want of funds—to seize your weapons and march against Corinthians and Megareans, and then to allow Philip to enslave Hellenic cities, because you cannot find rations for your troops.

21 These words do not spring from a wanton determination to court the ill-will of any party among you. I am neither so foolish nor so unfortunate as to desire unpopularity when I do not believe that I am doing any good. But a loyal citizen ought, in my judgement, to care more for the safety of his country's fortunes than for the popularity of his utterances. Such, I have heard, and perhaps you have heard it also, was the principle which the orators of our forefather's time habitually followed in public life—those orators who are praised by all who rise to address you, though they are far from imitating them—the great Aristides, and Nicias, and my own namesake, and Pericles. 22 But ever since these speakers have appeared who are always asking you, 'what would you like?' 'what may I propose for you?' 'what can I do to please you?' the interests of the city have been wantonly given away for the sake of the pleasure and gratification of the moment; and we see the consequences—the fortunes of the speakers prosper, while your own are in a shameful plight. 23 And yet consider, men of Athens, the main characteristics of the achievements of your forefathers' time, and those of your own. The description will be brief and familiar to you; for you need not have recourse to the history of others, when your own will furnish examples, by following

24 which you may achieve prosperity. Our forefathers, who were not courted and caressed by their politicians as you are by these persons to-day, were leaders of the Hellenes, with their goodwill, for forty-five years; they brought up into the Acropolis more than 10,000 talents; the king who then ruled Macedonia obeyed them as a foreigner ought to obey a Hellenic people; serving in person, they set up many glorious trophies for victories by land and sea; and alone of all mankind they left behind them, as the crown of their
25 exploits, a fame that is beyond the reach of envy. Such was the part they played in the Hellenic world: and now contemplate the manner of men they were in the city, both in public and in private life. As public men, they gave us buildings and objects of such beauty and grandeur, in the temples which they built and the offerings which they dedicated in them, that no room has been left for any of those that come after to surpass them: while in private life they
26 were so modest, so intensely loyal to the spirit of the constitution, that if any one actually knows what the house of Aristides, or Miltiades, or any other of the glorious men of that day, is like, he can see that it is no more imposing than those of their neighbours. For it was not to win a fortune that they undertook affairs of State; but each thought it his duty to add to the common weal. And thus, acting in a spirit of good faith towards the Hellenes, of piety towards the gods, and of equality towards one another, they naturally attained
27 great prosperity. Such was the national life of those times, when those whom I have mentioned were the foremost men in the State. How do matters stand to-day, thanks to these worthy persons? Is there any likeness, any resemblance, to old times? Thanks to them (and though I might say much,

I pass over all but this), when we had the field, as you see, completely open to us—when the Spartans had been ruined, and the Thebans had their hands full, and no other power could seriously dispute the supremacy with us on the field of battle—when we could have retained our own possessions in safety, and have stood as umpires of the rights of others—we have been deprived of our own territory; we have spent 28 more than 1,500 talents to no good purpose; the allies whom we had gained in the war, these persons have lost in time of peace; and we have trained Philip to be the powerful enemy to us that he is. Let any one rise and tell me how Philip has grown so strong, if we ourselves are not the source of his strength. 'But, my good Sir,' you say, 29 'if we are badly off in these respects, we are at any rate better off at home.' And where is the proof of this? Is it in the whitewashing of the battlements, the mending of the roads, the fountains, and all such trumperies? Look then at the men whose policy gives you these things. Some of them who were poor have become rich; others, who were unknown to fame, have risen to honour; some of them have provided themselves with private houses more imposing than our public buildings; and the lower the fortunes of the city have fallen, the higher theirs have risen.

What is the cause of all these things? Why is it that all 30 was well then, and all is amiss to-day? It is because then the people itself dared to act and to serve in the army; and so the people was master of its politicians; all patronage was in its own hands; any separate individual was content to receive from the people his share of honour or office or other emolument. The reverse is now the case. All patron- 31 age is in the hands of the politicians, while you, the people, emasculated, stripped of money and allies, have been reduced to the position of servile supernumeraries, content if they give you distributions of festival-money, or organize a procession at the Boedromia; and to crown all this bravery, you are expected also to thank them for giving you what is your own. They pen you up closely in the city; they entice you to these delights; they tame you till you come 32 to their hand. But a high and generous spirit can never, I believe, be acquired by men whose actions are mean and poor; for such as a man's practice is, such must his spirit be. And in all solemnity I should not be surprised if I suffered greater harm at your hands for telling you the things that I have told you, than the men who have brought them to pass. Even freedom of speech is not possible on all subjects in this place, and I wonder that it has been granted me to-day.

33 If, even now, you will rid yourselves of these habits, if you will resolve to join the forces and to act worthily of yourselves, converting the superfluities which you enjoy at home into resources to secure our advantage abroad, then it may be, men of Athens, it may be, that you will gain some great and final good, and will be rid of these your perquisites, which are like the diet that a physician gives a sick man—diet which neither puts strength into him nor lets him die. For these sums which you now share among yourselves are neither large enough to give you any adequate assistance, nor small enough to let you renounce them and go about your business; but these it is that[1] 34 increase the indolence of every individual among you. 'Is it, then, paid service that you suggest?' some one will ask. I do, men of Athens; and a system for immediate

[1] *ἔστι ταῦτα τά.*

enforcement which will embrace all alike; so that each, while receiving his share of the public funds may supply whatever service the State requires of him.[1] If we can remain at peace, then he will do better to stay at home, free from the necessity of doing anything discreditable through poverty. But if a situation like the present occurs, then supported by these same sums, he will serve loyally in person, in defence of his country. If a man is outside the military age, then let him take, in his place among the rest, that which he now receives irregularly and without doing any service, and let him act as an overseer and manager of business that must be done. In short, without adding or 35 subtracting anything, beyond a small sum, and only removing the want of system, my plan reduces the State to order, making your receipt of payment, your service in the army or the courts, and your performance of any duty which the age of each of you allows, and the occasion requires, all part of one and the same system. But it has been no part of my proposal that we should assign the due of those who act to those who do nothing; that we should be idle ourselves and enjoy our leisure helplessly, listening to tales of victories won by somebody's mercenaries; for this is what happens now. Not that I blame one who is doing some part of your 36 duty for you; but I require you to do for yourselves the things for which you honour others, and not to abandon the position which your fathers won through many a glorious peril, and bequeathed to you.

I think I have told you all that, in my belief, your interest demands. May you choose the course which will be for the good of the city and of you all!

[1] τοῦτο παρέχῃ.

ON THE PEACE (Or. V)

[*Introduction.* After the fall of Olynthus in 348, the Athenians, on the proposal of Eubulus, sent embassies to the Greek States in the Peloponnese and elsewhere, to invite them to join in a coalition against Philip. Aeschines went for this purpose to Megalopolis, and did his best to counteract Philip's influence in Arcadia. When the embassies proved unsuccessful, it became clear that peace must be made on such terms as were possible. Philip himself was anxious for peace, since he wished to cross the Pass of Thermopylae without such opposition from Athens as he had encountered in 352, and to be free from the attacks of hostile ships upon his ports. Even before the fall of Olynthus, informal communications passed between himself and Athens (see Speech on Embassy, §§ 12, 94, 315); and in consequence of these, Philocrates proposed and the Assembly passed a decree, under which ten ambassadors were appointed to go to Philip and invite him to send plenipotentiaries to Athens to conclude a peace. Demosthenes (who had strongly supported Philocrates) was among the ten, as well as Aeschines and Philocrates himself. Delighted with Philip's reception of them, and greatly attracted by his personality, the ambassadors returned with a letter from him, promising in general terms to confer great benefits upon Athens, if he were granted alliance as well as peace: in the meantime he undertook not to interfere with the towns allied to Athens in the Chersonese. Demosthenes proposed (in the Council, of which he was a member in the year 347–346) the usual complimentary resolution in honour of the ambassadors, and on his motion it was resolved to hold two meetings of the Assembly, on the 18th and 19th of the month Elaphebolion (i. e. probably just after the middle of April 346), when Philip's envoys would have arrived, to discuss the terms of peace. The envoys—Antipater, Parmenio, and Eurylochus—reached Athens shortly after this; and before the first of the two meetings was held, the Synod of the allies of Athens, now assembled in the city, agreed to peace on such terms as the Athenian people should decide, but added a proposal that it should be permitted to any Greek State to become a party to the Peace within three months. They said nothing of alliance. Of the two meetings of the Assembly, in view of the conflicting statements of Demosthenes and Aeschines, only a probable account can be given. At the first, Philocrates proposed that alliance as well as peace should be made by Athens and her allies with Philip and his allies, on the understanding that both parties should keep what they *de facto* possessed—a provision entailing the renunciation by Athens of Amphipolis and Poteidaea; but that the Phocians and the people of Halus should be excluded. Aeschines opposed this strongly; and both he and Demosthenes claim to have supported the resolution of the allies, which would have given the excluded peoples a chance of sharing the advantage of the Peace. The feeling of the Assembly was with them, although the Phocians had recently insulted the Athenians by declining to give up to Proxenus (the Athenian admiral) the towns guarding the approaches to Thermopylae, which they had themselves offered to place in the hands of Athens. But Philocrates obtained the postponement of the decision till the next day. On the next day, if not before, it became plain that Philip's envoys would not consent to forgo the exclusion of the Phocians and Halus; but in order that the Assembly might be induced to pass the resolution, the clause expressly excluding them was dropped, and peace and alliance were made between Athens and Philip, each with their allies.[1] Even this was not secured

[1] The term 'the allies of Athens' was ambiguous. It might be taken (as it was taken by Philip and his envoys) to include only the remaining members of the League (see p. 9), who were represented by the Synod then sitting, and whose policy Athens could control. But it was evidently possible to put a wider interpretation upon it, as the Assembly probably did and as Demosthenes often does (e.g. Speech on Embassy, § 278), and to understand it as including the Phocians and others

before Aeschines and his friends had deprecated rash attempts to imitate the exploits of antiquity by continuing the war, and had explained that Philip could not openly accept the Phocians as allies, but that when the Peace was concluded, he would satisfy all the wishes of the Athenians in every way; while Eubulus threatened the people with immediate war, involving personal service and heavy taxation, unless they accepted Philocrates' decree. A few days afterwards the Athenians and the representatives of the allies took the oath to observe the Peace: nothing was said about the Phocians and Halus: Cersobleptes' representative was probably not permitted to swear with the rest. The same ten ambassadors as before were instructed to receive Philip's oath, and the oaths of his allies, to arrange for the ransom of prisoners, and generally to treat with Philip in the interests of Athens. Demosthenes urged his colleagues (and obtained an instruction from the Council to this effect) to sail at once, in order that Philip, who was now in Thrace, might not make conquests at the expense of Athens before ratifying the Peace; but they delayed at Oreus, went by land, instead of under the escort of Proxenus by sea, and only reached Pella (the Macedonian capital) twenty-three days after leaving Athens. Philip did not arrive for twenty-seven days more. By this time he had taken Cersobleptes prisoner, and captured Serrhium, Doriscus, and other Thracian towns, which were held by Athenian troops sent to assist Cersobleptes. Demosthenes was now openly at variance with his colleagues. He had no doubt realized the necessity of peace, but probably regarded the exclusion of the Phocians as unwarrantable, and thought that the policy of his colleagues must end in Philip's conquest of all Greece. At Pella he occupied himself in negotiations for the ransom of prisoners. After taking the oath, Philip kept the ambassadors with him until he had made all preparations for his march southward, and during this time he played with them and with the envoys from the other

(such as Cersobleptes) with whom Athens had a treaty of alliance. Much of the trouble which followed arose out of this ambiguity.

Greek States who were present at the same time. His intention of marching to Thermopylae was clear; but he seems to have led all alike to suppose that he would fulfil their particular wishes when he had crossed the Pass. The ambassadors accompanied him to Pherae, where the oath was taken by the representatives of Philip's allies; the Phocians, Halus, and Cersobleptes were excluded from the Peace. (Halus was taken by Philip's army shortly afterwards.) The ambassadors of Athens then returned homewards, bearing a letter from Philip, but did not arrive at Athens before Philip had reached Thermopylae. On their return Demosthenes denounced them before the Council, which refused them the customary compliments, and (on Demosthenes' motion) determined to propose to the people that Proxenus with his squadron should be ordered to go to the aid of the Phocians and to prevent Philip from crossing the Pass. When the Assembly met on the 16th of Scirophorion (shortly before the middle of July), Aeschines rose first, and announced in glowing terms the intention of Philip to turn round upon Thebes and to re-establish Thespiae and Plataeae; and hinted at the restoration to Athens of Euboea and Oropus. Then Philip's letter was read, containing no promises, but excusing the delay of the ambassadors as due to his own request. The Assembly was elated at the promises announced by Aeschines; Demosthenes' attempt to contradict the announcement failed; and on Philocrates' motion, it was resolved to extend the Peace and alliance with Philip to posterity, and to declare that if the Phocians refused to surrender the Temple of Delphi to the Amphictyons, Athens would take steps against those responsible for the refusal. Demosthenes refused to serve on the Embassy appointed to convey this resolution to Philip: Aeschines was appointed, but was too ill to start. The ambassadors set out, but within a few days returned with the news that the Phocian army had surrendered to Philip (its leader, Phalaecus, and his troops being allowed to depart to the Peloponnese). The surrender had perhaps been accelerated by the news of the Athenian resolution. The Assembly, in alarm lest Philip should march southwards, now resolved to take measures of precaution and defence, and to send the same ambassadors to Philip, to do what they could. They went, Aeschines among them, and arrived in the midst of the festivities with which Philip was celebrating the success of his plans. The invitation which Philip sent to Athens—to send a force to join his own, and to assist in settling the affairs of Phocis—was (on Demosthenes' advice) declined by the Assembly; and soon afterwards another letter from Philip expressed surprise at the unfriendly attitude taken up by the Athenians towards him. Philip next summoned the Amphictyonic Council (the legitimate guardians of the Delphian Temple, on whose behalf the Thebans and Thessalians, aided by Philip, were now at war with the Phocians): and the Council, in the absence of many of its members, resolved to transfer the votes of the Phocians in the Council-meeting to Philip, to break up the Phocian towns into villages, disarming their inhabitants and taking away their horses, to require them to repay the stolen treasure to the temple by instalments, and to pronounce a curse upon those actually guilty of sacrilege, which would render them liable to arrest anywhere. The destructive part of the sentence was rigorously executed by the Thebans. In order to punish the former supporters of the Phocians, the right to precedence in consulting the oracle was transferred from Athens to Philip, by order of the Council, and the Spartans were excluded from the temple: Orchomenus and Coroneia were destroyed and their inhabitants enslaved; and Thebes became absolute mistress of all Boeotia. The Pythian games (at Delphi) in September 346 were celebrated under Philip's presidency; but both Sparta and Athens refused to send the customary deputation to them, and Philip accordingly sent envoys to Athens, along with representatives of the Amphictyons, to demand recognition for himself as an Amphictyonic power. Aeschines supported the demand, his argument being apparently to the effect that Philip had been forced to act as he had done by the Thebans and Thessalians; but the Assembly was very angry at the results (as they seemed to be) of Aeschines' diplomacy and the calamities of the Phocians; and it was only when Demosthenes, in the Speech on the Peace, advised compliance, that they were persuaded to give way. To have refused would have brought the united forces of the Amphictyonic States against Athens: and these she could not have resisted. It was therefore prudent to keep the Peace, though Demosthenes evidently regarded it only as an armistice.]

I SEE, men of Athens, that our present situation is one of great perplexity and confusion, for not only have many of our interests been sacrificed, so that it is of no use to make eloquent speeches about them; but even as regards what still remains to us, there is no general agreement in any single point as to what is expedient: some hold one view, and some another. Perplexing, moreover, and difficult as deliberation naturally is, men of Athens, you have made it far more difficult. For while all the rest of mankind are in the habit of resorting to deliberation before the event, you do not do so until afterwards: and consequently, during the whole time that falls within my memory, however high a reputation for eloquence one who upbraids you for all your errors may enjoy, the desired results and the objects of your deliberation pass out of your grasp. And yet I believe—and it is because I have convinced myself of this that I have risen—that if you resolve to abandon all clamour and contention, as becomes men who are deliberating on behalf of their country upon so great an issue, I shall be able to describe and recommend measures to you, by which the situation may be improved, and what we have sacrificed, recovered. 1 2 3

Now although I know perfectly well, men of Athens, that to speak to you about one's own earlier speeches, and about 4

oneself, is a practice which is always extremely repaying, I feel the vulgarity and offensiveness of it so strongly, that I shrink from it even when I see that it is necessary. I think, however, that you will form a better judgement on the subject on which I am about to speak, if I remind you of some few of the things which I have said
5 on certain previous occasions. In the first place, men of Athens, when at the time of the disturbances in Euboea you were being urged to assist Plutarchus, and to undertake an inglorious and costly campaign, I came forward first and unsupported to oppose this action, and was almost torn in pieces by those who for the sake of their own petty profits had induced you to commit many grave errors: and when only a short time had elapsed, along with the shame which you incurred and the treatment which you received—treatment such as no people in the world ever before experienced at the hands of those whom they went to assist—there came the recognition by all of you of the baseness of those who had urged you to this course, and of the excellence of
6 my own advice. Again, men of Athens, I observed that Neoptolemus the actor, who was allowed freedom of movement everywhere on the ground of his profession, and was doing the city the greatest mischief, was managing and directing your communications with Philip in Philip's own interest: and I came forward and informed you; and that, not to gratify any private dislike or desire to misrepresent
7 him, as subsequent events have made plain. And in this case I shall not, as before, throw the blame on any speakers or defenders of Neoptolemus—indeed, he had no defenders; it is yourselves that I blame. For had you been watching rival tragedies in the theatre, instead of discussing the vital

interests of a whole State, you could not have listened with more partiality towards him, or more prejudice against me. And yet, I believe, you have all now realized that though, 8 according to his own assertion, this visit to the enemy's country was paid in order that he might get in the debts owing to him there, and return with funds to perform his public service here; though he was always repeating the statement that it was monstrous to accuse those who were transferring their means from Macedonia to Athens; yet, when the Peace had removed all danger, he converted his real estate here into money, and took himself off with it to Philip. These then are two events which I have foretold— 9 events which, because their real character was exactly and faithfully disclosed by me, are a testimony to the speeches which I have delivered. A third, men of Athens, was the following; and when I have given you this one instance, I will immediately proceed to the subject on which I have come forward to speak. When we returned from the Embassy, after receiving from Philip his oath to maintain the Peace, there were some who promised that Thespiae and 10 Plataeae would be repeopled, and said that if Philip became master of the situation, he would save the Phocians, and would break up the city of Thebes into villages; that Oropus would be yours, and that Euboea would be restored to you in place of Amphipolis—with other hopes and deceptions of the same kind, by which you were seduced into sacrificing the Phocians in a manner that was contrary to your interest and perhaps to your honour also. But as for me, you will find that neither had I any share in this deception, nor yet did I hold my peace. On the contrary, I warned you plainly, as, I know you remember, that *I* had no knowledge and no expectations of this kind, and that I regarded such statements as nonsense.

11 All these plain instances of superior foresight on my part, men of Athens, I shall not ascribe to any cleverness, any boasted merits, of my own. I will not pretend that my foreknowledge and discernment are due to any causes but such as I will name; and they are two. The first, men of Athens, is that good fortune, which, I observe, is more 12 powerful than all the cleverness and wisdom on earth. The second is the fact that my judgement and reasoning are disinterested. No one can point to any personal gain in connexion with my public acts and words: and therefore I see what is to our interest undistorted, in the light in which the actual facts reveal it. But when you throw money into one scale of the balance, its weight carries everything with it; your judgement is instantly dragged down with it, and one who has acted so can no longer think soundly or healthily about anything.

13 Now there is one primary condition which must be observed by any one who would furnish the city with allies or contributions or anything else—he must do it without breaking the existing Peace: not because the Peace is at all admirable or creditable to you, but because, whatever its character, it would have been better, in the actual circumstances, that it should never have been made, than that having been made, it should now be broken through our action. For we have sacrificed many advantages which we possessed when we made it, and which would have rendered the war safer 14 and easier for us then than it is now. The second condition, men of Athens, is that we shall not draw on these self-styled Amphictyons, who are now assembled, until they have an

irresistible or a plausible reason for making a united war against us. My own belief is that if war broke out again between ourselves and Philip about Amphipolis or any such claim of our own, in which the Thessalians and Argives and Thebans had no interest, none of these peoples would go to war against us, least of all—and let no one raise a clamour before he hears 15 what I have to say—least of all the Thebans; not because they are in any pleasant mood towards us; not because they would not be glad to gratify Philip; but because they know perfectly well, however stupid one may think them, that if war springs up between themselves and you, *they* will get all the hardships of war for their share, while another will sit by, waiting to secure all the advantages; and they are not likely to sacrifice themselves for such a prospect, unless the origin and the cause of the war are such as concern all alike. Nor again should we, in my opinion, suffer at all, 16 if we went to war with Thebes on account of Oropus or any other purely Athenian interest. For I believe that while those who would assist ourselves or the Thebans would give their aid if their ally's own country were invaded, they would not join either in an offensive campaign. For this is the manner of alliances—such, at least, as are worth considering; and the relationship is naturally of this kind. The goodwill 17 of each ally—whether it be towards ourselves or towards the Thebans—does not imply the same interest in our conquest of others as in our existence. Our continued existence they would all desire for their own sakes; but none of them would wish that through conquest either of us should become their own masters. What is it then that I regard with apprehension? What is it that we must guard against? I fear lest a common pretext should be supplied for the coming war, a common charge against us, which will 18 appeal to all alike. For if the Argives and Messenians and Megalopolitans, and some of the other Peloponnesians who are in sympathy with them, adopt a hostile attitude towards us owing to our negotiations for peace with Sparta, and the belief that to some extent we are giving our approval to the policy which the Spartans have pursued: if the Thebans already (as we are told) detest us, and are sure to become even more hostile, because we are harbouring those whom they have exiled, and losing no opportunity of displaying our ill-will 19 towards them; and the Thessalians, because we are offering a refuge to the Phocian fugitives; and Philip, because we are preventing his admission to Amphictyonic rank; my fear is that, when each power has thus its separate reasons for resentment, they may unite in the war against us, with the decrees of the Amphictyons for their pretext: and so each may be drawn on farther than their several interests would carry them, just as they were in dealing with 20 the Phocians. For you doubtless realize that it was not through any unity in their respective ambitions, that the Thebans and Philip and the Thessalians all acted together just now. The Thebans, for instance, could not prevent Philip from marching through and occupying the passes, nor even from stepping in at the last moment to reap the credit 21 of all that they themselves had toiled for. For, as it is, though the Thebans have gained something so far as the recovery of their territory is concerned, their honour and reputation have suffered shamefully, since it now appears as though they would have gained nothing, unless Philip had crossed the Pass. This was not what they intended. They only submitted to all this in their anxiety to obtain

Orchomenus and Coroneia, and their inability to do so otherwise. And as to Philip, some persons, as you know, 22 are bold enough to say that it was not from any wish to do so that he handed over Orchomenus and Coroneia to Thebes, but from compulsion; and although I must part company with them there, I am sure that at least he did not want to do this *more* than he desired to occupy the passes, and to get the credit of appearing to have determined the issue of the war, and to manage the Pythian games by his own authority. These, I am sure, were the objects which he coveted most greedily. The Thessalians, again, did not desire to see either 23 the Thebans or Philip growing powerful; for in any such contingency they thought that they themselves were menaced. But they did desire to secure two privileges—admission to the Amphictyonic meeting, and the recovery of rights at Delphi; and in their eagerness for these privileges, they joined Philip in the actions in question. Thus you will find that each was led on, for the sake of private ends, to take action which they in no way desired to take. But this is the very thing against which we have now to be on our guard.

'Are we then, for fear of this, to submit to Philip? and 24 do *you* require this of us?' you ask me. Far from it. Our action must be such as will be in no way unworthy of us, and at the same time will not lead to war, but will prove to all our good sense and the justice of our position: and, in answer to those who are bold enough to think that we should refuse to submit to anything whatever,[1] and who cannot foresee the war that must follow, I wish to urge this consideration. We are allowing the Thebans to hold Oropus; and if any one asked us to state the reason honestly,

[1] οὐδ' ὁτιοῦν.

25 we should say that it was to avoid war. Again, we have just ceded Amphipolis to Philip by the Treaty of Peace; we permit the Cardians [n] to occupy a position apart from the other colonists in the Chersonese; we allow the Prince of Caria to seize the islands of Chios, Cos, and Rhodes, and the Byzantines to drive our vessels to shore —obviously because we believe that the tranquillity afforded by peace brings more blessings than any collision or contention over these grievances would bring: so that it would be a foolish and an utterly perverse policy, when we have behaved in this manner towards each of our adversaries individually, where our own most essential interests were concerned, to go now to war with all of them together, on account of this shadow at Delphi.

THE SECOND PHILIPPIC (Or. VI)

[*Introduction.* After settling affairs at Delphi in 346, Philip returned to Macedonia. During a considerable part of 345 and in the early months of 344 he was occupied with campaigns against the Illyrians, Dardani, and Triballi. But in the summer (probably) of 344 he resumed his activities in Greece, garrisoning Pherae and other towns of Thessaly with Macedonians, appropriating the revenues derived from the Thessalian ports, and establishing oligarchical governments throughout the country. At the same time negotiations were going on between himself and Athens with regard to the Thracian strongholds which he had captured in 346. He refused to give these up, though he offered to cut a canal across the Chersonese, for the protection of the Athenian allies there from the attacks of the Thracians. He also sent money and mercenaries to help the Messenians and Argives, who, like the Megalopolitans, were anxious to secure their independence of Sparta. Athens, which was on friendly terms with Sparta, sent envoys to the Peloponnesian states to counteract Philip's influence, and of these Demosthenes was one. In return, Argos and Messene complained to Athens of her interference with their attempt to secure freedom, and Philip sent envoys to deprecate the charges made against him by the Athenian ambassadors in the Peloponnese. He pointed out that he had not broken any promises made to Athens at the time of the Peace, for he had made none. (In fact, if Demosthenes' account is correct, he had confined himself to vague expressions of goodwill; the promises had been made by Aeschines.) The Second Philippic, spoken late in 344, proposes a reply to Philip, the text of which has unfortunately not come down to us. The Peloponnesian envoys appear also to have been in Athens at the time; and Philip's supporters had put forward various explanations of his conduct at the time when the Peace was made. To these also Demosthenes replies.]

1 In all our discussions, men of Athens, with regard to the acts of violence by which Philip contravenes the terms of the Peace, I observe that, although the speeches on our side are always manifestly just and sympathetic, and although those who denounce Philip are always regarded as saying what ought to be said, yet practically nothing is done which ought to be done, or which would make it worth while to 2 listen to such speeches. On the contrary, the condition of public affairs as a whole has already been brought to a point at which, the more and the more evidently a speaker can convict Philip both of transgressing the Peace which he made with you and of plotting against all the Hellenes, the harder 3 it is for him to advise you how you should act. The responsibility for this rests with us all, men of Athens. It is by deeds and actions, not by words, that a policy of encroachment must be arrested: and yet, in the first place, we who rise to address you will not face the duty of proposing or advising such action, for fear of unpopularity with you, though we dilate upon the character of Philip's acts, upon their atrocity, and so forth; and, in the second place, you who sit and listen, better qualified though you doubtless are than Philip for using the language of justice and appreciating it at the mouths of others, are nevertheless absolutely inert, when it is a question of preventing him from executing 4 the designs in which he is now engaged. It follows as the inevitable and perhaps reasonable consequence, that you are each more successful in that to which your time and your interest is given—he in actions, yourselves in words. Now if it is still enough for you, that your words are more just than his,

your course is easy, and no labour is involved in it. But if 5 we are to inquire how the evil of the present situation is to be corrected; if its advance is not still to continue, unperceived, until we are confronted by a power so great that we cannot even raise a hand in our own defence; then we must alter our method of deliberation, and all of us who speak, and all of you who listen, must resolve to prefer the counsels which are best, and which can save us, to those which are most easy and most attractive.

I am amazed, men of Athens, in the first place, that any 6 one who sees the present greatness of Philip and the wide mastery which he has gained, can be free from alarm, or can imagine that this involves no peril to Athens, or that it is not against you that all his preparations are being made. And I would beg you, one and all, to listen while I put before you in a few words the reasoning by which I have come to entertain the opposite expectation, and the grounds upon which I regard Philip as an enemy; that so, if my own foresight appears to you the truer, you may believe me; but if that of the persons who have no fears and have placed their trust in him, you may give your adhesion to them. Here then, men of Athens, is my argument. Of what, in 7 the first place, did Philip become master, when the Peace was concluded? Of Thermopylae, and of the situation in Phocis. Next, what use did he make of his power? He deliberately chose to act in the interests of Thebes, not in those of Athens. And why? He scrutinized every consideration in the light of his own ambition and of his desire for universal conquest: he took no thought for peace, or tranquillity, or justice; and he saw quite correctly that our 8 state and our national character being what they are, there was no attraction that he could offer, nothing that he could do, which would induce you to sacrifice any of the other Hellenes to him for your own advantage. He saw that you would take account of what was right; that you would shrink from the infamy attaching to such a policy; that you would exercise all the foresight which the situation demanded, and would oppose any such attempt on his part, as surely 9 as if you were at open war with him. But the Thebans, he believed—and the event proved that he was right—in return for what they were getting would let him do as he pleased in all that did not concern them; and far from acting against him, or preventing him effectively, would even join him in his campaign, if he bade them. His services to the Messenians and the Argives at the present moment are due to his having formed the same conception of them. And this, men of Athens, is the highest of all tributes to 10 yourselves: for these actions of his amount to a verdict upon you, that you alone of all peoples would never, for any gain to yourselves, sacrifice the common rights of the Hellenes, nor barter away your loyalty to them for any favour or benefit at his hands. This conception of you he has naturally formed, just as he has formed the opposite conception of the Argives and the Thebans, not only from his observation of the present, but also from his consideration of the past. 11 He discovers, I imagine, and is told, how when your forefathers might have been rulers of the rest of the Hellenes, on condition of submitting to the king themselves, they not only refused to tolerate the suggestion, on the occasion when Alexander, the ancestor of the present royal house, came as his herald to negotiate, but chose rather to leave their country and to face any suffering which they might have to endure; and how they followed up the refusal by those deeds which all are so eager to tell, but to which no one has ever been able to do justice; and for that reason, I shall myself forbear to speak of them, and rightly; for the grandeur of their achievements passes the power of language to describe. He knows, on the other hand, how the forefathers of the Thebans and Argives, in the one case, joined the barbarian army, in the other, offered no resistance to it. He knows, therefore, that both these people will 12 welcome what is to their own advantage, instead of considering the common interests of the Hellenes: and so he thought that, if he chose you for his allies, he would be choosing friends who would only serve a righteous cause; while if he joined himself to them, he would win accomplices who would further his own ambitions. That is why he chose them, as he chooses them now, in preference to you. For he certainly does not see them in possession of more ships than you; nor has he discovered some inland empire, and withdrawn from the seaboard and the trading-ports; nor does he forget the words and the promises, on the strength of which he was granted the Peace.

But some one may tell us, with an air of complete knowledge of the matter, that what then moved Philip to act 13 thus was not his ambition nor any of the motives which I impute to him, but his belief that the demands of Thebes were more righteous than your own. I reply, that this statement, above all others, is one which he cannot possibly make *now*. How can one who is ordering Sparta to give up Messene put forward his belief in the righteousness of the act, as his excuse for handing over Orchomenus and Coroneia to Thebes?

14 'But,' we are told (as the last remaining plea), 'he was forced to make these concessions, and did so against his better judgement, finding himself caught between the cavalry of Thessaly and the infantry of Thebes.' Admirable! And so, we are informed, he intends henceforth to be wary of the Thebans, and the tale goes round that he intends to fortify Elateia. 'Intends,' indeed! and I expect that it will
15 remain an intention! But the help which he is giving to the Messenians and Argives is no 'intention'; for he is actually sending mercenaries to them and dispatching funds, and is himself expected to arrive on the spot with a great force. Is he trying to annihilate the Spartans, the existing enemies of Thebes, and at the same time protecting the Phocians, whom he himself has ruined? Who will believe
16 such a tale? For if Philip had really acted against his will and under compulsion in the first instance—if he were now really intending to renounce the Thebans—I cannot believe that he would be so consistently opposing their enemies. On the contrary, his present course plainly proves that his former action also was the result of deliberate policy; and to any sound observation, it is plain that the whole of his plans are being organized for one end—the destruction of
17 Athens. Indeed, this has now come to be, in a sense, a matter of necessity for him. Only consider. It is empire that he desires, and you, as he believes, are his only possible rivals in this. He has been acting wrongfully towards you for a long time, as he himself best knows; for it is the occupation of your possessions that enables him to hold all his other conquests securely, convinced, as he is, that if he had let Amphipolis and Poteidaea go, he could not dwell
18 in safety even at home. These two facts, then, he well

knows—first, that his designs are aimed at you, and secondly, that you are aware of it: and as he conceives you to be men of sense, he considers that you hold him in righteous detestation: and, in consequence, his energies are roused: for he expects to suffer disaster, if you get your opportunity, unless he can anticipate you by inflicting it upon you. So 19 he is wide awake; he is on the alert; he is courting the help of others against Athens—of the Thebans and those Peloponnesians who sympathize with their wishes; thinking that their desire of gain will make them embrace the immediate prospect, while their native stupidity will prevent them from foreseeing any of the consequences. Yet there are examples, plainly visible to minds which are even moderately well-balanced —examples which it fell to my lot to bring before Messenian and Argive audiences, but which had better, perhaps, be laid before yourselves as well.

'Can you not imagine,' I said, 'men of Messenia, the 20 impatience with which the Olynthians used to listen to any speeches directed against Philip in those times, when he was giving up Anthemus to them—a city claimed as their own by all former Macedonian kings; when he was expelling the Athenian colonists from Poteidaea and presenting it to the Olynthians; when he had taken upon his own shoulders their quarrel with Athens, and given them the enjoyment of that territory? Did they expect, do you think, to suffer as they have done? if any one had foretold it, would they have believed him? And yet,' I continued, 'after enjoying 21 territory not their own for a very short time, they are robbed of their own by him for a great while to come; they are foully driven forth—not conquered merely, but betrayed by one another and sold; for it is not safe for a free state

22 to be on these over-friendly terms with a tyrant. What, again, of the Thessalians? Do you imagine,' I asked, 'that when he was expelling their tyrants, or again, when he was giving them Nicaea and Magnesia, they expected to see the present Council of Ten established in their midst? Did they expect that the restorer of their Amphictyonic rights would take their own revenues from them for himself? Impossible! And yet these things came to pass, as all men 23 may know. You yourselves,' I continued, 'at present behold only the gifts and the promises of Philip. Pray, if you are really in your right minds, that you may never see the accomplishment of his deceit and treachery. There are, as you know well,' I said, 'all kinds of inventions designed for the protection and security of cities—palisades, walls, trenches, 24 and every kind of defence. All these are made with hands, and involve expense as well. But there is one safeguard which all sensible men possess by nature—a safeguard which is a valuable protection to all, but above all to a democracy against a tyrant. And what is this? It is distrust. Guard this possession and cleave to it; preserve this, and you need 25 never fear disaster. What is it that you desire?' I said. 'Is it freedom? And do you not see that the very titles that Philip bears are utterly alien to freedom? For a king, a tyrant, is always the foe of freedom and the enemy of law. Will you not be on your guard,' I said, 'lest in striving to be rid of war, you find yourselves slaves?'

26 My audience heard these words and received them with a tumult of approbation, as well as many other speeches from the envoys, both when I was present and again later. And yet, it seems, there is still no better prospect of their 27 keeping Philip's friendship and promises at a distance. In

fact, the extraordinary thing is not that Messenians and certain Peloponnesians should act against their own better judgement, but that you who understand for yourselves, and who hear us, your orators, telling you, that there is a design against you, and that the toils are closing round you—that you, I say, by always refusing to act at once, should be about to find (as I think you will) that you have exposed yourselves unawares to the utmost peril: so much more does the pleasure and ease of the moment weigh with you, than any advantage to be reaped at some future date.

In regard to the practical measures which you must take, 28 you will, if you are wise, deliberate by yourselves later. But I will at once propose an answer which you may make to-day, and which it will be consistent with your duty to have adopted.

[*The answer is read.*]

Now the right course, men of Athens, was to have summoned before you those who conveyed the promises on the strength of which you were induced to make the Peace. For 29 I could never have brought myself to serve on the Embassy, nor, I am sure, would you have discontinued the war, had you imagined that Philip, when he had obtained peace, would act as he has acted. What we were then told was something very different from this. And there are others, too, whom you should summon. You ask whom I mean? After the Peace had been made, and I had returned from the Second Embassy, which was sent to administer the oaths, I saw how the city was being hoodwinked, and I spoke out repeatedly, protesting and forbidding you to sacrifice Thermopylae and the Phocians: and the men to whom I refer were those who 30 then said that a water-drinker like myself was naturally a fractious and ill-tempered fellow; while Philip, if only he crossed the Pass, would fulfil your fondest prayers; for he would fortify Thespiae and Plataeae; he would put an end to the insolence of the Thebans; he would cut a canal through the Chersonese at his own charges, and would repay you for Amphipolis by the restoration of Euboea and Oropus. All this was said from this very platform, and I am quite sure that you remember it well, though your memory 31 of those who injure you is but short. To crown your disgrace, with nothing but these hopes in view, you resolved that this same Peace should hold good for your posterity also; so completely had you fallen under their influence. But why do I speak of all this now? why do I bid you summon these men? By Heaven, I will tell the truth without reserve, 32 and will hold nothing back. My object is not to give way to abuse, and so secure myself as good a hearing as others in this place, while giving those who have come into collision with me from the first an opportunity for a further claim upon Philip's money. Nor do I wish to waste time in empty words. No; but I think that the plan which Philip is pursuing will some day trouble you more than the present 33 situation does; for his design is moving towards fulfilment, and though I shrink from precise conjecture, I fear its accomplishment may even now be only too close at hand. And when the time comes when you can no longer refuse to attend to what is passing; when you no longer hear from me or from some other that it is all directed against you, but all alike see it for yourselves and know it for a certainty; 34 then, I think, you will be angry and harsh enough. And I am afraid that because your envoys have withheld from you the guilty secret of the purposes which they have been bribed to forward, those who are trying to remedy in some degree the ruin of which these men have been the instruments will fall victims to your wrath. For I observe that it is the general practice of some persons to vent their anger, not upon the guilty, but upon those who are most within their grasp. While then the trouble is still to come, still in 35 process of growth, while we can still listen to one another's words, I would remind each of you once more of what he well knows—who it was that induced you to sacrifice the Phocians and Thermopylae, the control of which gave Philip command of the road to Attica and the Peloponnesus; who it was, I say, that converted your debate about your rights and your interests abroad into a debate about the safety of your own country, and about war on your own borders—a war which will bring distress to each of us personally, when it is at our doors, but which sprang into existence on that day. Had you not been misled by them, no trouble would 36 have befallen this country. For we cannot imagine that Philip would have won victories by sea which would have enabled him to approach Attica with his fleet, or would have marched by land past Thermopylae and the Phocians; but he would either have been acting straightforwardly—keeping the Peace and remaining quiet; or else he would have found himself instantly plunged into a war no less severe than that which originally made him desirous of the Peace. What 37 I have said is sufficient by way of a reminder to you. Heaven grant that the time may not come when the truth of my words will be tested with all severity: for I at least have no desire to see any one meet with punishment, however much he may deserve his doom, if it is accompanied by danger and calamity to us all.

ON THE EMBASSY (Or. XIX)

[*Introduction*. The principal events with which a reader of this Speech ought to be acquainted have already been narrated (see especially the Introductions to the last two Speeches). The influence of the anti-Macedonian party grew gradually from the time of the Peace onwards. In 346, within a month after the return of the Second Embassy, the ambassadors presented their reports before the Logistae or Board of Auditors (after a futile attempt on the part of Aeschines to avoid making a report altogether); and Timarchus, supported by Demosthenes, there announced his intention of taking proceedings against Aeschines for misconduct on the Second Embassy. But Timarchus' own past history was not above reproach: he was attacked by Aeschines for the immoralities of his youth, which, it was stated, disqualified him from acting as prosecutor, and though defended by Demosthenes, was condemned and disfranchised (345 B.C.). But early in 343 Hypereides impeached Philocrates for corruption as ambassador, and obtained his condemnation to death—a penalty which he escaped by voluntary exile before the conclusion of the trial; and, later in the same year, Demosthenes brought the same charge against Aeschines.

In the meantime (since the delivery of Demosthenes' Second Philippic) Philip had been making fresh progress. The Arcadians and Argives (for the Athenian envoys to the Peloponnese in 344 seem to have had little success) were ready to open their gates to him. His supporters in Elis massacred their opponents, and with them the remnant of the Phocians who had crossed over to Elis with Phalaecus. At Megara, Perillus and Ptoeodorus almost succeeded in bringing a force of Philip's mercenaries into the town, but the attempt was defeated, by the aid of an Athenian force under Phocion. In Euboea Philip's troops occupied Porthmus, where the democratic party of Eretria had taken refuge, owing to an overthrow of the constitution (brought about by Philip's intrigues) which resulted in the establishment of Cleitarchus as tyrant. In the course of the same year (343) occurred two significant trials. The first was that of Antiphon, who had made an offer to Philip to burn the Athenian dockyards at the Peiraeus. He was summarily arrested by order of Demosthenes (probably in virtue of some administrative office): Aeschines obtained his release, but he was re-arrested by order of the Council of Areopagus[1] and condemned to death. The other trial was held before the Amphictyonic Council on the motion of the people of Delos, to decide whether the Athenians should continue to possess the right of managing the Temple of Delos. The Assembly chose Aeschines as counsel for Athens; but the Council of Areopagus, which had been given power to revise the appointment, put Hypereides in his place. Hypereides won the case. Early in 343 (or at all events before the middle of the year), Philip sent Python of Byzantium to complain of the language used about him by Athenian orators, and to offer to revise and amend the terms of the Peace of Philocrates. In response, an embassy was sent, headed by Hegesippus, a violent opponent of Macedonia, to propose to Philip (1) that instead of the clause 'that each party shall retain possession of what they have', a clause, 'that each party shall possess what is their own,' should be substituted; and (2) that all Greek States not included in the Treaty of Peace should be declared free, and that Athens and Philip should assist them, if they were attacked. These proposals, if sanctioned, would obviously have reopened the question of Amphipolis, Pydna, and Poteidaea, as well as of Cardia and

[1] This body was composed of life-members, the archons passing into it annually at the conclusion of their term of office. A certain religious solemnity attached to it, and it was generally respected as a public-spirited and high-minded body.

the Thracian towns taken by Philip in 346. Hegesippus, moreover, was personally objectionable, and the embassy was dismissed with little courtesy by Philip, who even banished from Macedonia the Athenian poet Xenocleides for acting as host to the envoys. The feeling against Philip in Athens was evidently strong, when the prosecution of Aeschines by Demosthenes took place.

The trial was held before a jury (probably consisting of 1,501 persons), presided over by the Board of Auditors. Demosthenes spoke first, and Aeschines replied in a speech which is preserved. There is no doubt, on a comparison of the two speeches, that each, before it was published, received alterations and insertions, intended to meet the adversary's points, or to give a better colour to passages which had been unfavourably received. Probably not all the refutations 'in advance' were such in reality. But there is no sufficient reason to doubt that the speeches were delivered substantially as we have them. Aeschines was acquitted by thirty votes.

The question of the guilt or innocence of Aeschines will probably never be finally settled. A great part of his conduct can be explained as a sincere attempt to carry out the policy of Eubulus, or as the issue of a genuine belief that it was best for Athens to make terms with Philip and stand on his side. Even so the wisdom and the veracity of certain speeches which he had made is open to grave question; but this is a different thing from corruption. Moreover, to some of Demosthenes' arguments he has a conclusive reply. It is more difficult to explain his apparent change of opinion between the 18th and 19th of Elaphebolion, 346 (if Demosthenes' report of the debates is to be trusted); and some writers are disposed to date his corruption from the intervening night. Nor is it easy to meet Demosthenes' argument that if Aeschines had really been taken in by Philip, and believed the promises which he announced, or if he had actually heard Philip make the promises, he would have regarded Philip afterwards as a personal enemy, and not as a friend.

But even on these points Aeschines might reply (though he could not reply so to the Athenian people or jury) that though he did not trust the promises, he regarded the interest of Athens as so closely bound up with the alliance with Philip, that he considered it justifiable to deceive the people into making the alliance, or at least to take the risk of the promises which he announced proving untrue. In any case there is no convincing evidence of corruption; and it may be taken as practically certain that he was not bribed to perform particular services. It is less certain that he was not influenced by generous presents from Philip in forming his judgement of Philip's character and intentions. The standard of Athenian public opinion in regard to the receipt of presents was not that of the English Civil Service; and the ancient orators accuse one another of corruption almost as a matter of course. (We have seen that Demosthenes began the attack upon Eubulus' party in this form as early as the Speech for the Rhodians; it appears in almost every subsequent oration: and in their turn, his opponents make the same charge against him.) It is, in any case, remarkable that at a time when the people was plainly exasperated with the Peace and its authors, and very ill-disposed towards Philip, a popular jury nevertheless acquitted Aeschines; and the verdict is not sufficiently explained either by the fact that Eubulus supported Aeschines or by the jurors' memory of Demosthenes' own part in the earlier peace-negotiations, though this must have weakened the force of his attack. That Demosthenes himself believed Aeschines to have been bribed, and could himself see no other explanation of his conduct, need not be doubted; and although the speech contains some of those misrepresentations of fact and passages of irrelevant personal abuse which deface some of his best work, it also contains some of his finest pieces of oratory and narrative.

The second part of the speech is more broken up into short sections and less clearly arranged than the first; earlier arguments are repeated, and a few passages may be due (at least in their present shape) to revision after the trial: but the latter part even as it stands is successful in leaving the points of greatest importance strongly impressed upon the mind.

The following analysis of the speech may enable the reader to find his way through it without serious difficulty:—

INTRODUCTION (§§ 1–28)

(i) *Exordium* (§§ 1, 2). Impartiality requested of the jury, in view of Aeschines' attempt to escape by indirect means.

(ii) *Points of the trial* (§§ 3–8). An ambassador must (1) give true reports; (2) give good advice; (3) obey his instructions; (4) not lose time; (5) be incorruptible.

(iii) *Preliminary exposition of the arguments* (§§ 9–28).

(1) The previous anti-Macedonian zeal of Aeschines suddenly collapsed after the First Embassy.

(2) In the deliberations on the Peace, Aeschines supported Philocrates.

(3) After the Second Embassy, Aeschines prevented Athens from guarding Thermopylae and saving the Phocians, by false reports and promises.

(4) Such a change of policy is only explicable by corruption.

PART I (§§ 29–178)

The five points of Introduction (ii) are treated as three, or in three groups.

(i) The reports made by Aeschines on his return from the Second Embassy, and his advice, especially as to the ruin of the Phocians (§§ 29–97).

(1) The reports (*a*) to the Senate, (*b*) to the People, and their reception (§§ 29–46).

(2) Evidence that Aeschines conspired with Philip against the Phocians, whose ruin is described (§§ 47–71).

(3) Refutation of three anticipated objections, beginning at § 72, § 78, § 80 respectively (§§ 72–82).

(4) The danger to Athens from Aeschines' treachery (§§ 83–7).

(5) Request to confine the trial strictly to relevant points (§§ 88–97).

(ii) The corruption of Aeschines by the bribes of Philip (§§ 98–149).

(1) Arguments (beginning § 102, § 111, § 114, § 116) showing the corruption of Aeschines (§§ 98–119).

(2) Refutation of anticipated objections (beginning at § 120, § 134, § 147) (§§ 120–49).

(iii) Aeschines' loss of time, by which Philip profited, and disobedience to his instructions (§§ 150–77).

(1) Narrative of the Second Embassy (§§ 150–62).
(2) Comparison of the two Embassies (§§ 163–5).
(3) Comparison of Demosthenes' own conduct with that of the other ambassadors (§§ 167–77). Recapitulation of the points established (§§ 177, 178).

PART II (§§ 179–343)

(i) The injury done to Athens—
(*a*) by the loss of Thrace and the Hellespont;
(*b*) generally, by false reports from ambassadors (§§ 179–86).
(ii) Refutation of anticipated objections—
(*a*) 'It is not Philip's fault that he has not satisfied Athens' (§ 187).
(*b*) 'Demosthenes has no right to prosecute' (§§ 188–220): including a digression (§§ 192–200) on Aeschines' character and incidents in his life.
(iii) Demosthenes' object in prosecuting, passing into reproof of the laxity of Athens towards traitors (§§ 221–33).
(iv) Warning against any attempt by Aeschines to confuse the dates and incidents of the two Embassies (§§ 234–6.)
(v) Criticism of Aeschines' brothers and his prosecution of Timarchus (§§ 237–58).
(vi) The increasing danger from traitors, and the traditional attitude of Athens towards them (§§ 259–87).
(vii) Attack upon Eubulus for defending Aeschines (§§ 288–99).
(viii) Philip's policy and methods; proofs of Aeschines' complicity repeated (§§ 300–31).
(ix) Warnings to the jury against Aeschines' attempts to mislead them; and conclusion (§§ 331–43).]

How much interest this case has excited, men of Athens, and how much canvassing has taken place, must, I feel sure, have become fairly evident to you all, after the persistent overtures just now made to you, while you were drawing your lots. Yet I will make the request of you all—a request which ought to be granted even when unasked—that you will not allow the favour or the person of any man to weigh more with you than justice and the oath which each of you swore before he entered the court. Remember that what I ask is for your own welfare and for that of the whole State; while the entreaties and the eager interest 1 of the supporters of the accused have for their aim the selfish advantage of individuals: and it is not to confirm criminals in the possession of such advantages that the laws have called you together, but to prevent their attainment of them. 2 Now I observe that while all who enter upon public life in an honest spirit profess themselves under a perpetual responsibility, even when they have passed their formal examination, the defendant Aeschines does the very reverse. For before entering your presence to give an account of his actions, he has put out of the way one of those who appeared against him at his examination; and others he pursues with threats, thus introducing into public life a practice which is of all the most atrocious and most contrary to your interests. For if one who has transacted and managed any public business is to render himself secure against accusation by spreading terror round him, rather than by the justice of his case, your supremacy must pass entirely out of your hands.

3 I have every confidence and belief that I shall prove the defendant guilty of many atrocious crimes, for which he deserves the extreme penalty of the law. But I will tell you frankly of the fear which troubles me in spite of this confidence. It seems to me, men of Athens, that the issue of every trial before you is determined as much by the occasion as by the facts; and I am afraid that the length of time which has elapsed since the Embassy may have caused you to forget the crimes of Aeschines, or to be too familiar with 4 them. I will tell you therefore how, in spite of this, you may yet, as I believe, arrive at a just decision and give a true verdict to-day. You have, gentlemen of the jury, to inquire and to consider what are the points on which it is proper

to demand an account from an ambassador. He is responsible first for his report; secondly, for what he has persuaded you to do; thirdly, for his execution of your instructions; next, for dates; and, besides all these things, for the integrity or venality of his conduct throughout. And why is he 5 responsible in these respects? Because on his report must depend your discussion of the situation: if his report is true, your decision is a right one: if otherwise, it is the reverse. Again, you regard the counsels of ambassadors as especially trustworthy. You listen to them in the belief that they have personal knowledge of the matter with which they were sent to deal. Never, therefore, ought an ambassador to be convicted of having given you any worthless or pernicious advice. Again, it is obviously proper that he 6 should have carried out your instructions to him with regard to both speech and action, and your express resolutions as to his conduct. Very good. But why is he responsible for dates? Because, men of Athens, it often happens that the opportunity upon which much that is of great importance depends lasts but for a moment; and if this opportunity is deliberately and treacherously surrendered to the enemy, no subsequent steps can possibly recover it. But as to the 7 integrity or corruption of an ambassador, you would all, I am sure, admit that to make money out of proceedings that injure the city is an atrocious thing and deserves your heavy indignation. Yet the implied distinction was not recognized by the framer of our law. He absolutely forbade *all* taking of presents, thinking, I believe, that a man who has once received presents and been corrupted with money no longer remains even a safe judge of what is to the interest of the city. If then I can convict the defendant Aeschines by 8 conclusive proofs of having made a report that was utterly untrue, and prevented the people from hearing the truth from me; if I prove that he gave advice that was entirely contrary to your interests; that on his mission he fulfilled none of your instructions to him; that he wasted time, during which opportunities for accomplishing much that was of great importance were sacrificed and lost to the city; and that he received presents in payment for all these services, in company with Philocrates; then condemn him, and exact the penalty which his crimes deserve. If I fail to prove these points, or fail to prove them all, then regard me with contempt, and let the defendant go.

9 I have still to charge him, men of Athens, with many atrocious acts in addition to these—acts which would naturally call forth the execration of every one among you. But I desire, before all else that I am about to say, to remind you (though most of you, I know, remember it well) of the position which Aeschines originally took up in public life, and the speeches which he thought it right to address to the people against Philip; for I would have you realize that his own actions, his own speeches at the beginning of his career, are the 10 strongest evidence of his corruption. According to his own public declaration at that time, he was the first Athenian to perceive that Philip had designs against the Hellenes and was corrupting certain leading men in Arcadia. With Ischander, the son of Neoptolemus, to second him in his performance, he came before the Council and he came before the people, to speak on the subject: he persuaded you to send envoys in all directions to bring together a congress 11 at Athens to discuss the question of war with Philip: then, on his return from Arcadia, he reported to you those noble

and lengthy speeches which, he said, he had delivered on your behalf before the Ten Thousand at Megalopolis, in reply to Philip's spokesman, Hieronymus; and he described at length the criminal wrong that was done, not only to their own several countries, but to all Hellas, by men who took bribes and received money from Philip. Such was his policy 12 at that time, and such the sample which he displayed of his sentiments. Then you were induced by Aristodemus, Neoptolemus, Ctesiphon, and the rest of those who brought reports from Macedonia in which there was not an honest word, to send ambassadors to Philip and to negotiate for peace. Aeschines himself is appointed one of them, in the belief, not that he was one of those who would sell your interests, or had placed confidence in Philip, but rather one who would keep an eye on the rest. The speeches which he had already delivered, and his antipathy to Philip, naturally led you to take this view of him. Well, after this he came to me and 13 tried to make an agreement by which we should act in concert on the Embassy, and urged strongly that we should both keep an eye upon that abominable and shameless man Philocrates; and until we returned to Athens from the First Embassy, I at least, men of Athens, had no idea that he had been corrupted and had sold himself. For (not to mention the other speeches which, as I have told you, he had made on former occasions) at the first of the assemblies in which you debated about the Peace, he rose and delivered an exordium which I think I can repeat to you word for word as he uttered it at the meeting. 'If Philocrates,' he said, 'had spent a very 14 long time in studying how he could best oppose the Peace, I do not think he could have found a better device than a motion of this kind. The Peace which he proposes is one which I can never recommend the city to make, so long as a single Athenian remains alive. Peace, however, we ought, 15 I think, to make.' And he made a brief and reasonable speech in the same tone. But though he had spoken thus at the first meeting, in the hearing of you all, yet at the second meeting, when the Peace was to be ratified; when I was upholding the resolution of the allies and working for a Peace on just and equitable terms; when you in your desire for such a Peace would not even listen to the voice of the despicable Philocrates; then, I say, Aeschines rose and spoke in support of him, using language for which he deserves, 16 God knows, to die many deaths, saying that you must not remember your forefathers, nor tolerate speakers who recalled your trophies and your victories by sea; and that he would frame and propose a law, that you should assist no Hellene who had not previously assisted you. These words he had the callous shamelessness to utter in the very presence and hearing of the ambassadors whom you had summoned from the Hellenic states, in pursuance of the advice which he himself had given you, before he had sold himself.

17 You elected him again, men of Athens, to receive the oaths. How he frittered away the time, how cruelly he injured all his country's interests, and what violent mutual enmity arose between myself and him in consequence of his conduct and of my desire to prevent it, you shall hear presently. But when we returned from this Embassy which was sent to receive the oaths, and the report of which is now under examination; when we had secured nothing, either small or great, of all that had been promised and expected when you were making the Peace, but had been totally deceived; when they had again acted without regard to their instruc-

tions, and had conducted their mission in direct defiance of your decree; we came before the Council: and there are many who have personal knowledge of what I am about to tell you, for the Council-Chamber was crowded with spectators. Well, I came forward and reported to the Council 18 the whole truth: I denounced these men: I recounted the whole story, beginning with those first hopes, aroused in you by the report of Ctesiphon and Aristodemus, and going on to the speeches which Aeschines delivered during the time of the Peace-negotiations, and the position into which they had brought the city: as regards all that remained to you—I meant the Phocians and Thermopylae—I counselled you not to abandon these, not to be victims once more of the same mistake, not to let yourselves be reduced to extremities through depending upon a succession of hopes and promises: and I carried the Council with me. But 19 when the day of the Assembly came, and it was our duty to address you, the defendant Aeschines came forward before any of his colleagues—and I entreat you, in God's name, to follow me, and try to recollect whether what I tell you is true; for now we have come to the very thing which so cruelly injured and ruined your whole cause. He made not the remotest attempt to give any report of the results of the Embassy—if indeed he questioned the truth of my allegations at all—but instead of this, he made statements of such a character, promising you benefits so numerous and so magnificent, that he completely carried you away with him. For he said that, before his return, he had persuaded Philip 20 upon all the points in which the interests of the city were involved, in regard both to the Amphictyonic dispute and to all other matters: and he described to you a long speech which he professed to have addressed to Philip against the

Thebans, and of which he reported to you the substance, calculating that, as the result of his own diplomacy, you would within two or three days, without stirring from home or taking the field or suffering any inconvenience, hear that Thebes was being blockaded, alone and isolated from the

21 rest of Boeotia, that Thespiae and Plataeae were being repeopled, and that the debt due to the god was being exacted not from the Phocians, but from the Thebans who had planned the seizure of the temple. For he said that he gave Philip to understand that those who planned the act were no less guilty of impiety than those whose hands executed the plan; and that on this account the Thebans

22 had set a price upon his head. Moreover, he said that he heard some of the Euboeans, who had been thrown into a state of panic and confusion by the friendly relations established between Athens and Philip, saying to the ambassadors, 'You have not succeeded, gentlemen, in concealing from us the conditions on which you have made your Peace with Philip; nor are we unaware that while you have given him Amphipolis, he has undertaken to hand over Euboea to you.' There was, indeed, another matter which he had arranged as well, but he did not wish to mention this at present, since even

23 as it was some of his colleagues were jealous of him. This was an enigmatical and indirect allusion to Oropus. These utterances naturally raised him high in your estimation; he seemed to be an admirable speaker and a marvellous man; and he stepped down with a very lofty air. Then I rose and denied all knowledge of these things, and at the same time attempted to repeat some part of my report to the Council. But they now took their stand by me, one on this side, one on that—the defendant and Philocrates; they shouted, they

interrupted me, and finally they jeered, while you laughed. You would not hear, and you did not wish to believe anything 24 but what Aeschines had reported. Heaven knows, your feelings were natural enough; for who, that expected all these marvellous benefits, would have tolerated a speaker who said that the expectation would not be realized, or denounced the proceedings of those who made the promise? All else, of course, was of secondary importance at the time, in comparison with the expectations and the hopes placed before you; any contradiction appeared to be nothing but sheer obstruction and malignity, while the proceedings described seemed to be of incredible importance and advantage to the city.

Now with what object have I recalled these occurrences 25 to you before everything else, and described these speeches of his? My first and chief object, men of Athens, is that none of you, when he hears me speak of any of the things that were done and is struck by their unparalleled atrocity, may ask in surprise why I did not tell you at once and inform you of the facts; but may remember the promises which 26 these men made at each critical moment, and by which they entirely prevented every one else from obtaining a hearing; and that splendid pronouncement by Aeschines; and that you may realize that in addition to all his other crimes, you have suffered this further wrong at his hands—that you were prevented from learning the truth instantly, when you ought to have learned it, because you were deluded by hopes, deceits and promises. That is my first and, as I have said, 27 my chief object in recalling all these occurrences. But there is a second which is of no less importance than the first, and what is this? It is that you may remember the policy which he adopted in his public life, when he was still uncorrupted—

his guarded and mistrustful attitude towards Philip; and may consider the sudden growth of confidence and friendship 28 which followed; and then, if all that he announced to you has been realized, if the results achieved are satisfactory, you may believe that all has been done out of an honest interest in the welfare of Athens; but if, on the other hand, the issue has been exactly the opposite of that which he predicted: if his policy has involved the city in great disgrace and in grave perils, you may then be sure that his conversion was due to his own base covetousness and to his having sold the truth for money.

29 And now, since I have been led on to this subject, I desire to describe to you, before everything else, the way in which they took the Phocian question entirely out of your hands. And let none of you, gentlemen of the jury, when he looks at the magnitude of the transactions, imagine that the crimes with which the defendant is charged are on a grander scale than one of his reputation could compass. You have rather to observe that any one whom you would have placed in such a position as this—a position in which, as each critical moment arrived, the decision would be in his hands—could have brought about disasters equal to those for which Aeschines is responsible, if, like Aeschines, he had wished 30 to sell his services, and to cheat and deceive you. For however contemptible may be the men whom you frequently employ in the public service, it does not follow that the part which the world expects this city to play is a contemptible one. Far from it! And further, though it was Philip, of course, who destroyed the Phocian people, it was Aeschines and his party who seconded Philip's efforts. And so what you have to observe and consider is whether, so far as the preserva-

tion of the Phocians came within the scope of their mission, these men deliberately destroyed and ruined that whole cause. You have not to suppose that Aeschines ruined the Phocians by himself. How could he have done so?

(*To the clerk.*) Now give me the draft-resolution which the Council passed in view of my report, and the deposition of the clerk who wrote it. (*To the jury.*) For I would have you know that I am not repudiating to-day transactions about which I held my peace at the time, but that I denounced them at once, with full prevision of what must follow; and that the Council, which was not prevented from hearing the truth from me, neither voted thanks to the ambassadors, nor thought fit to invite them to the Town Hall. From the foundation of the city to this day, no body of ambassadors is recorded to have been treated so; nor even Timagoras, whom the people condemned to death. But these men have been so treated. (*To the clerk.*) First read them the deposition, and then the resolution. 31 32

[*The deposition and resolution are read.*]

Here is no expression of thanks, no invitation of the ambassadors to the Town Hall by the Council. If Aeschines asserts that there is any, let him point it out and produce it, and I give way to him. But there is none. Now on the assumption that we all fulfilled our mission in the same way, the Council had good reason not to thank any of us, for the transactions of all alike were in that case atrocious. But if some of us acted uprightly, while others did the reverse, it must, it seems, have been owing to the knavery of their colleagues that the virtuous were forced to take their share of this dishonour. How then can you all ascertain without 33 any difficulty who is the rogue? Recall to your minds who it is that has denounced the transaction from the outset. For it is plain that it must have been the guilty person who was well content to be silent, to stave off the day of reckoning for the moment, and to take care for the future not to present himself to give an account of his actions; while it must have been he whose conscience was clear to whom there occurred the thought of the danger, lest through keeping silence he might be regarded as a partner in such atrocious villany. Now it is I that have denounced these men from the outset, while none of them has accused me.

34 Such then was the resolution of the Council. The meeting of the Assembly took place when Philip was already at Thermopylae: for this was the first of all their crimes, that they placed Philip in command of the situation, so that, when you ought first to have heard the facts, then to have deliberated, and afterwards to have taken such measures as you had resolved upon, you in fact heard nothing until he was on the spot, and it was no longer easy to say what steps

35 you ought to take. In addition to this, no one read the resolution of the Council to the people, and the people never heard it; but Aeschines rose and delivered the harangue which I just now described to you, recounting the numerous and important benefits which he said he had, before his return, persuaded Philip to grant, and on account of which the Thebans had set a price upon his head. In consequence of this, appalled though you were at first at the proximity of Philip, and angry with these men for not having warned you of it, you became as mild as possible, having now formed the expectation that all your wishes would be realized; and you would not hear a word from me or from any one else.

After this was read the letter from Philip, which Aeschines 36 had written when we had left him behind, a letter which was nothing less than a direct and express defence in writing of the misconduct of the ambassadors. For in it is stated that Philip himself prevented them, when they were anxious to go to the several cities and receive the oaths, and that he retained them in order that they might help him to effect a reconciliation between the peoples of Halus and Pharsalus. He takes upon his own shoulders the whole of their misconduct, and makes it his own. But as to the Phocians and Thespiae, 37 and the promises contained in Aeschines' report to you—why, there is not the slightest mention of them! And it was no mere accident that the proceedings took this form. For the failure of the ambassadors to carry out or give effect to any of the instructions imposed upon them by your resolution—the failure for which you were bound to punish them—Philip makes himself responsible in their stead, and says that the fault was his; for you were not likely, of course, to be able to punish *him*. But the points in regard to which Philip wished 38 to deceive you and to steal a march upon the city were made the subject of the defendant's report, in order that you might be able to find no ground of accusation or reproach against Philip, since these points were not mentioned either in his letter or in any other part of the communications received from him. But (*to the clerk*) read the jury the actual letter—written by Aeschines, sent by Philip; and (*to the jury*) do you observe that it is such as I have described. (*To the clerk.*) Read on.

[*The letter is read.*]

You hear the letter, men of Athens; you hear how noble 39 and generous it is. But about the Phocians or the Thebans or the other subjects of the defendant's report—not a syllable.

Indeed, in this letter there is not an honest word, as you will very shortly see for yourselves. He says that he retained the ambassadors to help him reconcile the people of Halus: and such is the reconciliation that they have obtained, that they are exiles from their country, and their city is laid waste. And as to the prisoners, though he professed to be wondering what he could do to gratify you, he says that the idea of 40 procuring their release had not occurred to any one. But evidence has, as you know, been laid before you many times in the Assembly, to the effect that I myself went to ransom them, taking a talent[n] for the purpose; and it shall now be laid before you once more. It follows, therefore, that it was to deprive me of my laudable ambition that Aeschines persuaded Philip to insert this statement. But the strongest point of all is this. In his former letter—the letter which we brought back—he wrote, 'I should have mentioned expressly the great benefits that I propose to confer upon you, if I felt sure that you would grant me the alliance as well.' And yet when the alliance has been granted, he says that he does not know what he can do to gratify you. He does not even know what he had himself promised! Why, he must obviously have known that, unless he was trying to cheat you! To prove that he did write thus and in these terms, (*to the clerk*) take his former letter, and read the very passage, beginning at this point. Read on.

[*An extract from the letter is read.*]

41 Thus, before he obtained the Peace, he undertook to set down in writing the great benefits he would confer on the city, in the event of an alliance also being granted him. But as soon as he had obtained both his wishes, he says that

he does not know what he can do to gratify you, but that if you will inform him, he will do anything that will not involve any disgrace or stigma upon himself. Such are the excuses in which he takes refuge, to secure his retreat, in case you should actually make any suggestion or should be induced to ask any favour.

It would have been possible to expose this whole proceeding 42 at the time—and a great deal more—without delay; to inform you of the facts, and to prevent you from sacrificing your cause, had not the thought of Thespiae and Plataeae, and the idea that the Thebans were on the very point of paying the penalty, robbed you of the truth. While, however, there was good reason for mentioning these prospects, if the city was to hear of them and then be cheated, it would have been better, if their realization was actually intended, that nothing should have been said about them. For if matters had already reached a stage at which the Thebans would be no better off, even if they perceived the design against them, why was the design not fulfilled? But if its fulfilment was prevented because they perceived it in time, who was it that betrayed the secret? Must it not 43 have been Aeschines? Its fulfilment, however, was not in fact intended, nor did the defendant either desire or expect it; so that he may be relieved of the charge of betraying the secret. What was intended was that you should be hoodwinked by these statements, and should refuse to hear the truth from me; that you should not stir from home, and that such a decree should carry the day as would involve the destruction of the Phocians. Hence this prodigality in promises, and their proclamation in his speech to the people.

When I heard Aeschines making all these magnificent 44

promises, I knew perfectly well that he was lying; and I will tell you how I knew. I knew it first, because when Philip was about to take the oath in ratification of the Peace, the Phocians were openly excluded from it. This was a point which it would have been natural to pass over in silence, if the Phocians were really to be saved. And secondly, I knew it because the promises were not made by Philip's ambassadors or in Philip's letter, but by 45 the defendant. Accordingly, drawing my conclusions from these facts, I rose and came forward and attempted to contradict him; but as you were not willing to hear me, I held my peace, with no more than these words of solemn protest, which I entreat you, in Heaven's name, to remember. 'I have no knowledge of these promises,' I said, 'and no share in making them; and,' I added, 'I do not believe they will be fulfilled.' This last expression roused your temper, and I proceeded, 'Take care, men of Athens, that if any of these things comes to pass, you thank these gentlemen for it, and give your honours and crowns to them, and not to me. If, however, anything of an opposite character occurs, you must equally vent your anger on them: I decline all responsi-46 bility.' 'No, no!' interrupted Aeschines, 'do not decline responsibility now! Take care rather that you do not claim credit, when the time comes.' 'Indeed, it would be an injustice if I did so,' I replied. Then Philocrates arose with a most insolent air, and said, 'It is no wonder, men of Athens, that I and Demosthenes should disagree; for he drinks water, I drink wine.' And you laughed.

47 Now consider the decree which Philocrates proposed and handed in. An excellent resolution it sounds, as you hear it now. But when you take into account the occasion on

which it was proposed, and the promises which Aeschines was then making, you will see that their action amounts to nothing less than a surrender of the Phocians to Philip and the Thebans, and that, practically, with their hands tied behind their backs. (*To the clerk.*) Read the decree.

[*The decree is read.*]

There, men of Athens, is the decree, overflowing with 48 expressions of gratitude and auspicious language. 'The Peace,' it says, 'which is granted to Philip shall be granted on the same terms to his descendants, and also the alliance.' Again, we are 'to thank Philip for his promised acts of justice'. Yet Philip made no promises: so far was he from making promises that he said he did not know what he could do to gratify you. It was Aeschines who spoke in his name, and 49 made the promises. Then Philocrates took advantage of the enthusiasm which Aeschines' words aroused in you, to insert in the decree the clause, 'and unless the Phocians act as they are bound, and surrender the temple to the Amphictyons, the Athenian people will render their assistance against those who still stand in the way of such surrender.' Thus, 50 men of Athens, at a time when you were still at home and had not taken the field, when the Spartans had foreseen the deception and retired, and when none of the Amphictyons were on the spot but the Thessalians and Thebans, he proposes in the most innocent-sounding language in the world that they shall deliver up the temple to these. For he proposes that they shall deliver it up to the Amphictyons. But what Amphictyons? for there were none there but the Thessalians and Thebans. He does not propose that the Amphictyons should be convoked, or that they should wait until the Amphictyons met or that Proxenus should render assistance in Phocis, or that the Athenians should take the 51 field, or anything of the sort. Philip did indeed actually send two letters to summon you. But he did not intend you really to march from Athens. Not a bit of it! For he would not have waited to summon you until he had seen the time go by in which you could have set out; nor would he have tried to prevent me, when I wished to set sail and return hither; nor would he have instructed Aeschines to speak to you in the terms which would be least likely to cause you to march. No! he intended that you should fancy that he was about to fulfil your desires, and in that belief should abstain from any resolution adverse to him; and that the Phocians should, in consequence, make no defence or resistance, in reliance upon any hopes inspired by you, but should put themselves into his hands in utter despair. (*To the clerk.*) Read to the jury the letters of Philip.

[*The letters are read.*]

52 Now these letters summon you, and that, forsooth, instantly; and it was surely for Aeschines and his party, if the proceeding was in any way genuine, to support the summons, to urge you to march, and to propose that Proxenus, whom they knew to be in those parts, should render assistance at once. Yet it is plain that their action was of precisely the opposite character; and naturally so. For they did not attend to the terms of the letter, but to the intention with 53 which Philip wrote it. With this intention they co-operated, and to this they strove to give effect. As soon as the Phocians had learned the news of your proceedings in the Assembly, and had received this decree of Philocrates, and heard the defendant's announcement and his promises, everything

combined to effect their doom. Consider the circumstances. There were some of them who had the wisdom to distrust Philip. These were induced to trust him. And why? Because they believed that even if Philip were trying to deceive them ten times over, the ambassadors of Athens, at least, would never dare to deceive their own countrymen. This report which Aeschines had made to you must therefore be true: it was the Thebans, and not themselves, whose hour had come. There were others who 54 advocated resistance at all hazards; but these too were weakened in their resolution, now that they were persuaded that they could count upon Philip's favour, and that, unless they did as they were bidden, you, whose assistance they were hoping for, would march against them. There was also a third party, who thought that you repented of having made the Peace with Philip; but to these they pointed out that you had decreed that the same Peace should hold good for posterity also; so that on every ground, all assistance from you was despaired of. That is why they crowded all these points into one decree. And in this lies, I think, the 55 very greatest of all their crimes against you. To have made a Peace with a mortal man, whose power was due to the accidents of the moment—a Peace, whereby they covenanted that the disgrace brought upon the city should be everlasting; to have robbed the city, not only of all beside, but even of the benefits that Fortune might hereafter bestow: to have displayed such superabundant villany as to have done this wicked wrong not only to their countrymen now living, but also to all those who should ever thereafter be born—is it not utterly atrocious? And this last clause, by which the 56 Peace was extended to your descendants, you would certainly never have allowed to be added to the conditions of peace had you not then placed your trust in the promises announced by Aeschines, as the Phocians placed their trust in them and perished. For, as you know, they delivered themselves up to Philip; they gave their cities into his hands; and the consequences which befell them were the exact opposite of all that Aeschines had predicted to you.

57 That you may realize plainly that this calamity was brought about in the manner that I have described, and that they are responsible for it, I will go through the dates at which each separate event occurred; and if any one can contradict me on any point, I invite him to rise and speak in the time allotted to me. The Peace was made on the 19th of Elaphebolion, and we were away on the mission which was sent to receive the oaths three whole months.

58 All this time the Phocians remained unharmed. We returned from that mission on the 13th of Scirophorion. Philip had already appeared at Thermopylae, and was making promises to the Phocians, none of which they believed—as is proved, when you consider that otherwise they would not have appealed to you. Then followed the Assembly, at which, by their falsehoods and by the deception which they practised upon you, Aeschines and his party ruined the whole cause.

59 That was on the 16th of Scirophorion. Now I calculate that it was on the fifth day that the report of your proceedings reached the Phocians: for the Phocian envoys were here on the spot, and were deeply concerned to know what report these men would make, and what your resolution would be. That gives us the 20th as the date on which, as we calculate, the Phocians heard of your proceedings; for, counting from the 16th, the 20th is the fifth day. Then followed the 21st, the 22nd,

60 and the 23rd. On the latter day the truce was made, and the

ruin of the Phocians was finally sealed. This can be proved as follows. On the 27th you were holding an Assembly in the Peiraeus, to discuss the business connected with the dockyards, when Dercylus arrived from Chalcis with the news that Philip had put everything into the hands of the Thebans, and that this was the fifth day since the truce had been made. 23rd, 24th, 25th, 26th, 27th—the 27th is the fifth day precisely. Thus the dates, and their reports and their proposals—everything, in short, convicts them of having co-operated with Philip, and of sharing with him the responsibility for the overthrow of the Phocians. Again, the fact 61 that none of the towns in Phocis was taken by siege or by an attack in force, and that the utter ruin of them all was the direct consequence of their truce with Philip, affords the strongest evidence that it was the belief inspired in the Phocians by these men, that they would be preserved from destruction by Philip, which was the cause of their fate. Philip himself they knew well enough. (*To the clerk.*) Bring me our treaty of alliance with the Phocians, and the decrees under which they demolished their walls. (*To the jury.*) You will then realize what were the relations between themselves and you, upon which they relied, and what nevertheless was the fate which befell them through the action of these accursed men. (*To the clerk.*) Read.

[*The Treaty of Alliance between the Athenians and Phocians is read.*]

These, then, were the things for which they relied upon 62 you—friendship, alliance, and assistance. Now listen to what befell them, because Aeschines prevented your going to their assistance. (*To the clerk.*) Read.

[*The Agreement between Philip and the Phocians is read.*]

You hear it, men of Athens. 'An Agreement between Philip and the Phocians,' it runs—not between the Thebans and the Phocians, nor the Thessalians and the Phocians, nor the Locrians, nor any one else who was there. Again, 'the Phocians shall deliver up their cities to Philip'—not to the 63 Thebans or Thessalians or any one else. And why? Because the defendant's report to you was that Philip had crossed the Pass with a view to the preservation of the Phocians. Thus it was Aeschines in whom all their trust was placed; it was with him in their minds that they considered the whole situation; it was with him in their minds that they made the Peace. (*To the clerk.*) Now read the remainder. (*To the jury.*) And do you observe for what they trusted him, and what treatment they received. Does it show any resemblance or similarity to what Aeschines predicted in his report? (*To the clerk.*) Read on.

[*The decrees of the Amphictyons are read.*]

64 Men of Athens, the horror and the immensity of this calamity have never been surpassed in our day in the Hellenic world, nor even, I believe, in the time before us. Yet these great and dreadful events a single man has been given power to bring about, by the action of these men, while the city of Athens was still in being—Athens, whose traditional policy is to stand as the champion of the Hellenic peoples, and not to suffer anything like this to take place. The nature of the ruin which the unhappy Phocians have suffered may be seen, not only from these decrees, but also from the actual results of the action taken, and an awful and piteous sight it is, 65 men of Athens. For when recently we were on our way to

Delphi we could not help seeing it all—houses razed to the ground, cities stripped of their walls, the land destitute of men in their prime—only a few poor women and little children left, and some old men in misery. Indeed, no words can describe the distress now prevailing there. Yet this was the people, I hear you all saying, that once gave its vote against the Thebans, when the question of your enslavement was laid before them. What then, men of Athens, do you 66 think would be the vote, what the sentence, that your forefathers would give, if they could recover consciousness, upon those who were responsible for the destruction of this people? I believe that if they stoned them to death with their own hands, they would hold themselves guiltless of blood. Is it not utterly shameful—does it not, if possible, go beyond all shame—that those who saved us then, and gave the saving vote for us, should now have met with the very opposite fate through these men, suffering as no Hellenic people has ever suffered before, with none to hinder it? Who then is responsible for this crime? Who is the author of this deception? Who but Aeschines?

Of all the many reasons for which Philip might be con- 67 gratulated with good cause upon his fortune, the chief ground of congratulation is a piece of good fortune, to which, by every Heavenly Power, I cannot find any parallel in our days. To have captured great cities, to have reduced a vast expanse of territory to subjection, and all similar actions, are, of course, enviable and brilliant achievements—undeniably so. But many other persons might be mentioned who had achieved as much. The good fortune of which 68 I am about to speak is peculiar to Philip, and has never been given to any other. It is this—that when he needed scoundrels to do his work for him, he found even greater scoundrels than he wanted. For as such we have surely good reason to think of them. For when there were falsehoods which Philip himself, in spite of the immense interests which he had at stake, did not dare to utter on his own behalf—which he did not set down in any of his letters, and which none of his envoys uttered—these men sold their services for the purpose, and 69 undertook your deception. Antipater and Parmenio, servants of a master as they were, and unlikely ever to find themselves in your presence again, none the less secured for themselves that *they* should not be the instruments in your deception, while these men, who were Athenians, citizens of the most free city, and held an official position as your ambassadors—though they would have to meet you and look you in the face, and pass the remainder of their lives among you, and render before you an account of their actions—they, I say, undertook the task of deceiving you. How could vileness or desperation go further than this ?

70 But I would have you understand further that he is under your curse, and that you cannot, without violation of religion and piety, acquit him, when he has thus lied to you. (*To the clerk.*) Recite the Curse. Take it from me, and read it out of the law.

[*The Curse is read.*]

This imprecation is pronounced in your name, men of Athens, by the herald, at every meeting of the Assembly, as the law appoints ; and when the Council sits, it is pronounced again there. Nor can Aeschines say that he did not know it well. He was your under-clerk and servant to the Council, and used himself to read this law over to the 71 herald. Surely, then, you will have done a strange and monstrous thing, men of Athens, if to-day, when you have it in your power, you should fail to do for yourselves the thing which you enjoin upon the gods, or rather claim from them as your due; and should acquit a man whom you pray to the gods to destroy utterly—himself, his race and his house. You must not do this. You may leave it to the gods to punish one whom you cannot yourselves detect; but when you have yourselves caught the criminal, you must no longer lay the task of punishing him upon the gods.

72 Now I am told that he intends to carry his shamelessness and impudence so far, as to avoid all mention of his own proceedings—his report, his promises, the deception he has practised upon the city—as though his trial were taking place before strangers, instead of before you, who know all the facts; and that he intends to accuse first the Spartans, then the Phocians, and then Hegesippus. 73 That is mere mockery; or rather, it is atrocious shamelessness. For all that he will allege to-day against the Phocians or the Spartans or Hegesippus—their refusal to receive Proxenus, their impiety—let him allege what he will—all these allegations refer, as you know, to actions which were already past when these ambassadors returned to Athens, and which were no obstacle to the preservation of the Phocians—the admission is made by whom? By the defendant Aeschines himself. 74 For what was his report on that occasion? Not that if it had not been for their refusal to receive Proxenus, nor that if it had not been for Hegesippus, nor that if it had not been for such and such things, the Phocians would have been saved. No! he discarded all such qualifications, and stated expressly that before he returned he had persuaded Philip to save the Phocians, to repeople Boeotia, and to arrange matters to suit your convenience; that within two or three

days these things would be accomplished facts, and that for this reason the Thebans had set a price upon his head.
75 Refuse then, to hear or to tolerate any mention of what had already been done, either by the Spartans or by the Phocians, before he made his report; and do not let him denounce the rascality of the Phocians. It was not for their virtue that you once saved the Spartans, nor the Euboeans, that accursed people! nor many others; but because the interests of the city demanded their preservation, as they demanded that of the Phocians just now. And what wrong was done either by the Phocians or by the Spartans, or by yourselves, or by any one else in the world *after* he made those declarations, to prevent the fulfilment of the promises which he then made? Ask him that: for that is what he will
76 not be able to show you. It was within five days—five days and no more—that Aeschines made his lying report, that you believed him, that the Phocians heard of it, surrendered themselves and perished. This, I think, makes it as plain as it can possibly be, that the ruin of the Phocians was the result of organized deceit and trickery, and of nothing else. For so long as Philip was unable to proceed to Phocis on account of the Peace, and was only waiting in readiness to do so, he kept sending for the Spartans, promising to do all that they wished, in order that the Phocians might not win
77 them over to their side by your help. But when he had arrived at Thermopylae, and the Spartans had seen the trap and retired, he now sent Aeschines in advance to deceive you, in order that he might not, owing to your perceiving that he was playing into the hands of the Thebans, find himself once more involved in loss of time and war and delay, through the Phocians defending themselves and your going

to their assistance, but might get everything into his power without a struggle; and this is what has in fact happened. Do not, then, let the fact that Philip deceived the Spartans and Phocians as well as yourselves enable Aeschines to escape his punishment for deceiving you. That would not be just.

But if he tells you that, to compensate for the Phocians 78 and Thermopylae and all your other losses, you have retained possession of the Chersonese, do not, in Heaven's name, accept the plea! Do not tolerate the aggravation of all the wrong that you have suffered through his conduct as ambassador, by the reproach which his defence would bring upon the city—the reproach of having sacrificed the existence of your allies, in an underhand attempt to save part of your own possessions! You did not act thus; for when the Peace had already been made, and the Chersonese was no longer in danger, there followed four whole months during which the Phocians remained unharmed; and it was not until after this that the lying statements of Aeschines brought about their ruin by deceiving you. And further, you will 79 find that the Chersonese is in much greater danger now than it was then. For when do you think that we had the greater facilities for punishing Philip for any trespass against the Chersonese?—before he stole any of these advantages from the city, or now? For my part, I think we had far greater facilities then. What, then, does this 'retention of the Chersonese' amount to, when all the fears and the risks which attended one who would have liked to attack it have been removed?

Again, I am told that he will express himself to some such 80 effect as this—that he cannot think why he is accused by Demosthenes, and not by any of the Phocians. It is better that you should hear the true state of the case from me beforehand. Of the exiled Phocians, the best, I believe, and the most respectable, after being driven into banishment and suffering as they have suffered, are content to be quiet, and none of them would consent to incur an enmity which would fall upon himself, on account of the calamities of his people: while those who would do anything for money have no one 81 to give it to them. For assuredly *I* would never have given any one anything whatever to stand by my side here and cry aloud how cruelly they have suffered. The truth and the deeds that have been done cry aloud of themselves. And as for the Phocian people, they are in so evil and pitiable a plight, that there is no question for them of appearing as accusers at the examination of every individual ambassador in Athens. They are in slavery, in mortal fear of the Thebans and of Philip's mercenaries, whom they are compelled to support, broken up into villages as they are and stripped of 82 their arms. Do not, then, suffer him to urge such a plea. Make him prove to you that the Phocians are not ruined, or that he did not promise that Philip would save them. For the questions upon which the examination of an ambassador turns are these: 'What have you effected? What have you reported? If the report is true, you may be acquitted; if it is false, you must pay the penalty.' How can you plead the non-appearance of the Phocians, when it was you yourself, I fancy, that brought them, so far as it lay in your power, into such a condition that they could neither help their friends nor repel their enemies.

83 And further, apart from all the shame and the dishonour in which also these proceedings are involved, it is easy to show that in consequence of them the city has been beset

with grave dangers as well. Every one of you knows that it was the hostilities which the Phocians were carrying on, and their command of Thermopylae, that rendered us secure against Thebes, and made it impossible that either Philip or the Thebans should ever march into the Peloponnese or into Euboea or into Attica. But this guarantee of 84 safety which the city possessed, arising out of the position of Thermopylae and the actual circumstances of the time, you were induced to sacrifice by the deceptions and the lying statements of these ambassadors—a guarantee, I say, fortified by arms, by a continuous campaign, by great cities of allies, and by a wide tract of territory; and you have looked on while it was swept away. Fruitless has your first expedition to Thermopylae become—an expedition made at a cost of more than two hundred talents, if you include the private expenditure of the soldiers—and fruitless your hopes of triumph over Thebes! But of all the wicked 85 services which he has done for Philip, let me tell you of that which is in reality the greatest outrage of all upon Athens and upon you all. It is this—that when Philip had determined from the very first to do for the Thebans all that he has done, Aeschines, by reporting the exact opposite to you, and so displaying to the world your antagonism to Philip's designs, has brought about for you an increase in the enmity between yourselves and the Thebans, and for Philip an increase in their gratitude. How could a man have treated you more outrageously than this?

(*To the clerk.*) Now take and read the decrees of Dio- 86 phantus and Callisthenes; (*to the jury*) for I would have you realize that when you acted as you ought, you were thought worthy to be honoured with public thanksgivings and praises, both at home and abroad; but when once you had been driven astray by these men, you had to bring your children and wives in from the country, and to decree that the sacrifice to Heracles should take place within the walls, though it was a time of peace. And in view of this it is an amazing idea, that you should dismiss unpunished a man who even prevented the gods from receiving their worship from you after the manner of your fathers. (*To the clerk.*) Read the decree.

[*The decree of Diophantus is read.*]

This decree, men of Athens, was one which your conduct nobly deserved. (*To the clerk.*) Now read the next decree.

[*The decree of Callisthenes is read.*]

87 This decree you passed in consequence of the action of these men. It was not with such a prospect in view that you made the Peace and the alliance at the outset, or that you were subsequently induced to insert the words which extended them to your posterity. You expected their action to bring you benefits of incredible value. Aye, and besides this, you know how often, after this, you were bewildered by the report that Philip's forces and mercenaries were threatening Porthmus or Megara. You have not then to reflect contentedly that Philip has not yet set foot in Attica. You have rather to consider whether their action has not given him power to do so when he chooses. It is that danger that you must keep before your eyes, and you must execrate and punish the man who is guilty of putting such power into Philip's hands.

88 Now I am aware that Aeschines will eschew all defence

of the actions with which he is charged, and that, in his desire to lead you as far away as possible from the facts, he will enumerate the great blessings which Peace brings to all mankind, and will set against them the evils that follow in the train of war. His whole speech will be a eulogy of peace, and in that will consist his defence. But such an argument actually incriminates the defendant further. If peace, which brings such blessings to all other men, has been the source of such trouble and confusion to us, what explanation can be found, except that they have taken bribes and have cruelly marred a thing by nature so fair? 'What?' he may say, 89 'have you not to thank the Peace for three hundred ships, with their fittings, and for funds which remain and will remain yours?' In answer to this, you are bound to suppose that, thanks to the Peace, Philip's resources too have become far more ample—aye, and his command of arms, and of territory, and of revenues, which have accrued to him to such large amounts. We, too, have had some increase of revenue. 90 But as for power and alliances, by the establishment of which all men retain their advantages, either for themselves or their masters, ours have been sold by these men —ruined and enfeebled; while Philip's have become more formidable and extensive by far. Thus it is not fair that while Philip has been enabled by their action to extend both his alliances and his revenue, all that would in any case have been ours, as the result of the Peace, should be set off against what they themselves sold to Philip. The former did not come to us in exchange for the latter. Far from it! For had it not been for them, not only should we have had the former, as we have now, but we should have had the latter as well.

91 You would doubtless admit, men of Athens, in general terms, that, on the one hand, however many and terrible the disasters that have befallen the city, your anger cannot justly be visited upon Aeschines, if none of them has been caused by him; and that, on the other hand, Aeschines is not entitled to be acquitted on account of any satisfactory results that may have been accomplished through the action of others. You must examine the acts of Aeschines himself, and then show him your favour if he is worthy of it, or your resentment, on the other hand, if his acts prove to be deserving of that. 92 How, then, can you solve this problem fairly? You will do so if, instead of allowing him to confound all questions with one another—the criminal conduct of the generals, the war with Philip, the blessings that flow from peace—you consider each point by itself. For instance, were we at war with Philip? We were. Does any one accuse Aeschines on that ground? Does any one wish to bring any charge against him in regard to things that were done in the course of the war? No one whatever. He is therefore acquitted in regard to such matters, and must not say anything about them; for the witnesses and the proofs which a defendant produces must bear upon the matters which are in dispute; he must not deceive you by offering a defence upon points which are not disputed. Take care, then, that you say nothing about the war; for no one charges you with any responsibility for that. 93 Later on we were urged by certain persons to make peace. We consented; we sent ambassadors; and the ambassadors brought commissioners to Athens who were to conclude the Peace. Once more, does any one blame Aeschines for this? Does any one allege that Aeschines introduced the proposal of peace, or that he committed any

crime in bringing commissioners here to make it? No one whatever. He must therefore say nothing in regard to the fact that the city made peace; for he is not responsible for that. 'Then what *is* your assertion, sir?' I may be asked. 94 'At what point *do* your charges begin?' They begin, men of Athens, from the time when the question before you was not whether you should make peace or not (for that had already been settled), but what sort of peace you should make—when Aeschines opposed those who took the side of justice, supported for a bribe the hireling mover of the decree, and afterwards, when he had been chosen to receive the oaths, failed to carry out every one of your instructions, destroyed those of your allies who had passed unscathed through the war, and told you falsehoods whose enormity and grossness has never been surpassed, either before or since. At the outset, before Philip was given a hearing in regard to the Peace, Ctesiphon and Aristodemus took the leading part in the work of deception; but when the time had come for action, they surrendered their rôle to Philocrates and Aeschines, who took it up and ruined everything. And 95 then, when he is bound to answer for his actions and to give satisfaction for them—like the unscrupulous God-forsaken clerk that he is—he will defend himself as though it were the Peace for which he was being tried. Not that he wishes to account for more than is charged against him—that would be lunacy. No! He sees rather that in all his own proceedings no good can be found—that his crimes are his whole history; while a defence of the Peace, if it has no other merits, has at least the kindly sound of the name to recommend it. I fear, indeed, 96 men of Athens, I fear that, unconsciously, we are enjoying this Peace like men who borrow at heavy interest. The guarantees of its security—the Phocians and Thermopylae—they have betrayed. But, be that as it may, it was not through *Aeschines* that we originally made it; for, paradoxical as it may seem, what I am about to say is absolutely true—that if any one is honestly pleased at the Peace, it is the generals, who are universally denounced, that he must thank for it: for had they been conducting the war as you desired them to do, 97 you would not have tolerated even the name of peace. For peace, then, we must thank the generals; but the perilous, the precarious, the untrustworthy nature of the Peace is due to the corruption of these men. Cut him off, then, cut him off, I say, from all arguments in defence of the Peace! Set him to defend his own actions! Aeschines is not being tried on account of the Peace. On the contrary, the Peace stands discredited owing to Aeschines. And here is evidence of the fact:—if the Peace had been made, and if no subsequent deception had been practised upon you, and none of your allies had been ruined, who on earth would have been hurt by the Peace, except in so far as it was inglorious? And for its inglorious character the defendant in fact shares the responsibility, for he spoke in support of Philocrates. At least no irreparable harm would have been done; whereas now, I believe, much has been done, and the guilt rests with the defendant.

98 That these men have been the agents in this shameful and wicked work of ruin and destruction, I think you all know. Yet so far am I, gentlemen of the jury, from putting any unfair construction upon these facts or asking you to do so, that if it has been through stupidity or simplicity, or ignorance in any form whatever, that such results have been so brought about, I acquit Aeschines myself, and I 99 recommend you also to acquit him. At the same time

none of these excuses is either constitutional or justifiable. For you neither command nor compel any one to undertake public business; but when any one has satisfied himself of his own capacity and has entered political life, then, like good-hearted, kindly men, you welcome him in a friendly and ungrudging manner, and even elect him to office and place your own interests in his hands. Then, if a man succeeds, 100 he will receive honour and will so far have an advantage over the crowd. But if he fails, is he to plead palliations and excuses? That is not fair. It would not satisfy our ruined allies, or their children, or their wives, or the rest of the victims, to know that it was through my stupidity—not to speak of the stupidity of the defendant—that they had suffered such a fate. Far from it! Nevertheless, I bid you 101 forgive Aeschines for these atrocious and unparalleled crimes if he can prove that it was simplicity of mind, or any form of ignorance whatever, which led him to work such ruin. But if it was the rascality of a man who had taken money and bribes—if he is plainly convicted of this by the very facts themselves—then, if it be possible, put him to death; or if not, make him, while he lives, an example to others.

And now give your thoughts to the proof by which he is convicted on these points, and observe how straightforward it will be.

If the defendant Aeschines was not deliberately deceiving 102 you for a price, he must necessarily, I presume, have had one of two reasons for making the statements in question to you, in regard to the Phocians and Thespiae and Euboea. Either he must have heard Philip promise in express terms that such would be his policy and the steps he would take;

or else he must have been so far bewitched and deluded by Philip's generosity in all other matters as to conceive these further hopes of him. There is no possible alternative 103 besides these two. Now in both these cases he, more than any living man, ought to detest Philip. And why? Because, so far as Philip could bring it about, all that is most dreadful and most shameful has fallen upon him. He has deceived you; his reputation is gone [he is rightly ruined]; he is on his trial; aye, and were the course of the proceedings in any way that which his conduct called for, he would long 104–109 ago have been impeached; whereas now, thanks to your innocence and meekness, he presents his report, and that at the time which suits his own wishes. I ask, then, if there is one among you who has ever heard Aeschines raise his voice in denunciation of Philip—one, I say, who has seen Aeschines exposing him or saying a word against him? Not one! All Athens denounces Philip before Aeschines does so. Every one whom you meet does so, though not one of them has been injured by him—I mean, of course, personally. On the assumption that Aeschines had not sold himself, I should have expected to hear him use some such expressions as these—'Men of Athens, deal with *me* as you will. I trusted Philip; I was deceived; I was wrong; I confess my error. But beware of *him*, men of Athens. He is faithless—a cheat, a knave. Do you not see how he has treated me? how he 110 has deceived me?' But I hear no such expressions fall from him, nor do you. And why? Because he was *not* misled; he was *not* deceived; he made these statements, he betrayed all to Philip, because he had sold his services and received the money for them; and gallantly and loyally has he behaved—as Philip's hireling. But as your ambassador, as your fellow citizen, he is a traitor who deserves to die, not once, but thrice.

111 This is not the only evidence which proves that all those statements of his were made for money. For, recently, the Thessalians came to you, and with them envoys from Philip, demanding that you should decree the recognition of Philip as one of the Amphictyons. Who then, of all men, should naturally have opposed the demand? The defendant Aeschines. And why? Because Philip had acted in a manner precisely contrary to the announcement which Aeschines had made to you. 112 Aeschines declared that Philip would fortify Thespiae and Plataeae; that he intended, not to destroy the Phocians, but to put down the insolence of Thebes. But in fact Philip has raised the Thebans to an undue height of power, while he has utterly destroyed the Phocians; and instead of fortifying Thespiae and Plataeae, he has brought Orchomenus and Coroneia into the same bondage with them. How could any contradiction be greater than this? Aeschines did *not* oppose the demand. He neither opened his lips nor uttered a sound in opposition to it. 11 But even this, monstrous as it is, is not yet the worst. For he, and he alone, in all Athens, actually supported the demand. This not even Philocrates dared to do, abominable as he was; it was left for the defendant Aeschines. And when you raised a clamour and would not listen to him, he stepped down from the platform, and, showing off before the envoys who had come from Philip, told them that there were plenty of men who made a clamour, but few who took the field when it was required of them—you remember the incident, no doubt—being himself, of course, a marvellous soldier, God knows!

114 Again, if we had been unable to prove that any of the ambassadors had received anything—if the fact were not patent to all—we might then have resorted to examination by torture, and other such methods. But if Philocrates not only admitted the fact frequently in your presence at the Assembly, but used actually to make a parade of his guilt—selling wheat, building houses, saying that he was going whether you elected him or not, importing timber, changing Macedonian gold openly at the bank—it is surely impossible for *him* to deny that he received money, when he himself

115 confesses and displays his guilt. Now, is any human being so senseless or so ill-starred that, in order that Philocrates might receive money, while he himself incurred infamy and disgrace, he would want to fight against those upright citizens in whose ranks he might have stood, and to take the side of Philocrates and face a trial? I am sure that there is no such man; but in all these considerations, if you examine them aright, you will find strong and evident signs of the corruption of the defendant.

116 Consider next an incident which occurred last in order of time, but which is second to none as an indication that Aeschines had sold himself to Philip. You doubtless know that in the course of the recent impeachment of Philocrates by Hypereides, I came forward and expressed my dissatisfaction with one feature of the impeachment—namely, the idea that Philocrates alone had been responsible for all these monstrous crimes, and that the other nine ambassadors had no share in them. I said that it was not so, for Philocrates by himself would have been nowhere, had he not had some

117 of them to co-operate with him. 'And therefore,' I said, 'in order that I may not personally acquit or accuse any one,

and that the guilty may be detected, and those who have had no share in the crime acquitted by the evidence of their own conduct, let any one who wishes to do so rise and come forward into your midst, and let him declare that he has no share in it, and that the actions of Philocrates are displeasing to him. Any one who does this,' I said, 'I acquit.' You remember the incident, I am sure. Well, 118 no one came forward or showed himself. Each of the others has some excuse. One was not liable to examination; another, perhaps, was not present; a third is related to Philocrates. But Aeschines has no such excuse. No! So completely has he sold himself, once for all—so plain is it that his wages are not for past services only, but that, if he escapes now, Philip can equally count upon his help against you in the future—that to avoid letting fall even a word that would be unfavourable to Philip, he does not accept his discharge even when you offer to discharge him, but chooses to suffer infamy, to stand his trial and to endure any treatment in this court, rather than to take a step that would not please Philip. But what is the meaning of this 119 partnership, this careful forethought for Philocrates? For if Philocrates had by his diplomacy accomplished the most honourable results and achieved all that your interest required, and yet admitted (as he did admit) that he had made money by his mission, this very fact was one by which an uncorrupted colleague should have been repelled and set him on his guard, and led to protest to the best of his power. Aeschines has not acted in this way. Is it not all clear, men of Athens? Do not the facts cry aloud and tell you that Aeschines has taken money, that he is a rascal for a price, and that consistently—not through stupidity, or ignorance, or bad luck?

120 'But where is the witness who testifies to my corruption?' he asks. Why, this is the finest thing of all! The witnesses, Aeschines, are facts; and they are the surest of all witnesses: none can assert or allege against them, that they are influenced by persuasion or by favour to any one: what your treachery and mischief have made them, such, when examined, they must appear. But, besides the facts, you shall at once bear witness against yourself. Come, stand up and answer me! Surely you will not plead that you are so inexperienced as not to know what to say. For when, under the ordinary limitations of time, you prosecute and win cases that have all the novelty of a play—cases, too, that have no witness to support them—you must plainly be a speaker of tremendous genius.

121 Many and atrocious as are the crimes of the defendant Aeschines, and great as is the wickedness which is implied by them (as I am sure you also feel) there is none which is more atrocious than that of which I am about to speak to you, and none which will afford more palpable proof that he has taken bribes and sold everything. For when once more, for the third time, you sent the ambassadors to Philip on the strength of those high and noble expectations which the defendant's promises had roused, you elected both Aeschines and myself, and most of those whom you had previously

122 sent. For my part I came forward and declined upon oath to serve; and though some raised a clamour and bade me go, I declared that I would not; but the defendant had already been elected. Afterwards, when the Assembly had risen, he and his party met and discussed whom they should leave behind in Athens. For while everything was still in suspense, and the future doubtful, there were all kinds

of gatherings and discussions in the market-place. They were afraid, no doubt, that a special meeting of the Assembly might suddenly be called, and that you might then hear the truth from me, and pass some of the resolutions which it was your duty to pass in the interest of the Phocians, and that so Philip's object might slip from his grasp. For had you merely passed a resolution and shown them the faintest ray of hope of any kind, the Phocians would have been saved. It was absolutely impossible for Philip to stay where he was, unless you were misled. There was no corn in the country, for, owing to the war, the land had not been sown; and to import corn was impossible so long as your ships were there and in command of the sea; while the Phocian towns were many in number, and difficult to take except by a prolonged siege. Even assuming that he were taking a town a day, there are two and twenty of them. For all these reasons they left Aeschines in Athens, to guard against any alteration of the course which you had been deluded into taking. Now to decline upon oath to serve, without any cause, was a dangerous and highly suspicious proceeding. 'What?' he would have been asked, 'are you not going on the mission which is to secure all those wonderful good things which you have foretold?' Yet he was bound to remain. How could it be done? He pleads illness. His brother took with him Execestus the physician, came before the Council, swore that Aeschines was too ill to serve, and was himself elected in his place. Five or six days later the ruin of the Phocians had been accomplished, and Aeschines' contract—a mere matter of business—had been fulfilled. Dercylus turned back, and on his arrival here from Chalcis announced to you the destruction of the Phocians, while you were holding an Assembly

123 124 125

in the Peiraeus. On hearing the news you were naturally struck with sympathy for them, and with terror for yourselves. You passed resolutions to bring in your children and wives from the country, to repair the garrison-forts, to fortify the Peiraeus, and to celebrate the sacrifice to 126 Heracles within the city walls: and in the midst of all this, in the midst of the confusion and the tumult which had fallen upon the city, this learned and able speaker, so loud of voice, though not elected either by the Council or by the people, set off as ambassador to the man who had wrought the destruction, taking no account of the illness which he had previously made his excuse, upon oath, for not serving, nor of the election of another ambassador in his place, nor of the law which imposes the penalty of death for such offences; 127 nor yet reflecting how utterly atrocious it was, that after announcing that the Thebans had placed a price on his head, he should choose the moment when the Thebans had (in addition to all Boeotia, which they already possessed) become masters of the territory of the Phocians as well, to go into the very midst of Thebes, and into the very camp of the Thebans. But so beside himself was he, so utterly bent upon his profits and his bribe, that he ruled out and overlooked all such considerations, and took his departure.

128 Such was the nature of this transaction; and yet his proceedings when he arrived at his destination are far worse. All of you who are present, and all other Athenians as well, thought the treatment of the unhappy Phocians so atrocious and so cruel that you sent to the Pythian games neither the official deputation from the Council, nor the Thesmothetae, but abandoned that ancient representation of yourselves at the festival. But Aeschines went to the

triumphal feast with which the Thebans and Philip were celebrating the victory of their cause and their arms. He joined in the festival: he shared in the libations and the prayers which Philip offered over the ruined walls and country and arms of your allies: with Philip he set garlands on his head, and raised the paean, and drank the loving-cup. Nor 129 is it possible for the defendant to give a different version of the facts from that which I have given. As regards his sworn refusal to serve, the facts are in your public records in the Metroon, guarded by your officer; and a decree stands recorded with express reference to the name of Aeschines. And as for his conduct there, his fellow ambassadors, who were present, will bear witness against him. They told me the story; for I was not with them on this Embassy, having entered a sworn refusal to serve.

(*To the clerk.*) Now read me the resolution [and the 130 record], and call the witnesses.

[*The decree is read, and the witnesses called.*]

What prayers, then, do you imagine Philip offered to the gods, when he poured his libation, or the Thebans? Did they not ask them to give success in war, and victory, to themselves and their allies, and the contrary to the allies of the Phocians? In these prayers, therefore—in these imprecations upon his own country—Aeschines joined. It is for you to return them upon his own head to-day.

His departure, then, was a contravention of the law which 131 imposes the penalty of death for the offence, and it has been shown that on his arrival he acted in a manner for which he deserves to die again and again, while his former proceedings and the work which he did as ambassador, in their interest, would justly slay him. Ask yourselves what penalty can be found, which will adequately atone for all these 132 crimes ? It would surely be shameful, men of Athens, that while all of you, and the whole people, denounce publicly all the consequences of the Peace ; while you decline to take part in the business of the Amphictyons ; while your attitude towards Philip is one of vexation and mistrust, because the deeds that have been done are impious and atrocious, instead of righteous and advantageous to you ; that nevertheless, when you have come into court as the sworn representatives of the State, to sit in judgement upon the report of these proceedings, you should acquit the author of all the evil, when you have taken him red-handed in actions like these. 133 Who is there of all your fellow citizens—nay, who of all the Hellenes—that would not have good cause for complaint against you, when he saw that though you were enraged against Philip, who in making peace after war was merely purchasing the means to his end from those who offered them for sale—a very pardonable transaction—you were yet acquitting Aeschines, who sold your interests in this shameful manner, notwithstanding the extreme penalties which the laws appoint for such conduct ?

134 Now it is possible that an argument may also be used by the other side to some such effect as this—that the condemnation of those whose diplomacy brought about the Peace will mean the beginning of enmity with Philip. If this is true, then, I can imagine, upon consideration, no more serious charge that I could bring against the defendant, than this. If Philip, who spent his money on the Peace which he wished to obtain, has become so formidable, so powerful, that you have already ceased to regard your oaths and the

justice of the case, and are seeking how you can gratify Philip, what penalty, that those who are responsible for this could suffer, would be adequate to the offence? I believe, however, 135 that I shall actually show you that it would more probably mean the beginning of a friendship, advantageous to you. For you must be well assured, men of Athens, that Philip does not despise your city; nor was it because he regarded you as less serviceable than the Thebans, that he preferred them to you. No! He had been instructed by these men and had heard from them, what I once told you in the Assembly, 136 without contradiction from any of them, that the People is the most unstable thing in the world, and the most incalculable, inconstant as a wave of the sea, stirred by any chance wind. One comes, another goes; but no one cares for the public interest, or remembers it. Philip needs (he is told) friends upon whom he can rely to execute and manage his business with you—such friends, for instance, as his informant. If this were secured for him, he would easily effect all that he desired in Athens. Now if he heard that 137 those who had used such language to him had immediately upon their return been beaten to death, he would doubtless have behaved as the Persian king did. And how was this? He had been deceived by Timagoras, and had given him, it is said, forty talents; but when he heard that Timagoras had been put to death here, and had not even power to secure his own life, much less to carry out the promises he had made to him, he recognized that he had not paid the price to the man who had the power to effect his object. For first, as you know, he sent a dispatch, acknowledging once more your title to Amphipolis, which he had previously described as in alliance and friendship with himself; and secondly, he thenceforward wholly abstained from giving money to any 138 one. This is exactly what Philip would have done, if he had seen that any of these men had paid the penalty, and what, if he sees it, he will still do. But when he hears that they address you, and enjoy a high reputation with you, and prosecute others, what is he to do? Is he to seek to spend much, when he can spend less? or to desire to court the favour of all, when he need but court two or three? That would be madness. For even those public benefits which Philip conferred upon the Thebans he conferred not from choice—far from it—but because he was induced to do so by their 139 ambassadors; and I will tell you how. Ambassadors came to him from Thebes just at the time when we were there upon our mission from you. Philip wished to give them money, and that (so they said) in very large amounts. The Theban ambassadors would not accept or receive it. After that, while drinking at a sacrificial banquet and displaying his generosity towards them, Philip offered, as he drank to them, presents of many kinds—captives and the like—and finally he offered them goblets of gold and silver. All these they steadily refused, declining to put themselves in his power 140 in any way. At last Philo, one of the ambassadors, made a speech, men of Athens, which was worthy to be made in the name, not of Thebes, but of yourselves. For he said that it gave them pleasure and delight to see the magnanimous and generous attitude of Philip towards them; but for their own personal part, they were already his good friends even without these presents; and they begged him to apply his generosity to the existing political situation of their country, and to do something worthy of himself and Thebes, promising that, if he did so, their whole city, as well as themselves, would become attached to him. And 141 now observe what the Thebans have gained by this, and what consequences have followed; and contemplate in a real instance the advantages of refusing to sell your country's interests. First of all, they obtained peace when they were already distressed and suffering from the war, in which they were the losing side. Next, they secured the utter ruin of their enemies, the Phocians, and the complete destruction of their walls and towns. And was this all? No, indeed! For besides all this they obtained Orchomenus, Coroneia, Corsia, the Tilphossaeum, and as much of the territory of the Phocians as they desired. This then was what the Thebans 142 gained by the Peace; and surely no more could they have asked even in their prayers. And the ambassadors of Thebes gained—what? Nothing but the credit of having brought this good fortune to their country; and a noble reward it was, men of Athens, a proud record on the score of merit and honour—that honour which Aeschines and his party sold for money. Let us now set against one another the consequences of the Peace to the city of Athens and to the Athenian ambassadors respectively; and then observe whether its effects have been similar in the case of the city and of these men personally. The city has surrendered all 143 her possessions and all her allies; she has sworn to Philip that even if another approaches them to preserve them for her, you will prevent him; that you will consider any one who wishes to give them up to you as your enemy and foe, and the man who has robbed you of them as your ally and friend. That is the resolution which Aeschines supported, and which 144 was moved by his accomplice Philocrates; and although on the first day I was successful, and had persuaded you to ratify the decree of the allies and to summon Philip's envoys, the defendant forced an adjournment of the question till the next day, and persuaded you to adopt the resolution of Philocrates, in which these proposals, and many others even 145 more atrocious, are made. These were the consequences of the Peace to Athens. It would not be easy to devise anything more shameful. What were the consequences to the ambassadors who brought these things about? I say nothing of all that you have seen for yourselves—the houses, the timber, the wheat. But they also possess properties and extensive estates in the country of your ruined allies, bringing in incomes of a talent to Philocrates and thirty 146 minae to the defendant. Yet surely, men of Athens, it is an atrocious and a monstrous thing, that the calamities of your allies should have become sources of revenue to your ambassadors, and that the same Peace which to the city that sent them meant the ruin of her allies, the surrender of her possessions, and shame in the place of honour, should have created for the ambassadors who brought these things to pass against their country, revenue, affluence, property, and wealth, in the place of abject poverty. To prove, however, that what I am telling you is true (*to the clerk*) call me the witnesses from Olynthus.

[*The witnesses are called.*]

147 Now I should not wonder if he even dared to make some such statement as this—that the Peace which we were making could not have been made an honourable one, or such as I demanded, because our generals had mismanaged the war. If he argues thus, then remember, in Heaven's name, to ask him whether it

was from some other city that he went as ambassador, or from this city itself? If it was from some other, to whose success in war and to whose excellent generals he can point, then it was natural for him to take Philip's money: but if it was from Athens itself, why do we find him taking presents as part of a transaction which involved the surrender of her possessions by the city which sent him? For in any honest transaction the city that sent the ambassadors ought to have shared the same fortune as the ambassadors whom she sent. 148 Consider also this further point, men of Athens. Do you think that the successes of the Phocians against the Thebans in the war, or the successes of Philip against you, were the more considerable? Those of the Phocians against the Thebans, I am quite certain. At least, they held Orchomenus and Coroneia and the Tilphossaeum; they had intercepted the Theban garrison at Neones; they had slain two hundred of them on Hedyleum; a trophy had been raised, their cavalry were victorious, and a whole Iliad of misfortunes had beset 149 the Thebans. You were in no such position as this, and may you never be so in the future! Your most serious disadvantage in your hostilities with Philip was your inability to inflict upon him all the damage that you desired; you were completely secure against suffering any harm yourselves. How is it then that, as the result of one and the same Peace, the Thebans, who were being so badly worsted in the war, have recovered their own possessions and, in addition, have gained those of their enemies; while you, the Athenians, have lost under the Peace even what you retained safely through the war? It is because their ambassadors did not sell their interests, while these men have sold yours. [Ah! he will say, but the allies were exhausted by the war . . .].

That this is how these things were accomplished, you will realize still more clearly from what I have yet to say.

150 For when this Peace was concluded—the Peace of Philocrates, which Aeschines supported—and when Philip's envoys had set sail, after receiving the oaths from us—and up to this time nothing that had been done was irreparable, for though the Peace was disgraceful and unworthy of Athens, still we were to get those marvellous good things in return—then I say, I asked and told the ambassadors to sail as quickly as possible to the Hellespont, and not to sacrifice any of our positions there, nor allow Philip to occupy them in the in-

151 terval. For I knew very well that everything that is sacrificed when peace is in process of being concluded after war, is lost to those who are so neglectful; since no one who had been induced to make peace with regard to the situation as a whole ever yet made up his mind to fight afresh for the sake of possessions which had been left unsecured; such possessions those who first take them keep. And, apart from this, I thought that, if we sailed, the city could not fail to secure one of two useful results. Either, when we were there and had received Philip's oath according to the decree, he would restore the possessions of Athens which he had taken, and

152 keep his hands off the rest; or, if he did not do so, we should immediately report the fact to you here, and so, when you saw his grasping and perfidious disposition in regard to those your remoter and less important interests, you would not in dealing with greater matters close at hand—in other words, with the Phocians and Thermopylae—let anything be lost. If he failed to forestall you in regard to these, and you were not deceived, your interests would be completely secured, and he would give you your rights without hesitation.

And I had good reason for such expectations. For if the 153 Phocians were still safe and sound, as they then were, and were in occupation of Thermopylae, Philip would have had no terror to brandish before you, which could make you overlook any of your rights. For he was not likely either to make his way through by land, or to win a victory by sea, and so reach Attica; while if he refused to act as was right, you would instantly close his ports, reduce him to straits for money and other supplies, and place him in a state of siege; and in that case it would be he, and not you, to whom the advantages of peace would be the overmastering consideration. And that I am not inventing this or claiming wisdom 154 after the event—that I knew it at once, and, with your interest in view, foresaw what must happen and told my colleagues—you will realize from the following facts. When there was no longer any meeting of the Assembly available (since you had used up all the appointed days) and still the ambassadors did not depart, but wasted time here, I proposed a decree as a member of the Council, to which the people had given full powers, that the ambassadors should depart directly, and that the admiral Proxenus should convey them to any district in which he should ascertain Philip to be. My proposal was just what I now tell you, couched expressly in those terms. (*To the clerk.*) Take this decree and read it.

[*The decree is read.*]

I brought them away, then, from Athens, sorely against 155 their will, as you will clearly understand from their subsequent conduct. When we reached Oreus and joined Proxenus, instead of sailing and following their instructions, they made a circuitous journey by land, and before we reached Macedonia we had spent three and twenty days. All the rest of the time, until Philip's arrival, we were sitting idle at Pella; and this, with the journey, brought the time up to 156 fifty days in all. During this interval, in a time of peace and truce, Philip was taking Doriscus, Thrace, the district towards the Walls, the Sacred Mountain—everything, in fact, and making his own arrangements there; while I spoke out repeatedly and insistently, first in the tone of a man giving his opinion to his colleagues, then as though I were informing the ignorant, till at last I addressed them without any concealment as men who had sold themselves and were 157 the most impious of mankind. And the man who contradicted me openly and opposed everything which I urged and which your decree enjoined, was Aeschines. Whether his conduct pleased all the other ambassadors as well, you will know presently; for as yet I allege nothing about any of them, and make no accusation: no one of them need appear an honest man to-day because I oblige him to do so, but only of his own free will, and because he was no partner in Aeschines' crimes. That the conduct in question was disgraceful, atrocious, venal, you have all seen. Who were the partners in it, the facts will show.

158 'But of course, during this interval they received the oaths from Philip's allies, or carried out their other duties.' Far from it! For though they had been absent from home three whole months, and received 1,000 drachmae from you for their expenses, they did not receive the oaths from a single city, either on their journey to Macedonia, or on the way back. It was in the inn before the temple of the Dioscuri—any one who has been to Pherae will understand me—when Philip was already on the march towards Athens at the head of an army, that the oaths were taken, in a fashion which

was disgraceful, men of Athens, and insulting to you. To 159 Philip, however, it was worth anything that the transaction should have been carried out in this form. These men had failed in their attempt to insert among the terms of the Peace the clause which excluded the people of Halus and Pharsalus; Philocrates had been forced by you to expunge the words, and to write down expressly 'the Athenians and the allies of the Athenians'; and Philip did not wish any of his own allies to have taken such an oath; for then they would not join him in his campaign against those possessions of yours which he now holds, but would plead their oaths in excuse; nor did he wish them to be witnesses of the 160 promises on the strength of which he was obtaining the Peace. He did not wish it to be revealed to the world that the city of Athens had not, after all, been defeated in the war, and that it was Philip who was eager for peace, and was promising to do great things for Athens if he obtained it. It was just to prevent the revelation of these facts that he thought it inadvisable that the ambassadors should go to any of the cities; while for their part, they sought to gratify him in everything, with ostentatious and extravagant obsequiousness. But when 161 all this is proved against them—their waste of time, their sacrifice of your position in Thrace, their complete failure to act in accordance either with your decree or your interests, their lying report to you—how is it possible that before a jury of sane men, anxious to be true to their oath, Aeschines can be acquitted? To prove, however, that what I say is true (*to the clerk*), first read the decree, under which it was our duty to exact the oaths, then Philip's letter, and then the decree of Philocrates and that of the people.

[*The decrees and letter are read.*]

162 And now, to prove that we should have caught Philip in the Hellespont, had any one listened to me, and carried out your instructions as contained in the decrees, (*to the clerk*) call the witnesses who were there on the spot.

[*The witnesses are called.*]

(*To the clerk.*) Next read also the other deposition—Philip's answer to Eucleides,[n] who is present here, when he went to Philip afterwards.

[*The deposition is read.*]

163 Now listen to me, while I show that they cannot even deny that it was to serve Philip's interest that they acted as they did. For when we set out on the First Embassy—that which was to discuss the Peace—you dispatched a herald in advance to procure us a safe conduct. Well, on that occasion, as soon as ever they had reached Oreus, they did not wait for the herald, or allow any time to be lost; but though Halus was being besieged, they sailed there direct, and then, leaving the town again, came to Parmenio, who was besieging it, set out through the enemy's camp to Pagasae, and, continuing their journey, only met the herald at Larissa: with such eager 164 haste did they proceed. But at a time when there was peace and they had complete security for their journey and you had instructed them to make haste, it never occurred to them either to quicken their pace or to go by sea. And why? Because on the former occasion Philip's interest demanded that the Peace should be made as soon as possible; whereas now it required that as long an interval as possible 165 should be wasted before the oaths were taken. To prove

that this is so, (*to the clerk*) take and read this further deposition.

[*The deposition is read.*]

How could men be more clearly convicted of acting to serve Philip's interest throughout, than by the fact that they sat idle, when in your interest they ought to have hurried, on the very same journey over which they hastened onward, without even waiting for the herald, when they ought not to have moved at all?

166 Now observe how each of us chose to conduct himself while we were there, sitting idle at Pella. For myself, I chose to rescue and seek out the captives, spending my own money and asking Philip to procure their ransom with the sums which he was offering us in the form of presents. How Aeschines passed his whole time you shall hear presently. 167 What then was the meaning of Philip's offering money to us in common? He kept sounding us all—for this too I would have you know. And how? He sent round privately to each of us, and offered us, men of Athens, a very large sum in gold. But when he failed in a particular case (for I need not mention my own name myself, since the proceedings and their results will of themselves show to whom I refer), he thought that we should all be innocent enough to accept what was given to us in common; and then, if we all alike had a share, however small, in the common present, those who had sold themselves privately would be secure. 168 Hence these offers, under the guise of presents to his guest-friends. And when I prevented this, my colleagues further divided among themselves the sum thus offered. But when I asked Philip to spend this sum on the prisoners, he could neither, without discredit, denounce my colleagues, and say, 'But So-and-so has the

money, and So-and-so,' nor yet evade the expense. So he gave the promise, but deferred its fulfilment, saying that he would send the prisoners home in time for the Panathenaea. (*To the clerk.*) Read the evidence of Apollophanes, and then that of the rest of those present.

[*The evidence is read.*]

169 Now let me tell you how many of the prisoners I myself ransomed. For while we were sitting waiting there at Pella, before Philip's arrival, some of the captives—all, in fact, who were out on bail—not trusting, I suppose, my ability to persuade Philip to act as I wished, said that they wished to ransom themselves, and to be under no obligation to Philip for their freedom: and they borrowed, one three minae, another five, and another—whatever the amount of 170 the ransom was in each case. But when Philip had promised that he would ransom the rest, I called together those to whom I had advanced the money; I reminded them of the circumstances; and, lest they should seem to have suffered by their impatience, and to have been ransomed at their own cost, poor men as they were, when all their comrades expected to be set free by Philip, I made them a present of their ransom. To prove that I am speaking the truth, (*to the clerk*) read these depositions.

[*The depositions are read.*]

171 These, then, are the sums which I excused them, and gave as a free gift to fellow citizens who had met with misfortune. And so, when Aeschines says presently, in his speech to you, 'Demosthenes, if, as you say, you knew, from the time when I supported Philocrates' proposal, that we were acting altogether dishonestly, why did you go again as our colleague

on the subsequent mission to take the oaths, instead of entering a sworn excuse?' remember this, that I had promised those whose freedom I had procured that I would bring them their ransom, and deliver them to the best of my power. It would have been a wicked thing to break my word and 172 abandon my fellow citizens in their misfortune; while, on the other hand, if I had excused myself upon oath from service, it would not have been altogether honourable, nor yet safe, to make a tour there in a private capacity. For let destruction, utter and early, fall upon me, if I would have joined in a mission with these men for a very large sum of money, had it not been for my anxiety to rescue the prisoners. It is a proof of this, that though you twice elected me to serve on the Third Embassy, I twice swore an excuse. And all through the journey in question my policy was entirely opposed to theirs. All, then, that it was within my own 173 power to decide in the course of my mission resulted as I have described; but wherever in virtue of their majority they gained their way, all has been lost. And yet, had there been any who listened to me, all would have been accomplished in a manner congruous with my own actions. For I was not so pitiful a fool as to give away money, when I saw others receiving it, in my ambition to serve you, and yet not to desire what could have been accomplished without expense, and would have brought far greater benefits to the whole city. I desired it intensely, men of Athens; but, of course, they had the advantage over me.

Come now and contemplate the proceedings of Aeschines 174 and those of Philocrates, by the side of my own; for the comparison will bring out their character more vividly. Well, they first pronounced the exclusion from the Peace of the Phocians and the people of Halus, and of Cersobleptes, contrary to your decree and to the statements made to you. Then they attempted to tamper with and alter the decree, which we had come there as ambassadors to execute. Then they entered the Cardians as allies of Philip and voted against sending the dispatch which I had written to you, sending in its stead an utterly unsound dispatch of their

175 own composition. And then the gallant gentleman asserted that I had promised Philip that I would overthrow your constitution, because I censured these proceedings, not only from a sense of their disgracefulness, but also from fear lest through the fault of these men I might have to share their ruin: while all the time he was himself having incessant private interviews with Philip. And, to pass over all besides, Dercylus (not I) watched him through the night at Pherae, along with my slave who is here present; and as the slave came out of Philip's tent he took him and bade him report what he had seen, and remember it himself; and finally, this disgusting and shameless fellow was left behind with

176 Philip for a night and a day, when we went away. And to prove that I am speaking the truth, I will myself give evidence which I have committed to writing, so as to put myself in the position of a responsible witness; and after that I call upon each of the other ambassadors, and I will compel them to choose their alternative—either to give evidence, or to swear that they have no knowledge of the matter. If they take the latter course, I shall convict them of perjury beyond doubt.

[*Evidence is read.*]

177 You have seen now by what mischief and trouble I was hampered, throughout our absence from home. For what

must you imagine their conduct to have been there, with their paymaster close at hand, when they act as they do before your very eyes, though you have power either to confer honour or, on the other hand, to inflict punishment upon them?

I wish now to reckon up from the beginning the charges which I have made, in order to show you that I have done all that I undertook to do at the beginning of my speech. I have 178 proved that there was no truth in his report—that, on the contrary, he deceived you—by the evidence not of words but of the actual course of events. I have proved that he was the cause of your unwillingness to hear the truth from my mouth, captivated as you were at the time by his promises and undertakings; that he gave you advice which was the exact opposite of that which he ought to have given, opposing the Peace which was suggested by the allies, and advocating the Peace of Philocrates; that he wasted time, in order that you might not be able to march to the aid of the Phocians, even if you wished to do so; and that he has done many atrocious deeds during his absence from home; for he has betrayed and sold everything, he has taken bribes, and has left no form of rascality untried. These are the points which I promised at the outset to prove, and I have proved them. Observe, then, what follows; for what I have 179 now to say to you has already become a simple matter. You have sworn that you will vote according to the laws and the decrees of the people and the Council of Five Hundred. The defendant is proved, in all his conduct as ambassador, to have acted in contravention of the laws, of the decrees, and of justice. He ought, therefore, to be convicted in any court composed of rational men. Even if there were no other crimes at his door, two of his actions are sufficient to slay him; for he betrayed to Philip not 180 only the Phocians but also Thrace. Two places in the whole world of greater value to Athens than Thermopylae on land, and the Hellespont over sea, could not possibly be found; and both these places these men have shamefully sold, and placed in Philip's hands to be used against you. The enormity of this crime alone—the sacrifice of Thrace and the Walls—apart from all the rest, might be proved in countless ways, and it is easy to point out how many men have been executed or fined vast sums of money by you for such offences—Ergophilus, Cephisodotus, Timomachus, Ergocles long ago, Dionysius, and others; all of whom together, I may almost say, have done the city less harm than the defendant.

181 But in those days, men of Athens, you still guarded against danger by calculation and forethought; whereas now you overlook any danger which does not annoy you from day to day, or cause you pain by its immediate presence, and then pass such resolutions here as 'that Philip shall take the oath in favour of Cersobleptes also,' 'that we will not take part in the proceedings of the Amphictyons,' 'that we must amend the Peace.' But none of these resolutions would have been required, had Aeschines then been ready to sail and to do what was required. As it is, by urging us to go by land, he has lost all that we could have saved by sailing; and by lying, all that could have been saved by speaking the truth.

182 He intends, I am told, to express immediately his indignation that he alone of all the speakers in the Assembly should have to render an account of his words. I will not urge that all speakers would reasonably be called upon to

render such an account, if any of their words were spoken for money; I only say this. If Aeschines in his private capacity has spoken wildly on some occasion or committed some blunder, do not be over-strict with him, but let it pass and grant him pardon: but if as your ambassador he has deliberately deceived you for money, then do not let him go, or tolerate the plea that he ought not to be called to account for what he *said*. Why, for what, if not for his 183 words, is an ambassador to be brought to justice? Ambassadors have no control over ships or places or soldiers or citadels—no one puts such things in their hands—but over words and times. As regards times, if he did not cause the times of the city's opportunities to be lost, he is not guilty; but if he did so, he has committed crime. And as to his words, if the words of his report were true or expedient, let him escape; but if they were at once false, venal, and disastrous, let him be convicted. No greater wrong can a man do you, 184 than is done by lying speeches. For where government is based upon speeches, how can it be carried on in security, if the speeches are not true? and if, in particular, a speaker takes bribes and speaks to further the interests of the enemy, how can you escape real danger? For to rob you of your opportunities is not the same thing as to rob an oligarchy or a tyrant. Far from it. Under such govern- 185 ments, I imagine, everything is done promptly at a word of command. But with you the Council must first hear about everything, and pass its preliminary resolution—and even that not at any time, but only when notice has been given of the reception of heralds and embassies: then you must convoke an Assembly, and that only when the time comes for one, as ordained by law: then those who speak for your true good have to master and overcome those who, through ignorance or wickedness, oppose

186 them. Besides all this, even when a measure is resolved upon, and its advantages are already plain, time must be granted to the impecuniosity of the majority, in which they may procure whatever means they require in order to be able to carry out what has been resolved. And so he who causes times so critical to be lost, in a state constituted as ours is, has not caused you to lose times, but has robbed you absolutely of the realization of your aims.

187 Now all those who are anxious to deceive you are very ready with such expressions as 'disturbers of the city,' 'men who prevent Philip from conferring benefits on the city.' In reply to these, I will use no argument, but will read you Philip's letters, and will remind you of the occasion on which each piece of deception took place, that you may know that Philip has got beyond this exaggerated title of 'benefactor', of which we are so sickened, in his attempts to take you in by it.

[*Philip's letters are read.*]

188 Now although his work as ambassador has been so shameful, so detrimental to you in many—nay, in all points, he goes about asking people what they think of Demosthenes, who prosecutes his own colleagues. I prosecute you indeed, whether I would or no, because throughout our entire absence from home you plotted against me as I have said, and because now I have the choice of only two alternatives: either I must appear to share with you the responsibility

189 for such work as yours, or I must prosecute you. Nay, I deny that I was ever your colleague in the Embassy. I say that

your work as ambassador was an atrocious work, while my own was for the true good of those present here. It is Philocrates that has been your colleague, as you have been his, and Phrynon. For your policy was the same as theirs, and you all approved of the same objects. But 'where are the salt, the table, the libations that we shared?' So he asks everywhere in his theatrical style—as though it were not the criminals, but the upright, that were false to such pledges! I am certain that though all the Prytanes offer 190 their common sacrifice on each occasion, and join one with another in their meal and their libation, the good do not on this account copy the bad; but if they detect one of their own number in crime they report the fact to the Council and the people. In the very same way the Council offers its inaugural sacrifice and feasts together, and joins in libations and sacred rites. So do the generals, and, one may practically say, every body of magistrates. Does that mean that they grant an indemnity to any of their number who is guilty of crime? Very far from it. Leon accuses Timagoras, 191 after being his fellow ambassador for four years: Eubulus accuses Tharrex and Smicythus, after sharing the banquet with them: the great Conon, the elder, prosecuted Adeimantus,[n] though they were generals together. Which sinned against the salt and the libation, Aeschines—the traitors and the faithless ambassadors and the hirelings, or their accusers? Plainly those who violated, as you have done, the sanctity, not of private libations, but of libations poured in the name of the whole country.

That you may realize that these men have been the most 192 worthless and wicked not only of all who have ever gone to Philip in a public capacity, but even of those who have gone as private persons, and indeed of all mankind, I ask you to listen to me while I describe briefly an incident which falls outside the story of this Embassy. When Philip took Olynthus he celebrated Olympian games, and gathered together all the 193 artists to the sacrifice and the festal gathering. And while he was entertaining them at a banquet, and crowning the victors, he asked Satyrus, the well-known comic actor, why he alone requested no favour of him. Did he see any meanness in him, or any dislike towards himself? Satyrus answered (so the story goes) that he happened to stand in no need of the things for which the rest were asking, but that the boon which he would like to ask was a favour which it would be very easy indeed for Philip to bestow; only he was afraid 194 that he might fail to obtain it. Philip bade him name his request, declaring with some spirit that there was nothing that he would not do for him. Satyrus is then said to have stated that Apollophanes of Pydna was formerly his friend and guest-friend, and that when he had perished by a treacherous assassination, his kinsman had, in alarm, conveyed his daughters, then little children, to Olynthus secretly. 'These girls,' said Satyrus, 'have been taken prisoners at the capture of the city; they are with you, and they are 195 now of marriageable age. It is these girls that I beg and entreat you to give to me. But I should like you to hear and understand what sort of present you will be giving me, if you really give it. I shall gain nothing by receiving it: I shall give them in marriage, and a dowry with them, and shall not allow them to suffer anything unworthy of us or of their father.' When those who were present at the feast heard this, there was such applause and cheering and approbation on all hands, that Philip was moved and granted the request, although the Apollophanes who was spoken of was one of the murderers of Alexander, Philip's brother. Now let us 196 examine side by side with this banquet of Satyrus, that in which these men took part in Macedonia. Observe what likeness and resemblance there is between the two! For these men were invited to the house of Xenophron, the son of Phaedimus, who was one of the Thirty, and went. I did not go. But when it came to the time for wine, he brought in an Olynthian woman—good-looking, but well-bred and modest, as the event proved. At first, I believe (according to the account 197 which Iatrocles gave me the next day), they only forced her to drink a little wine quietly and to eat some dessert; but as the feast proceeded and they waxed warm, they bade her recline and even sing a song. And when the poor creature, who was in great distress, neither would nor could do as they bade her, Aeschines and Phrynon declared that it was an insult and quite intolerable, that a captive woman—one of those god-forsaken devils the Olynthians—should give herself airs. 'Call a slave,' they cried, 'and let some one bring a strap.' A servant came with a lash; they had been drinking, I imagine, and were easily annoyed; and as soon as she said something and burst into tears, the servant tore open her dress and gave her a number of cuts across the back. Beside herself with the pain and the sense of her position, 198 the woman leaped up and fell before the knees of Iatrocles, overturning the table as she did so. And had he not rescued her, she would have perished as the victim of a drunken debauch; for the drunkenness of this abominable creature is something horrible. The case of this woman was also mentioned in Arcadia before the Ten Thousand, and Diophantus reported to you what I shall now force him to testify; for the matter was much talked of in Thessaly and everywhere.

199 Yet with all this on his conscience this unclean creature will dare to look you in the face, and will very soon be speaking to you of the life he has lived, in that magnificent voice of his. It chokes me to hear him! Does not the jury know how at first you used to read over the books to your mother at her initiations, and wallow amid bands of drunken 200 men at their orgies, while still a boy? and how you were afterwards under-clerk to the magistrates, and played the rogue for two or three drachmae? and how at last, in recent days, you thought yourself lucky to get a parasitic living in the training-rooms of others, as a third-rate actor? What then is the life of which you propose to speak? Where have you lived it? For the life which you have really lived has been what I have described. And how much does he take upon himself! He brought another man to trial here for unnatural offences! But I leave this point for the moment. (*To the clerk.*) First, read me these depositions.

[*The depositions are read.*]

201 So many, then, and so gross, gentlemen of the jury, being the crimes against you of which he stands convicted—and what wickedness do they not include? he is corrupt, he is a minion, he is under the curse, a liar, a betrayer of his own people; all the most heinous offences are there—he will not defend himself against a single one of these charges, and will have no defence to offer that is either just or straightforward. But the statement which, I am told, he intends to make, borders on madness; though perhaps a man who has no other plea to offer must contrive anything that he can.

For I hear that he is to say that I, forsooth, have been 202 a partner in everything of which I accuse him; that at first I used to approve of his policy and to act with him; and that I have suddenly changed my mind and become his accuser. As a defence of his conduct such assertions are, of course, neither legitimate nor to the point, though they do imply some kind of charge against myself; for, of course, if I have acted thus, I am a worthless person. But the conduct itself is no better for that. Far from it! At the same time, 203 I think it is proper for me to prove to you both the points in question—first, that if he makes such an assertion he will be lying; and secondly, what is the just line of defence. Now a just and straightforward defence must show either that the acts charged against him were not committed, or that having been committed, they are to the advantage of the city. But Aeschines cannot do either of these things. For I pre- 204 sume that it is not possible for him to say that it is to the advantage of the city that the Phocians have been ruined, that Thermopylae is in Philip's hands, that Thebes is powerful, that there are soldiers in Euboea and plotting against Megara, and that the Peace should not have been sworn to, when on the former occasion he announced the very contrary of all these things to you in the guise of advantages, and advantages about to be realized? Nor will he be able to persuade you that these things have not been done, when you yourselves have seen them and know the facts well. It 205 remains for me, therefore, to show you that I have had no share in any of their proceedings. Shall I then dismiss everything else from consideration—all that I have said against them in your presence, all my collisions with them during our absence, all my antagonism to them from first to last—and produce my opponents themselves as witnesses to the fact that my conduct and theirs have been absolutely contrary the one to the other—that they have taken money to your detriment, and that I refused to receive it? Then mark what I say.

206 Who, would you say, was of all men in Athens the most offensive, most overflowing with effrontery and contemptuousness? I am sure that none of you, even by mistake, would name any other than Philocrates. And who, would you say, possessed the loudest voice and could enunciate whatever he pleased most clearly? Aeschines the defendant, I am sure. Who is it then that these men describe as cowardly and timid before a crowd, while I call him cautious? It is myself; for I have never annoyed you or forced myself upon you against 207 your will. Now at every meeting of the Assembly, as often as a discussion has arisen upon these subjects, you hear me accusing and convicting these men, declaring explicitly that they have taken money and have sold all the interests of the city. And not one of them has ever to this day contradicted the statement, when he heard it, or opened his mouth, or 208 shown himself. What then is the reason, why the most offensive men in the city, the men with the loudest voices, are so cowed before me, the timidest of men, whose voice is no louder than any other? It is because Truth is strong; while to them, on the other hand, the consciousness of having sold public interests is a source of weakness. It is this that steals away the boldness of these men, this that binds down their tongues and stops their mouths—chokes them, and 209 makes them silent. You remember, of course, how at the recent meeting in the Peiraeus, when you would not have him for your representative, he was shouting that he would

impeach me and indict me, and crying, 'Oh! Oh!' But such steps are the beginning of long and numerous trials and speeches; whereas the alternative was but to utter perhaps two or three words, which even a slave purchased yesterday could have pronounced—'Men of Athens, this is utterly atrocious. Demosthenes is accusing me here of crimes in which he himself was a partner; he says that I have taken money, when he has taken money, or shared it, himself.' But no such words, no such sound, did he utter, nor did one **210** of you hear him do so; he only uttered threats to a different effect. And why? Because he knew that he had done what he was charged with doing; he was abjectly afraid to use any such expressions; his resolution could not rise to them, but shrank back; for it was in the grip of his conscience; whereas there was nothing to hinder him from uttering irrelevant abuse and slander. But here is the strongest **211** proof of all, and it consists not in words, but in fact. For when I was anxious to do what it was right to do, namely, to make a second report to you, after serving a second time as ambassador, Aeschines came before the Board of Auditors with a number of witnesses, and forbade them to call me before the court, since I had rendered my account already, and was no longer liable to give it. The incident was extremely ridiculous. And what was the meaning of it? He had made his report with reference to the First Embassy, against which no one brought any charge, and did not wish to go before the court again with regard to the Second Embassy, with reference to which he now appears before you, and within which all his crimes fell. But if I came before **212** you twice, it became necessary for him also to appear again; and so he tried to prevent them from summoning me. But this action of his, men of Athens, plainly proves to you two things—first, that he had so condemned himself that none of you can now acquit him without impiety; and secondly, that he will not speak a word of truth about me. Had he anything true to assert, he would have been found asserting it and accusing me then; he would certainly not have tried 213 to prevent my being summoned. To prove the truth of what I say, (*to the clerk*) call me the witnesses to the facts.

But further, if he makes slanderous statements against me which have nothing to do with the Embassy, there are many good reasons for your refusing to listen to him. For I am not on my trial to-day, and when I have finished my speech I have no further time allotted to me. What can such statements mean, except that he is bankrupt of legitimate arguments? For who that was on his trial and had any 214 defence to make, would prefer to accuse another? And consider also this further point, gentlemen of the jury. If I were on my trial, with the defendant Aeschines for accuser and Philip for judge; and if, being unable to disprove my guilt, I abused Aeschines and tried to sully his character, do you not think that Philip would be indignant at the very fact of a man abusing *his* benefactors in his own presence? Do not *you* then prove worse than Philip; but force Aeschines to defend himself against the charges which are the subject of the trial. (*To the clerk.*) Read the deposition.

[*The deposition is read.*]

215 So for my part, because I had nothing on my conscience, I felt it my duty to render an account and submit all the information that the laws required, while the defendant took the opposite view. How then can his conduct and mine have been

the same? or how can he possibly assert against me now things of which he has never even accused me before? It is surely impossible. And yet he will assert these things, and, Heaven knows, it is natural enough. For you doubtless know well that ever since the human race began and trials were instituted, no one was ever convicted admitting his crime: they brazen it out, they deny it, they lie, they make up excuses, they take every means to escape paying the penalty. *You* must not 216 let any of these devices mislead you to-day; your judgement must be given upon the facts, in the light of your own knowledge; you must not attend to words, whether mine or his, still less to the witnesses whom he will have ready to testify anything, since he has Philip to pay his expenses—you will see how glibly they will give evidence for him; nor must you care whether his voice is fine and loud, or whether mine is poor. For it is no trial of orators or of 217 speeches that you have to hold to-day, if you are wise men. You have rather, in the name of a cause shamefully and terribly ruined, to thrust off the present disgrace on to the shoulders of the guilty, after a scrutiny of those results which are known to you all. And these results, which you 218 know and do not require us to tell you of—what are they? If the consequences of the Peace have been all that they promised you; if you admit that you were so filled with an unmanly cowardice, that, though the enemy was not in your land, though you were not blockaded by sea, though your city was menaced by no other danger whatever, though, on the contrary, the price of corn was low and you were in other respects as well off as you are to-day, though you knew before- 219 hand on the information of these men that your allies were about to be ruined and Thebes to become powerful, that

Philip was about to occupy the Thracian strongholds and to establish a basis of operations against you in Euboea, and that all that has now happened was about to come to pass, you nevertheless made peace cheerfully;—if that is so, then acquit Aeschines, and do not add perjury to all your disgrace. For in that case he is guilty of no crime against you; it is I that am mad and brainsick to accuse him now.

220 But if what they told you was altogether the reverse of this, if it was a tale of great generosity—of Philip's love for Athens, of his intention to save the Phocians, to check the insolence of the Thebans, and beside all this (if he obtained the Peace) to confer on you benefits that would more than compensate for Amphipolis, and to restore to you Euboea and Oropus; if, I say, they stated and promised all this, and have now totally deceived and cheated you, and have all but robbed you of Attica itself, then condemn him, and do not, in addition to all the outrages—I know not what other word to use—that you have suffered, carry with you to your homes, through upholding their corruption, the curse and the guilt of perjury.

221 Again, gentlemen of the jury, ask yourselves what reason I could have had for choosing to accuse these men, if they had done no wrong? You will find none. Is it pleasant to have many enemies? Pleasant? It is not even safe. Was there any quarrel between me and Aeschines? None. What then? 'You were afraid for yourself, and in your cowardice thought to save yourself this way:' for that, I have heard, is what he says. What? I was afraid, when, according to your own statement, there was nothing to be afraid of, and no crime had been committed? If he repeats such an assertion, men of Athens, consider what these men themselves,

the actual criminals, ought to suffer for their offences, if I, who am absolutely guiltless, was afraid of being ruined owing to them. But what *is* my motive for accusing you ? 222 I am an informer, of course, and want to get money out of you! And which was the easier course for me— to get money out of Philip, who offered a large sum—to get as much as any of these men, and to have not only Philip for my friend, but also my opponents (for they would assuredly have been friends, had I been partner with them, since even now they have no inherited quarrel against me, but only the fact that I refused to join in their actions) ; or to beg them for a share of their gains, and be regarded with hostility both by Philip and by them ? Is it likely that when I was ransoming the prisoners at such cost to myself, I should ask to receive a paltry sum from these men, in a disgraceful manner and with their enmity accompanying it ? Impossible! 223 My report was true. I abstained from taking money for the sake of justice and truth and my own future. For I thought, as others among you have thought, that my own uprightness would receive its reward, and that I must not barter my ambition to stand well with you for gain of any kind. And I abhor these men, because I saw that they were vile and impious in the conduct of their mission, and because I have been robbed of the objects of my own ambition, owing to their corruption, now that you have come to be vexed with the Embassy as a whole. And it is because I foresee what must happen that I now accuse him, and appear to challenge his report ; for I would have it decided here, in a trial before a jury, that my conduct has been the opposite of his. And I am afraid—afraid, I say, for I will speak all my 224 mind to you—that though when the time comes you may drag me in spite of my entire innocence to the same ruin with them, you are now utterly supine. For, men of Athens, you appear to me to be altogether unstrung, waiting to suffer the horrors which others are suffering before your eyes, and taking no precautions, no thought for the city, which for so long has 225 been exposed to destruction in many a dreadful form. Is it not, think you, dreadful and preternatural? For even where I had resolved upon silence, I am driven to speak. You doubtless know Pythocles here, the son of Pythodorus. I had been on very kindly terms with him, and to this day there has been no unpleasantness between us. He avoids me now, when he meets me—ever since he visited Philip—and if he is obliged to encounter me anywhere, he starts away immediately, lest any one should see him talking with me. But with Aeschines he walks all round the market-226 place, discussing their plans. Now is it not a terrible and shocking thing, men of Athens, that those who have made it their choice to foster Philip's interests should be able to rely upon so accurate a discrimination on Philip's part, that all that any one of them does here can no more be hid from Philip (so they believe) than if he were standing by their side, and that his friends and foes alike are those that Philip chooses; while those whose life is lived for *your* good, who are greedy of honour at *your* hands, and have not betrayed you, should be met by such deafness, such blindness, on your part, that to-day I have to wrestle with these devils incarnate on equal terms, and that before you, who know the 227 whole truth? Would you know or hear the cause of these things? I will tell you, and I beg that none of you be angry with me for speaking the truth. It is, I imagine, that Philip has but one body and one soul, and it is with all his heart that he cherishes those who do him good and detests those who do him evil: whereas each of you, in the first place, has no feeling that the good or the evil which is being done to the city, is being done to himself; other feelings are of 228 more consequence, and often lead you astray—pity, envy, anger, favour towards the suppliant, and an infinite number of other motives: while if a man has actually escaped all these, he will still not escape from those who do not want such a man to exist at all. And so the error due to each of these single causes steals on little by little, till the state is exposed to the whole accumulated mischief.

Do not fall victims to any such error to-day, men of 229 Athens: do not let the defendant go, when he has done you all this wrong. For honestly, if you let him go, what will be said of you? 'Certain men,' it will be said, 'went as ambassadors to Philip yonder—Philocrates, Aeschines, Phrynon, and Demosthenes; and, what happened? One of them not only gained nothing by his mission, but ransomed the prisoners at his private expense; another, with the money for which he sold the interests of his country, went about purchasing harlots and fish. One of them, the abominable 230 Phrynon, sent his son to Philip before he had registered him as an adult; the other did nothing unworthy of himself or his city. One, though serving as choregus and trierarch, felt it his duty voluntarily to incur that further expense [to ransom the prisoners] rather than see any of his fellow citizens suffering misfortune for want of means; the other, so far from rescuing any of those who were already in captivity, joined in bringing a whole district, and more than 10,000 infantry and 1,000 cavalry with them, the forces of the actual allies of his country, into captivity to Philip. What

231 followed? When the Athenians got them into their hands (for they had long known the truth) what did they do? They let go the men who had received bribes and had disgraced themselves, and their city, and their children; they thought that these were wise men, and that all was well with the city; and as for their accuser, they thought him thunderstruck—a man who did not understand his country, 232 and did not know where to fling his money away.' And who, men of Athens, with this example before his eyes, will be willing to offer you his honest service? who will act as ambassador for nothing, if he is not only to gain nothing by it, but is not to be more trustworthy in your eyes than those who have taken money? You are not only trying these men to-day, but you are laying down a law for all future time—a law which will declare whether your ambassadors are to serve the enemy for a price, or to act disin-233 terestedly for your true good and to take no bribe? On all the other points you require no evidence; but to prove that Phrynon sent his son, (*to the clerk*) call me the witnesses to the facts.

Aeschines then did not prosecute Phrynon, for sending his own son to Philip for a disgraceful purpose. But because a man, who in his youth was above the average in appearance, did not foresee the suspicion which his good looks might entail, and afterwards lived a somewhat fast life, he has prosecuted him for unnatural offences.

234 Now let me speak of the banquet and the decree; for I had almost overlooked what I was especially bound to tell you. In drawing up the resolution of the Council with reference to the First Embassy, and again in addressing the people, at the assemblies in which you were to discuss the

question of peace, not a single word or act of a criminal nature on the part of these men having so far come to light, I followed the ordinary custom, and proposed to accord them a vote of thanks, and to invite them to the Town Hall. And I did, of course, entertain Philip's ambassadors as well, 235 and on a very splendid scale, men of Athens. For when I saw that in their own country they prided themselves even on things like these, as showing their prosperity and splendour, I thought that I must begin by outdoing them in this respect, and displaying even greater magnificence. These incidents Aeschines will shortly bring forward to prove that 'Demosthenes himself voted thanks to us, and gave a banquet to the ambassadors', without telling you the precise time when the incidents occurred. For these things belong to 236 a time before any injury had been done to the city, and before it was evident that they had sold themselves. The ambassadors had only just arrived on their first visit; the people had still to hear what they proposed; and there was nothing as yet to show that Aeschines would support Philocrates, or that Philocrates would make such proposals as he did. If, then, Aeschines uses any such argument, remember that the dates of the incidents are earlier than those of his crimes. But since then there has been no friendliness between myself and them, and no common action. (*To the clerk.*) Read the deposition.

[*The deposition is read.*]

Now perhaps his brother Philochares will support him, 237 and Aphobetus. There is much that you may fairly urge in reply to both; and I am obliged, men of Athens, to speak to you quite freely and without any reserve. You, Philochares, are a painter of vase-cases and drums; your brothers are under-clerks and quite ordinary men—not that there is any harm in these things, but at the same time they do not qualify a man to be a general. And yet, Aphobetus and Philochares, we thought you worthy to be ambassadors and 238 generals, and to receive the highest honours; so that even if none of you were guilty of any crime, we should owe no gratitude to you; you would rather owe gratitude to us for your preferment. For we passed by many others, more deserving of such honours than you were, and exalted you instead. But if in the enjoyment of these very honours one of you has actually committed crimes, and crimes of such a nature, how much more deserving are you of execration than of acquittal? Much more, I am sure. Perhaps they will force their claims upon you, for they are loud-voiced and shameless, and they have taken to themselves the motto 239 that 'it is pardonable for brother to help brother'. But you must not give way. Remember that if it is right for them to think of Aeschines, it is for you to think of the laws and the whole State, and, above all, of the oath which you yourselves, who sit here, have taken. Yes, and if they have entreated some of you to save the defendant, then ask yourselves whether you are to save him if he is proved innocent of crime, or even if he is proved guilty. If they ask you to do so, should he be innocent, I too say that you must acquit him. But if you are asked to acquit him, whatever he has done, then they have asked you to commit perjury. For though your vote is secret, it will not be hidden from the gods; and the framer of our law [which enjoins secret voting] was absolutely right, when he saw that though none of these men will know which of you has granted his request, the gods will know, and the unseen powers, who has given the unjust vote. And it is better for a man to lay up, for his children 240 and himself, those good hopes which *they* can bestow, by giving the decision that is just and right, than to win credit from these men for a favour of whose reality they can have no certain knowledge, and to acquit the defendant, when his own testimony condemns him. For what stronger testimony can I produce, Aeschines, to prove how terrible your work as ambassador has been, than your own testimony against yourself? For when you thought it necessary to involve in so great and dreadful a calamity one who wished to reveal some of your actions as ambassador, it is plain that you expected your own punishment to be a terrible one, if your countrymen learned what you had done.

That step, if you are wise, he will prove to have taken to 241 his own detriment; not only because it is an overwhelming proof of the nature of his conduct as ambassador, but also because of those expressions which he used in the course of the prosecution, and which are now at our disposal against himself. For the principles of justice, as defined by you when you were prosecuting Timarchus, must, I presume, be no less valid when used by others against yourself. His words 242 to the jury on that occasion were these. 'Demosthenes intends to defend Timarchus, and to denounce my acts as ambassador. And then, when he has led you off the point by his speech, he will brag of it, and go about saying, "Well? what do you think?[1] Why I led the jury right away from the point, and stole the case triumphantly out of their hands."' Then you at least must not act thus, but must make your defence with reference to the real points of your case, though, when you were prosecuting

[1] πῶς; τί;

Timarchus on that occasion, you permitted yourself to make any charges and assertions that you chose.

243 But there were verses too, which you recited before the jury, in your inability to produce any witness to the charges on which you were prosecuting Timarchus :—

> Rumour, the voice of many folk, not all
> Doth die, for Rumour too a goddess is.[1]

Well, Aeschines, all those who are present say that you have made money out of your mission ; and so it holds true against you, I suppose, that 'Rumour, the voice of many 244 folk, not all doth die'. For observe how easily you can ascertain how much larger a body of accusers appears in your case than in his. Timarchus was not known even to all his neighbours ; while there is not a man, Hellene or foreigner, but says that you and your fellow ambassadors made money out of your mission. And so, if the rumour is true, then the rumour which is the voice of many folk is against you ; and you have yourself laid down that such a rumour is to be believed, that 'Rumour too a goddess is', and that the poet who composed these lines was a wise man.

245 Then, you remember, he collected some iambic verses, and recited the whole passage ; for instance :—

> Whoso in evil company delights
> Of him I ne'er enquired, for well I trow,
> As is his company, such is the man.[2]

And 'when a man goes to the cockpit and walks about with Pittalacus'—he added more to the same effect—'surely,' said he, 'you know what to think of him.' Well, Aeschines,

[1] Hesiod, *Works and Days*, 761.
[2] Euripides, *Phoenix* fragment.

these same verses will now exactly serve my turn against you, and if I quote them to the jury, the quotation will be true and apposite. 'But whoso in the company delights' of Philocrates, and that when he is an ambassador, 'Of him I ne'er enquired, for well I trow' that he has taken money, as did Philocrates who does not deny it.

He attempts to insult others by labelling them hack- 246 writers and sophists. He shall himself be proved liable to these very imputations. The verses he quoted are derived from the *Phoenix* of Euripides—a play which has never to this day been acted either by Theodorus or Aristodemus, the actors under whom Aeschines always played third-rate parts, though it was performed by Molon, and no doubt by other actors of former times. But the *Antigone* of Sophocles has often been acted by Theodorus and often by Aristodemus; and in this play there are some admirable and instructive verses, which he must know quite well by heart, since he has often delivered them himself, but which he has omitted to quote. For you know, I am sure, that in 247 every tragedy it is, as it were, the special privilege of third-rate actors to play in the rôle of tyrants and sceptred kings. Consider, then, these excellent lines, placed by the poet in the mouth of our Creon-Aeschines in this play—lines which he neither repeated to himself to guide him as an ambassador, nor yet quoted to the jury. (*To the clerk.*) Read the passage.

Verses from the 'Antigone' of Sophocles.

To learn aright the soul and heart and mind
Of any man—for that, device is none,
Till he be proved in government and law,
And so revealed. For he who guides the State,

Yet cleaves not in his counsels to the best,
But from some fear in prison locks his tongue,
Is in mine eyes, as he hath ever been,
Vilest of men. And him, who sets his friend
Before his land, I count of no esteem.
For I—be it known to God's all-viewing eye—
Would ne'er keep silence, seeing the march of doom
Upon this city—doom in safety's stead,
Nor ever take to me as mine own friend
My country's foe. For this I know, that she,
Our country, is the ship that bears us safe,
And safe aboard her, while she sails erect,
We make good friends.

248 None of these lines did Aeschines ever repeat to himself during his mission. Instead of preferring his country he thought that to be friend and guest-friend of Philip was much more important and profitable for himself, and bade a long farewell to the wise Sophocles. He saw the 'march of doom' draw near, in the campaign against the Phocians; but he gave no warning, no announcement of what was to come. On the contrary, he helped to conceal it, he helped to carry out the doom, he prevented those who would have 249 given warning—not remembering that 'Our country is the ship that bears us safe, and safe aboard her' his mother with the help of her initiations and purifications and the property of the clients, on whom she lived, reared up these sons of hers to their destined greatness; while his father, who kept an elementary school, as I am told by my elders, near the temple of the Hero-Physician, made a living, such as he could indeed, but still on the same ship. The sons,

who had received money as under-clerks and servants in all the magistrates' offices, were finally elected clerks by you, and for two years continued to get their living in the Round Chamber; and Aeschines was just now dispatched as your ambassador—from this same ship. He regarded none of these things. He took no care that the ship should sail erect. 250 Nay, he capsized her; he sank the ship; he did all that he could to bring her into the power of the enemy. What then? Are you not a sophist? Aye, and a villanous one. Are you not a hack? Aye, and one detested of Heaven—for you passed over the scene which you had so often performed and knew well by heart, while you sought out a scene which you had never acted in your life, and produced the passage in the hope of injuring one of your fellow citizens.

And now examine his speech about Solon. He told us that 251 the statue of Solon, with his hand concealed in the drapery of his robe, was erected as an illustration of the self-restraint of the orators of that day. (This was in the course of a scurrilous attack upon the impetuosity of Timarchus.) But the Salaminians tell us that this statue was erected less than fifty years ago, whereas some two hundred and forty years have passed between the time of Solon and the present day; so that not only was the artist, who modelled him in this attitude, not living in Solon's day, but even his grandfather was not. That then is what he told the jury, copying the attitude as 252 he did so. But that which it would have done his country far more good to see—the soul and the mind of Solon—he did not copy. No, he did the very reverse. For when Salamis had revolted from Athens and the death-penalty had been decreed against any one who proposed to attempt its recovery, Solon, by singing, at the risk of his own life, a lay which he had composed, won back the island 253 for his country, and wiped out her disgrace: while Aeschines, when the king and all the Hellenes had decided that Amphipolis was yours, surrendered and sold it, and supported Philocrates, who proposed the resolution for this purpose. It is indeed worth his while (is it not?) to remember Solon! Nor was he content with acting thus in Athens; for when he had gone to Macedonia, he did not even mention the name of the place which it was the object of his mission to secure. This, in fact, he reported to you himself, in words which doubtless you remember: 'I too had something to say about Amphipolis; but in order that Demosthenes might have an opportunity of speaking upon the subject, I left 254 it to him.' Upon which I came forward and denied that Aeschines had left to me anything which he was anxious to say to Philip; he would rather have given any one a share in his lifeblood than in his speech. The truth is, I imagine, that he had taken money; and as Philip had given him the money in order that he might not have to restore Amphipolis, he could not speak in opposition to Philip's case. Now (*to the clerk*) take this lay of Solon's and read it; and (*to the jury*) then you will know how Solon used to hate all such men as this.

255 It is not when you are speaking, Aeschines, but when you are upon an embassy, that you should keep your hand within your robe. But on the Embassy you held out your hand, and held it open; you brought shame to your countrymen: and do you here assume a solemn air and recite in those practised tones the miserable phrases that you have learned by heart, and expect to escape the penalty for all your

heinous crimes—even if you do go round with a cap on your head, uttering abuse against me? (*To the clerk.*) Read the verses.

Solon's Lay.

The Father's voice hath spoken,
  Whose word is Destiny,
And the blest Gods have willed it,
  The Gods who shall not die;
That ne'er shall the Destroyer
  Prevail against our land;
The Dread Sire's valiant Daughter
  Guards us with eye and hand.
Yet her own sons, in folly,
  Would lay their country low,
For pelf; and in her leaders
  An heart of sin doth grow.
For them—their pride's fell offspring—
  There waiteth grievous pain;
For sated still, they know not
  Their proud lust to contain.
Not theirs, if mirth be with them,
  The decent, peaceful feast;
To sin they yield, and sinning
  Rejoice in wealth increased.
No hallowed treasure sparing,
  Nor people's common store,
This side and that his neighbour
  Each robs with havoc sore.
The holy law of Justice
  They guard not Silent she,

Who knows what is and hath been,
  Awaits the time to be.
Then cometh she to judgement,
  With certain step, tho' slow;
E'en now she smites the city,
  And none may 'scape the blow.
To thraldom base she drives us,
  From slumber rousing strife,—
Fell war of kin, destroying
  The young, the beauteous life.
The foemen of their country
  In wicked bands combine,
Fit company; and stricken
  The lovely land doth pine.
These are the Wrong, the Mischief,
  That pace the earth at home;
But many a beggared exile
  To other lands must roam—
Sold, chained in bonds unseemly;
  For so to each man's hall
Comes home the People's Sorrow,
  And leaps the high fence-wall.
No courtyard door can stay it;
  It follows to his side,
Flee tho' he may, and crouching
  In inmost chamber hide.
Such warning unto Athens
  My spirit bids me sound,
That Lawlessness in cities
  Spreads evil all around;

But Lawfulness and Order
Make all things good and right,
Chaining Sin's hands in fetters,
Quenching the proud soul's light,
Smoothing the rough, the sated
Staying, and withering
The flowers, that, fraught with ruin,
From fatal seed upspring.
The paths of crooked justice
Are turned into straight;
The ways of Pride grow gentle,
The ways of Strife and Hate;
Then baleful Faction ceases,
Then Health prevails alway,
And Wisdom still increases,
Beneath Law's wholesome sway.

You hear, men of Athens, how Solon speaks of men like 25 these, and of the gods, who, he says, preserve the city. It is my belief and my hope that this saying of his, that the gods preserve our city, is true at all times; but I believe that all that has happened in connexion with the present examination is, in a sense, a special proof of the goodwill of some unseen power towards the city. Consider what has happened. 25 A man who as ambassador did a work of great wickedness, and has surrendered countries in which the gods should have been worshipped by yourselves and your allies, has disfranchised one who accepted the challenge to prosecute him. To what end? To the end that he himself might meet with no pity or mercy for his own iniquities. Nay, more; while prosecuting his victim he deliberately set himself to speak evil of me; and again, before the People, he threatened to enter an indictment against me, and said more to the same effect. And to what end? To the end that I, who had the most perfect knowledge of all his acts of villany, and had followed them closely throughout, might have your full indulgence 258 in prosecuting him. Aye, and through postponing his appearance before you continually up to the present moment, he has been insensibly brought to a time when, on account of what is coming upon us, if for no other reason, it is neither possible nor safe for you to allow him (after his corruption) to escape unscathed. For though, men of Athens, you ought always to execrate and to punish those who are traitors and corrupt, to do so at this time would be more than ever seasonable, and would confer a benefit upon all mankind in 259 common. For a disease, men of Athens, an awful disease has fallen upon Hellas—a disease hard to cope with, and requiring abundant good fortune, and abundant carefulness on your own part. For the most notable men in their several cities, the men who claim to lead in public affairs, are betraying their own liberty—unhappy men!—and bringing upon themselves a self-chosen servitude, under the milder names of friendship and companionship with Philip, and other such phrases; while the other citizens, and the sovereign bodies in each city, however composed, whose duty it was to punish these men and slay them out of hand, are so far from taking any such action, that they admire and envy them, and every one would be glad to be in the same 260 case. Yet it is from this very cause—it is through entertaining ambitions like these—that the Thessalians, who up to yesterday or the day before had lost thereby only their paramount position and their dignity as a state, are now already being stripped of their very liberty; for there are Macedonian garrisons in some of their citadels. This same disease it is which has invaded the Peloponnese and brought about the massacres in Elis, infecting the unhappy people of that country with such insanity and frenzy, that in order to be lords over one another and to gratify Philip, they murder their kinsmen and fellow citizens. Not even here has the **261** disease been stayed: it has penetrated Arcadia and turned it upside-down; and now many of the Arcadians, who should be no less proud of liberty than yourselves—for you and they alone are indigenous peoples—are declaring their admiration for Philip, erecting his image in bronze, and crowning him; and, to complete the tale, they have passed a resolution that, if he comes to the Peloponnese, they will receive him within their walls. The Argives have acted in exactly the **262** same way. These events, I say it in all solemnity and earnestness, call for no small precautions: for this plague, men of Athens, that is spreading all around us, has now found its way to Athens itself. While then we are still safe, ward it off, and take away the citizenship of those who first introduced it. Beware lest otherwise you realize the worth of the advice given you this day, only when there is no longer anything that you can do. Do you not perceive, men of **263** Athens, how vivid and plain an example has been afforded you by the unhappy Olynthians? The destruction of those wretched men was due to nothing so much as to conduct like that of which I speak. You can test this clearly if you review their history. For at a time when they possessed only 400 cavalry, and numbered not more than 5,000 men in all, since the Chalcidians were not yet all united under one government, the Spartans came against them with a large **264** force, including both army and fleet (for you doubtless remember that at that period the Spartans were virtually masters both of land and sea); and yet, though this great force came against them, the Olynthians lost neither the city nor any single fortress, but won many battles, killed three of the enemy's commanders, and finally concluded the war on their 265 own terms. But when some of them began to take bribes, and the people as a whole were foolish enough, or rather unfortunate enough, to repose greater confidence in these men than in those who spoke for their own good; when Lasthenes roofed his house with the timber which came from Macedonia, and Euthycrates was keeping a large herd of cattle for which he had paid no one anything; when a third returned with sheep, and a fourth with horses, while the people, to whose detriment all this was being done, so far from showing any anger or any disposition to chastise men who acted so, actually gazed on them with envy, and paid them honour and regarded 266 them as heroes—when, I say, such practices were gaining ground in this way, and corruption had been victorious; then, though they possessed 1,000 cavalry and numbered more than 10,000 men; though all the surrounding peoples were their allies; though you went to their assistance with 10,000 mercenaries and 50 ships, and with 4,000 citizen-soldiers as well, none of these things could save them. Before a year of the war had expired they had lost all the cities in Chalcidice, while Philip could no longer keep pace with the invitations of the traitors, and did not know which place 267 to occupy first. Five hundred horsemen were betrayed by their own commanders and captured by Philip, with their arms—a larger number than were ever before captured by any one. And the men who acted thus were not ashamed to face the sun or the earth—the soil of their native land—on which they stood, or the temples, or the sepulchres of the dead, or the disgrace which was bound to follow upon such deeds afterwards. Such is the madness and distraction which corruption engenders. So it is for you—for you, the People—to be wise, to refuse to suffer such things, and to visit them with public chastisement. For it would be monstrous indeed, if, after the terrible condemnation which you passed upon those who betrayed the Olynthians, it were seen that you allowed the criminals who are in your very midst to go unpunished. (*To the clerk.*) Read the decree passed with reference to the Olynthians.

[*The decree is read.*]

This decree, gentlemen of the jury, is one which in the eyes of all, Hellenes and foreigners alike, it was right and honourable in you to have passed in condemnation of traitors and men detested of Heaven. And so, since the taking of the bribe is the step which precedes such actions, and it is the bribe that prompts the traitor's deeds, whenever, men of Athens, you find a man receiving a bribe, you must count him a traitor as well. That one man betrays opportunities, and another affairs of state, and another soldiers, means only, I imagine, that each works mischief in the particular department over which he has control; but there should be no distinction in your execration of all such men. You, men of Athens, are the only people in the world who can draw from your own history examples which bear upon this matter, and who have those ancestors, whom you rightly praise, to imitate in your actions. You may not be able, at the present time, to imitate them in the battles, the 268 269 campaigns, the perils in which they distinguished themselves, since at the present moment you are at peace; but at least 270 you can imitate their wisdom. For of wisdom there is need everywhere; and a right judgement is no more laborious or troublesome a thing than a wrong one. Each of you need sit here no longer, in order to judge and vote on the question before him aright, and so to make his country's position a better one, and worthy of our ancestors, than he must in order to judge and vote wrongly, and so make it worse and unworthy of our ancestors. What then were their sentiments on this matter? (*To the clerk.*) Take this, clerk, and read it: (*to the jury*) for I would have you see that the acts towards which you are so indifferent are acts for which your forefathers voted death to the doers. (*To the clerk.*) Read.

[*An inscription is read.*]

271 You hear the inscription, men of Athens, declaring that Arthmius of Zeleia, son of Pythonax, is a foe and a public enemy to the people of Athens and their allies—both he and all his house. And why? Because he brought the gold from the foreigner to the Hellenes. Apparently, therefore, we may judge from this, that your ancestors sought to ensure that no one, not even a stranger, should work mischief against Hellas for money; whereas you do not even seek to prevent any of your fellow citizens from injuring his own 272 city. 'But,' it may be said, 'the inscription occupies a quite unimportant position.' On the contrary, although all yonder Acropolis is sacred and there is no lack of space upon it, this inscription stands on the right hand of the great bronze statue of Athena, the prize of valour in the war against the barbarians, set up by the State with funds which the

Hellenes had presented to her. In those days, therefore, uprightness was so sacred, and such merit was attached to the punishment of actions like these, that the sentences passed upon such crimes were thought to deserve the same position as the prize-statue of the goddess. And now, unless you, in your turn, set a check upon this excess of licence, the result must be ridicule, impunity, and shame.[1] You would do well, I think, men of Athens, 273 to imitate your forefathers, not in this or that point alone, but continuously, and in all that they did. Now I am sure that you have all heard the story of Callias, the son of Hipponicus, to whose diplomacy was due the Peace which is universally celebrated, and which provided that the king should not come down by land within a day's ride of the sea, nor sail with a ship of war between the Chelidonian islands and the Cyanean rocks. He was thought to have taken bribes on his mission; and your forefathers almost put him to death, and actually fined him, at the examination of his report, a sum of 50 talents. True it is, that 274 no more honourable peace can be mentioned than this, of all which the city ever made before or afterwards. But it was not to this that they looked. The nature of the Peace they attributed to their own prowess and the glory of their city: but whether the transaction was disinterested or corrupt, depended upon the character of the ambassador; and they expected the character displayed by one who took part in public affairs to be upright and incorruptible. Your ances- 275 tors, then, regarded corruption as so inimical, so unprofitable, to the state, that they would not admit it in connexion with any single transaction or any single man; while you,

[1] ἄδεια, αἰσχύνη.

men of Athens, though you have seen that the Peace which has laid low the walls of your own allies is building the houses of your ambassadors—that the Peace which has robbed the city of her possessions has secured for them more than they had ever before hoped for even in their dreams—you, I say, instead of putting them to death of your own accord, need a prosecutor to assist you; and when all can see their crimes in very deed, you are making their trial a trial of words.

276 It is not, however, by the citation of ancient history, nor by these examples alone, that one may stimulate you to vengeance: for even within the lifetime of yourselves, who are here and still living, many have paid the penalty. All the rest of these I will pass over; but I will mention one or two of those who were punished with death, on returning from a mission whose results have been far less disastrous to the city than those of the present Embassy. (*To the clerk.*) Take then this decree and read it.

[*The decree is read.*]

277 In this decree, men of Athens, you passed sentence of death upon those ambassadors, one of whom was Epicrates, a good man, as I am told by my elders, and one who had in many ways been of service to his country—one of those who brought the people back from the Peiraeus, and who was generally an upholder of the democracy. Yet none of these services helped him, and rightly. For one who claims to manage affairs of such magnitude has not merely to be half honest; he must not secure your confidence and then take advantage of it to increase his power to do mischief; he must do absolutely no wrong against you of his own will.

278 Now if there is one of the things for which those men were

sentenced to death, that these men have not done, you may put me to death without delay. Observe what the charges were. 'Since they conducted their mission,' says the decree, 'contrary to the terms of the resolution'—that is the first of the charges. And have not these men contravened the terms of the resolution? Does not the decree speak of peace 'for the Athenians and the allies of the Athenians?' and did they not exclude the Phocians from the treaty? Does not the decree bid them administer the oath to the magistrates in the several cities? and did they not administer it to men sent to them by Philip? Does not the resolution forbid them 'to meet Philip anywhere alone?' and did they not incessantly do business with him privately? Again I read, 'And 279 some of them have been convicted of making a false report before the Council.' But these men have been convicted of doing so before the People as well. And convicted by whom? for this is the splendid thing. Convicted by the actual facts; for all that has happened, as you know, has been the exact reverse of what they announced. 'And,' the decree goes on, 'of not sending true dispatches.' Nor did these men. 'And of accusing our allies falsely and taking bribes.' Instead of 'accusing falsely', say, 'of having utterly ruined'—surely a far more heinous thing than a false accusation. And as for the charge of taking bribes, if it had been denied, it would still have required proof; but since they admitted it, a summary procedure was surely the proper one. What 280 then will you do, men of Athens? You are the offspring of that generation, and some of you are actually survivors from it; and will you endure it, that Epicrates, the benefactor of the people, one of the men from the Peiraeus, should have been exiled and punished; that Thrasybulus, again, the

son of the great Thrasybulus, the People's friend, who brought the people back from Phyle, should recently have been fined ten talents; and that the descendant of Harmodius, and of those who achieved for you the greatest of blessings, and whom, for the benefits which they conferred upon you, you have caused to share in the libations and the bowls outpoured, in every temple where sacrifice is offered, singing of them and honouring them as you honour heroes and gods—
281 that all these, I say, should have undergone the penalty ordained by the laws, and that no feeling of compassion or pity, nor the tears of their children who bore the names of our benefactors, nor aught else, should have availed them anything: and yet, when you have to do with the son of Atrometus the schoolmaster, and Glaucothea, who used to hold those meetings of the initiated, a practice for which another priestess was put to death—when you have in your hands the son of such parents, a man who never did a single service to his country—neither himself, nor his father, nor
282 any of his house—will you let him go? Where is the horse, the trireme, the military service, the chorus, the burden undertaken for the state, the war-contribution, the loyal action, the peril undergone, for which in all their lifetime the city has had to thank him or his? Aye, and even if all these stood to his credit, and those other qualifications, of uprightness and integrity in his mission, were not also to be found in him, it would surely have been right that he should perish. But when neither the one nor the other are to be
283 found, will you not avenge yourselves upon him? Will you not call to mind his own words, when he was prosecuting Timarchus—that there was no help for a city which had no sinews to use against the criminal, nor for a constitution

in which compassion and solicitation were more powerful than the laws—that it was your duty not to pity the aged mother of Timarchus, nor his children, nor any one else, but to attend solely to one point, namely, that if you abandoned the cause of the laws and the constitution, you would look in vain for any to have pity on yourselves. Is that 284 unhappy man to have lost his rights as a citizen, because he witnessed the guilt of Aeschines, and will you then suffer Aeschines to escape unscathed? On what ground can you do so? for if Aeschines demanded so heavy a penalty from those whose sins were against their own persons, what must be the magnitude of the penalty which *you* should require—you, the sworn judges of the case—from those who have sinned so greatly against their country's interests, and of whom Aeschines is convincingly proved to be one? 'But,' we are 285 told, 'that was a trial which will raise the moral standard of our young men.' Yes, and this trial will raise that of our statesmen, upon whose character the supreme interests of the city are staked. For your care ought to extend to them also. But you must realize that his real motive for ruining Timarchus himself was not, Heaven knows, to be found in any anxiety for the virtue of your sons. Indeed, men of Athens, they are virtuous even now; for I trust that the city will never have fallen so low, as to need Aphobetus and Aeschines to reform the morals of the young. No! the reason 286 was that Timarchus had proposed in the Council, that if any one was convicted of conveying arms or fittings for ships of war to Philip, the penalty should be death. And here is a proof. How long had Timarchus been in the habit of addressing you? For a long time. Now throughout all this time Aeschines was in Athens, and never showed any vexation or indignation at the fact of such a man addressing you, until he had been to Macedonia and made himself a hireling. (*To the clerk.*) Come, take the actual decree which Timarchus proposed, and read it.

[*The decree is read.*]

287 So the man who proposed on your behalf the resolution which forbade, on pain of death, the supply of arms to Philip during the war, has been ruined and treated with contumely; while Aeschines, who had surrendered the arms of your very allies to Philip, was his accuser, and charged him—I call Heaven and Earth to witness—with unnatural offences, although two of his own kinsmen stood by his side, the very sight of whom would call forth a cry of protest from you—the disgusting Nicias, who went to Egypt and hired himself to Chabrias, and the accursed Cyrebion, who joins in processions, as a reveller, without a mask. Nay, why mention these things? His own brother Aphobetus was there before his eyes! In very truth all the words that were spoken on that day about unnatural offences were water flowing up stream.

288 And now, to show you the dishonour into which the villainy and mendacity of the defendant have brought our country, passing by all besides, I will mention a fact known to you all. Formerly, men of Athens, all the other Hellenes used to watch attentively, to see what had been resolved in your Assembly; but now we are already going about and inquiring what others have decided—trying to overhear what the Arcadians are doing, or the Amphictyons, or where Philip will be next, and whether he is alive or dead.
289 We do this, do we not? But for me the terrible question

is not whether Philip is alive, but whether in this city the habit of execrating and punishing criminals is dead. Philip has no terrors for me, if your own spirit is sound; but the prospect that you may grant security to those who wish to receive their wages from him—that they may be supported by some of those whom you have trusted, and that those who have all along denied that they were acting in Philip's interests may now mount the platform in their defence—that is the prospect which terrifies me. Tell me, Eubulus, why **290** it was, that at the recent trial of your cousin Hegesilaus, and of Thrasybulus, the uncle of Niceratus, when the primary question was before the jury, you would not even respond when they called upon you; and that when you rose to speak on the assessment of the penalty, you uttered not a word in their defence, but only asked the jury to be indulgent to you? Do you refuse to ascend the platform in defence of kinsmen and relations, and will you then do so in defence of **291** Aeschines, who, when Aristophon was prosecuting Philonicus, and in accusing him was denouncing your own acts, joined with him in accusing you, and was found in the ranks of your enemies? You frightened your countrymen here by saying that they must either march down to the Peiraeus at once, and pay the war-tax, and convert the festival-fund into a war-fund, or else pass the decree advocated by Aeschines and proposed by the shameless Philocrates—a decree, of which **292** the result was that the Peace became a disgraceful instead of a fair one, and that these men have ruined everything by their crimes: and have you, after all this, become reconciled to him? You uttered imprecations upon Philip, in the presence of the people, and swore by the life of your children that you would be glad if perdition seized him; and will you now come to the aid of Aeschines? How can perdition seize Philip, when you are trying to save those who take bribes 293 from him? Why is it that you prosecuted Moerocles for misappropriating 20 drachmae out of the sums paid by each of the lessees of the mines, and indicted Ctesiphon for the theft of sacred moneys, because he paid 7 minae into the bank three days too late; and yet, when men have taken money and confess it, and are convicted, by being caught in the very act, of having done so in order to bring about the ruin of our allies, you do not prosecute them, but even 294 command their acquittal? But the appalling character of these crimes and the great watchfulness and caution that they call for, and the triviality of the offences for which you prosecuted those other men, may further be seen in this way. Were there any men in Elis who stole public funds? It is very likely indeed. Well, had any of them anything to do with the overthrow of the democracy there? Not one of them. Again, while Olynthus was standing, were there others of the same character there? I am sure that there were. Was it then through them that Olynthus was destroyed? No. Again, do you not suppose that in Megara there was some one who was a thief and who embezzled public funds? There must have been. Well, has any such person been shown 295 to be responsible for the recent crisis there? Not one. But of what sort *are* the men who commit crimes of such a character and magnitude? They are those who count themselves worthy to be styled friends and guest-friends of Philip, who would fain be generals, who claim to be leaders, who must needs be exalted above the people. Was not Perillus put on his trial lately before the Three Hundred at Megara, because he went to Philip's court; and did not Ptoeodorus, the first man in Megara in wealth, family, and distinction, come forward and beg him off, and send him back again to Philip? and was not the consequence that the one came back at the head of the mercenaries, while the other was churning the butter at home? For there is nothing, 296 nothing, I say, in the world, which you must be so careful not to do, as not to allow any one to become more powerful than the People. I would have no man acquitted or doomed, to please any individual. Only let us be sure that the man whose actions acquit or condemn him will receive from you the verdict he deserves. That is the true democratic principle. 297 And further, it is true that many men have come to possess great influence with you at particular times—Callistratus, and again Aristophon, Diophantus, and others before them. But where did each of these exercise his primacy? In the Assembly of the People. But in the law-courts no man has ever, to this day, carried more influence than the laws and the juror's oath. Do not then allow the defendant to have such influence to-day. To prove to you that there is good reason for you not to trust, but to beware of such influence, I will read you an oracle of the gods, who always protect the city far better than do its foremost citizens. (*To the clerk.*) Read the oracles.

[*The oracles are read.*]

You hear, men of Athens, the warnings of the gods. If 298 these responses were given by them when you were at war, they mean that you must beware of your generals, since in war it is the generals who are leaders; but if they were uttered after you had made peace, they must refer to those who are at the head of your government; for these are the leaders whom you obey, and it is by these that you are in danger of being led astray. 'And hold the state together' [says the oracle] 'until all are of one mind, and afford no joy 299 to their foes.' Which event then, men of Athens, do you think would afford joy to Philip—the acquittal of one who has brought about all this evil, or his punishment? His acquittal, I am sure. But the oracle, you see, says that we should so act as not to afford joy to our foes; and therefore, by the mouth of Zeus, of Dione, and of all the gods, is this exhortation given to us all, that with one mind we chastise those who have done any service to our enemies. Without are those who are plotting against us, within are their confederates. The part of the plotters is to offer the bribe; that of their confederates is to receive it, and to save from condemnation those who have received it.

300 And further, it needs no more than human reason to arrive at the conclusion that nothing can be more hateful and dangerous than to allow your first citizen to be intimate with those whose objects are not those of the People. Consider by what means Philip has become master of the entire situation, and by what means he has accomplished the greatest of his successes. It has been by purchasing the opportunities for action from those who offered them for sale—by corrupting and exciting the aspirations of the leaders of their several 301 cities. These have been the means. Now both of these methods it is in your power, if you wish it, to render futile to-day, if you will refuse to listen to prominent persons who speak in defence of such practices, and will thus prove that they have no power over you—for now they assert that they have you under their control—while at the same time you punish the man who has sold himself, and let all the world see what 302 you have done. For you would have reason enough, men of Athens, for being angry with any man who had acted so,

and had betrayed your allies and your friends and your opportunities (for with these are bound up the whole prosperity or adversity of every people), but with no one more than with Aeschines, or with greater justice. After taking up a position as one of those who mistrusted Philip—after being the first and the only man to perceive that Philip was the common enemy of all the Hellenes—he deserted, he betrayed you; he suddenly became Philip's supporter. Surely he deserves to die many times over! Nay, he himself 303 will not be able to deny that these things are so. For who was it that brought Ischander forward before you originally, stating that he had come from the friends of Athens in Arcadia? Who was it that cried out that Philip was organizing Hellas and the Peloponnese against you, while you were asleep? Who was it that delivered those long and noble orations to the people, that read to you the decrees of Miltiades and Themistocles, and the oath of the young soldiers in the temple of Aglaurus? Was it not the defen- 304 dant? Who was it that persuaded you to send embassies almost as far as the Red Sea, on the ground that Philip was plotting against Hellas, and that it was for you to foresee this and not to sacrifice the interests of the Hellenes? Was it not Eubulus who proposed the decree, while the ambassador to the Peloponnese was the defendant Aeschines? What expressions he used in his address to the people, after he arrived there, is best known to himself: but I know you all remember what he reported to you. Many a time in the 305 course of his speech he called Philip 'barbarian' and 'devil'; and he reported the delight of the Arcadians at the thought that Athens was now waking up and attending to public affairs. One thing he told us, which caused him, he said, more distress than anything else. As he was leaving, he met Atrestidas, who was travelling home from Philip's court, and with him were walking some thirty women and children. Wondering at this, he asked one of the travellers who the 306 man was, and what this crowd was along with him; and on hearing that it was Atrestidas, who was on his way home, and that these with him were captives from Olynthus whom Philip had given him as a present, he was struck with the atrocity of the thing and burst into tears, and lamented the unhappy condition of Hellas, that she should allow such tragedies to pass unnoticed. At the same time he counselled you to send representatives to Arcadia to denounce Philip's agents, saying that his friends told him that if Athens took notice of the matter and sent envoys, Philip's agents would 307 be punished. Such, men of Athens, was the tenor of his speeches then; and very noble they were, and worthy of this city. But when he had been to Macedonia, and had seen the enemy of himself and of the Hellenes, were his speeches couched any more in the same or a similar tone? Far from it! He told you that you must neither remember your forefathers nor mention your trophies, nor go to the aid of any one. He was amazed, he said, at those who urged you to confer with the rest of the Hellenes in regard to the Peace with Philip, as though there was any need to convince some one else 308 about a matter which was purely your own affair. And as for Philip, 'Why, good gracious!' said he, 'Philip is the most thorough Hellene in the world, a most able speaker, and most friendly towards Athens: only there are certain persons in Athens so unreasonable and so churlish, that they are not ashamed to slander him and call him "barbarian".' Now is it possible that the man who had formerly spoken as Aeschines did, should now have dared to speak in such a way, if he had not been corrupted? What? Is there a man 309 who after conceiving such detestation for Atrestidas, owing to those children and women from Olynthus, could have endured to act in conjunction with Philocrates, who brought freeborn Olynthian women here to gratify his lust, and is so notorious for his abominable living, that it is unnecessary for me now to use any offensive or unpleasant expression about him; for if I say that Philocrates brought women here, the rest will be understood by all of you and of the bystanders, and you will, I am sure, pity the poor unhappy creatures—though Aeschines felt no pity for them, and shed no tears for Hellas at the sight of them, or at the thought of the outrages they were suffering among their own allies at the hands of our ambassadors. No! he will shed tears on his 310 own behalf—he whose proceedings as ambassador have had such results—and perhaps he will bring forward his children, and mount them upon the platform. But, gentlemen of the jury, when you see the children of Aeschines, remember that the children of many of your allies and friends are now vagabonds, wandering in beggary, owing to the cruel treatment they have suffered in consequence of his conduct, and that these deserve your compassion far more than those whose father is a criminal and a traitor. Remember that your own children have been robbed even of their hopes by these men, who inserted among the terms of the Peace the clause which extended it to posterity. And when you see the tears of Aeschines, remember that you have now before you a man who urged you to send representatives to Arcadia to denounce the agents of Philip. Now to-day you need send no embassy 311 to the Peloponnese; you need take no long journey; you need incur no travelling expenses. Each of you need only come as far as this platform, to deposit the vote which piety and justice demand of him, on behalf of your country; and to condemn the man who—I call Earth and Heaven to witness!—after originally delivering the speeches which I described, speaking of Marathon and of Salamis, and of your battles and your trophies, suddenly—so soon as he had set foot in Macedonia—changed his tone completely, and told you that you must not remember your forefathers, nor recount your trophies, nor go to the aid of any one, nor take common counsel with the Hellenes—who all but told

312 you that you must pull down your walls. Never throughout all time, up to this day, have speeches more shameful than these been delivered before you. What Hellene, what foreigner, is so dense, or so uninstructed, or so fierce in his hatred of our city, that if one were to put to him this question, and say, 'Tell me now; of all Hellas, as it now is—all this inhabited country—is there any part which would have been called by this name, or inhabited by the Hellenes who now possess it, unless those who fought at Marathon and Salamis, our forefathers, had displayed that high prowess on their behalf?' Why, I am certain that not one would answer 'Yes': they would say that all these regions must have been

313 conquered by the barbarians. If then no single man, not even one of our enemies, would have deprived them of these their panegyrics and praises, does Aeschines forbid you to remember them—you their descendants—in order that he himself may receive money? In all other blessings, moreover, the dead have no share; but the praises which follow their noble deeds are the peculiar possession of those who have died thus; for then even envy opposes them no longer. Of these praises Aeschines would deprive them; and justly,

therefore, would he now be deprived of his privileges as as a citizen, and justly, in the name of your forefathers, would you exact from him this penalty. Such words you used, nevertheless, in the wickedness of your heart, to despoil and traduce the deeds of our forefathers, and by your word you ruined all our interests in very deed. And then, as the 314 outcome of this, you are a landed gentleman, and have become a personage of consequence! For this, too, you must notice. Before he had wrought every kind of mischief against the city he acknowledged that he had been a clerk; he was grateful to you for having elected him, and behaved himself modestly. But since he has wrought countless evils, he has drawn up his eyebrows, and if any one speaks of 'Aeschines the late clerk', he is his enemy at once, and declares that he has been insulted: he walks through the market-place with his cloak trailing down to his ankles, keeping step with Pythocles, and puffing out his cheeks—already one of Philip's friends and guest-friends, if you please—one of those who would be rid of the democracy, and who regard the established constitution as so much tempestuous madness—he who was once the humble servant of the Round Chamber.

I wish now to recapitulate to you summarily the ways in 315 which Philip got the better of you in policy, when he had taken these heaven-detested men to aid him. It is well worth while to review and contemplate the course of his deception as a whole. It began with his anxiety for peace; for his country was being plundered, and his ports were closed, so that he could enjoy none of the advantages which they afforded; and so he sent the messengers who uttered those generous sentiments on his behalf—Neoptolemus, Aristodemus, and Ctesiphon. But so soon as we went to 316 him as your ambassadors, he immediately hired the defendant to second and co-operate with the abominable Philocrates, and so get the better of those who wished to act uprightly; and he composed such a letter to you as he thought would 317 be most likely to help him to obtain peace. But even so, he had no better chance than before of effecting anything of importance against you, unless he could destroy the Phocians. And this was no easy matter. For he had now been reduced, as if by chance, to a position in which he must either find it impossible to effect any of his designs, or else must perforce lie and forswear himself, and make all men, whether Hellenes 318 or foreigners, witnesses of his own baseness. For if, on the one hand, he received the Phocians as allies, and administered the oath to them together with yourselves, it at once became necessary for him to break his oaths to the Thessalians and Thebans; for he had sworn to aid the latter in the reduction of Boeotia, and the former in the recovery of their place in the Amphictyonic Council; but if, on the other hand, he refused to receive them (as in fact he did reject them), he thought that you would not let him cross the Pass, but would rally to Thermopylae—and so you would have done, had you not been misled; and if this happened, he calculated that he would be unable to march across. 319 Nor had he to learn this from others; he had already the testimony of his own experience. For on the occasion of his first defeat of the Phocians, when he destroyed their mercenaries and their leader and general, Onomarchus, although not a single human being, Hellene or foreigner, came to the aid of the Phocians, except yourselves, so far was he from crossing the Pass and thereafter carrying out any of his designs, 320 that he could not even approach near it. He realized,

I imagine, quite clearly, that at a time when the feelings of the Thessalians were turning against him, and the Pheraeans (to take the first instance) refused to accompany him—when the Thebans were being worsted and had lost a battle, and a trophy had been erected to celebrate their defeat—it was impossible for him to cross the Pass, if you rallied to its defence; and that if he made the attempt he would regret it, unless some cunning could be called in to aid him. How then, he asked, can I avoid open falsehood, and yet accomplish all that I wish without appearing perjured? How can it be done? It can be done, if I can get some of the Athenians to deceive the Athenians. In that case the discredit no longer falls to my share. And so Philip's own envoys first 321 informed you that Philip declined to receive the Phocians as allies; and then these men took up the tale, and addressed you to the effect that it was inconvenient to Philip to receive the Phocians as your allies openly, on account of the Thebans and the Thessalians; but if he gets command of the situation, they said, and is granted the Peace, he will do just what we should now request him to promise to do. So they obtained the Peace from you, by holding out these 322 seductive hopes, without including the Phocians. But they had still to prevent the expedition to Thermopylae, for the purpose of which, despite the Peace, your fifty ships were still lying ready at anchor, in order that, if Philip marched, you might prevent him. How then could it be done? what 323 cunning could be used in regard to this expedition in its turn? They must deprive you of the necessary time, by bringing the crisis upon you suddenly, so that, even if you wished to set out, you might be unable to do so. So this, it appears, was what these men undertook to do; while for my part, as you have often been told, I was unable to depart in advance of them, and was prevented from sailing even 324 when I had hired a boat for the purpose. But it was further necessary that the Phocians should come to believe in Philip and give themselves up to him voluntarily, in order that there might be no delay in carrying out the plan, and that no hostile decree whatever might issue from you. 'And therefore,' said he, 'the Athenian ambassadors shall announce that the Phocians are to be preserved from destruction, so that even if any one persists in distrusting me, he will believe them, and put himself in my hands. We will summon the Athenians themselves, so that they may imagine that all that they want is secured, and may pass no hostile decree: but the ambassadors shall make such reports about us, and give such promises, as will prevent them from moving under any circumstances.' 325 It was in this way, and by such trickery as this, that all was ruined, through the action of these doomed wretches. For immediately afterwards, as you know, instead of seeing Thespiae and Plataeae repeopled, you heard that Orchomenus and Coroneia had been enslaved; instead of Thebes being humbled and stripped of her insolence and pride, the walls of your own allies were being razed, and it was the Thebans who were razing them—the Thebans who, according to Aeschines' 326 story, were as good as broken up into villages. Instead of Euboea being handed over to you in exchange for Amphipolis, Philip is making new bases of operations against you in Euboea itself, and is plotting incessantly against Geraestus and Megara. Instead of the restoration of Oropus to you, we are making an expedition under arms to defend Drymus and the country about Panactum —a step which we never took 327 so long as the Phocians remained unharmed. Instead of the restoration of the ancestral worship in the temple, and the exaction of the debt due to the god, the true Amphictyons are fugitives, who have been banished and their land laid desolate; and Macedonians, foreigners, men who never were Amphictyons in the past, are now forcing their way to recognition; while any one who mentions the sacred treasures is thrown from the rocks, and our city has been deprived of her right to precedence in consulting the oracle. Indeed, 328 the story of all that has happened to the city sounds like a riddle. Philip has spoken no falsehood, and has accomplished all that he wished: you hoped for the fulfilment of your fondest prayers, and have seen the very opposite come to pass; you suppose yourselves to be at peace, and have suffered more terribly than if you had been at war; while these men have received money for all this, and up to this very day have not paid the penalty. For that the situation has been 329 made what it is solely by bribery, and that these men have received their price for it all, has, I feel sure, long been plain to you in many ways; and I am afraid that, quite against my will, I may long have been wearying you by attempting to prove with elaborate exactness what you already know for yourselves. Yet this one point I ask you still to listen to. 330 Is there, gentlemen of the jury, one of the ambassadors whom Philip sent, whose statue in bronze you would erect in the market-place? Nay, one to whom you would give maintenance in the Town Hall, or any other of those complimentary grants with which you honour your benefactors? I think not. And why? For you are of no ungrateful or unfair or mean disposition. You would reply, that it is because all that they did was done in the interest of Philip, and nothing in your own; and the reply would be true and

331 just. Do you imagine then that, when such are your sentiments, Philip's are not also such? Do you imagine that he gives all these magnificent presents because your ambassadors conducted their mission honourably and uprightly with a view to *your* interest? Impossible. Think of Hegesippus, and the manner in which he and the ambassadors who accompanied him were received by Philip. To go no further, he banished Xenocleides, the well-known poet, by public proclamation, because he received the ambassadors, his own fellow citizens. For so it is that he behaves to men who honestly say what they think on your behalf: while to those who have sold themselves he behaves as he has to these men. Do we then need witnesses? do we need stronger proofs than these to establish my conclusions? Will any one be able to steal these conclusions from your minds?

332 Now I was told a most extraordinary thing just now by some one who accosted me in front of the Court, namely, that the defendant is prepared to accuse Chares, and that by such methods and such arguments as that, he hopes to deceive you. I will not lay undue stress on the fact that Chares, subjected to every form of trial, was found to have acted on your behalf, so far as was in his power, with faithfulness and loyalty, while his frequent shortcomings were due to those who, for money, were cruelly injuring your cause. But I will go much further. Let it be granted that all that the defendant will say

333 of Chares is true. Even so it is utterly absurd that Aeschines should accuse him. For I do not lay the blame on Aeschines for anything that was done in the course of the war—it is the generals who have to account for all such proceedings—nor do I hold him responsible for the city's having made peace. So far I acquit him of everything. What then do I allege, and at what point does my accusation begin? I accuse him of having

supported Philocrates, at the time when the city was making peace, instead of supporting those who proposed what was for your real good. I accuse him of taking bribes, and subsequently, on the Second Embassy, of wasting time, and of not carrying out any of your instructions. I accuse him of cheating the city, and ruining everything, by the suggestion of hopes that Philip would do all that we desired; and then I accuse him of speaking afterwards in defence of one of whom all warned him to beware, on account of the great crimes of which he had been guilty. These are my charges, and these are what 334 you must bear in mind. For a Peace that was honest and fair, and men that had sold nothing and had told no falsehoods afterwards, I would even have commended, and would have bidden you crown them. But the injuries which some general may have done you have nothing to do with the present examination. Where is the general who has caused the loss of Halus? or of the Phocians? or of Doriscus? or of Cersobleptes? or of the Sacred Mountain? or of Thermopylae? Who has secured Philip a road to Attica that leads entirely through the country of allies and friends? who has given Coroneia and Orchomenus and Euboea to others? who has all but given Megara to the enemy, only recently? who has made the Thebans powerful? Not one of all these heavy losses was the 335 work of the generals; nor does Philip hold any of these places because you were persuaded to concede it to him by the treaty of peace. The losses are due to these men and to their corruption. If then he evades these points, and tries to mislead you by speaking of every other possible subject, this is how you must receive his attempt. 'We are not sitting in judgement upon any general,' you must say, 'nor are you on your trial for the things of which you speak.

Do not tell us whether some one else may not also be responsible for the ruin of the Phocians: prove to us that no responsibility attaches to yourself. Why do you tell us *now* of the alleged iniquities of Demosthenes, instead of accusing him when his report was under examination? For such an 336 omission alone you deserve to perish. Do not speak of the beauty of peace, nor of its advantages. No one holds you responsible for the city's having made peace. But show that it was not a shameful and discreditable peace; that we have not since been deceived in many ways; that all was not lost. It is for all these things that the responsibility has been proved to be yours. And why, even to this hour, do you praise the man who has done us all this evil?' If you keep a watch upon him thus, he will have nothing to say; and then he will lift up his voice here, in spite of all his vocal exercises, to no purpose.

337 And yet perhaps it is necessary for me to speak about his voice also. For of this too, I am told, he is extremely proud, and expects to carry you away by his declamation. But seeing that you used to drive him away and hiss him out of the theatre and almost stone him, when he was performing the tragic story of Thyestes or of the Trojan War, so that at last he gave up his third-rate playing, you would be acting in the most extraordinary way if, now that he has wrought countless ills, not on the stage, but in the most important affairs in the public life of the state, you listened to him 338 for his fine voice. By no means must you do this, or give way to any foolish sentiment. Rather reflect, that if you were testing the qualifications of a herald, you would then indeed look for a fine voice; but when you are testing those of an ambassador, or a man who claims the administration

of any public business, you must look for an upright man—a man who bears himself proudly indeed, as your representative, but seeks no more than equality with yourselves—as I myself refused to pay respect to Philip, but did pay respect to the captives, whom I saved, and never for a moment drew back; whereas Aeschines rolled at Philip's feet, and chanted his paeans, while he looks down upon you. And further, 339 whenever you notice that cleverness or a good voice or any other natural advantage has been given to an honest and public-spirited man, you ought all to congratulate him and help him to cultivate his gift; for the gift is an advantage in which you all share, as well as he. But when the gift is found in a corrupt and villainous man, who can never resist the chance of gain, then you should exclude him from your presence, and give a harsh and hostile reception to his words: for villainy, which wins from you the reputation of ability, is the enemy of the State. You see what great troubles have 340 fallen upon the city, through those qualities which have brought renown to Aeschines. But whereas all other faculties are more or less independent, the gift of eloquence, when it meets with hostility from you who listen, is a broken thing. Listen, then, to the defendant as you would listen to a corrupt villain, who will not speak a single word of truth.

Observe also that the conviction of the defendant is in 341 every way expedient, not only on all other grounds, but even when you consider our relations with Philip himself. For if ever Philip finds himself compelled to give the city any of her rights, he will change his methods. As it is, he has chosen to deceive the people as a whole, and to show his favours to a few persons; whereas, if he learns that these men have perished, he will prefer for the future to act in the

interest of yourselves collectively, in whose hands all power
342 rests. If, however, he intends to persist in his present domineering and outrageous insolence, you will, by getting rid of these men, have rid the city of those who would do anything in the world for him. For when they have acted as they have done, with the expectation of having to pay the penalty in their minds, what do you think they will do, if you relax your severity towards them? Where is the Euthycrates, or the Lasthenes, or the traitor of any de-
343 scription, whom they will not outdo? And who among all the rest will not be a worse citizen, when he sees that, for those who have sold themselves, the friendship of Philip serves, in consequence, for revenue, for reputation, and for capital; while to those who have conducted themselves uprightly, and have spent their own money as well, the consequences are trouble, hatred, and ill will from a certain party. Let it not be so. It is not for your good—whether you regard your reputation or your duty towards Heaven or your safety or any other object, that you should acquit the defendant; but rather that you should avenge yourselves upon him, and make him an example in the eyes of all your fellow citizens and of the whole Hellenic world.

ON THE CHERSONESE (Or. VIII)

[*Introduction.* Late in the year 343 (some time after the acquittal of Aeschines) Philip invaded Epirus, made Alexander, brother of his wife Olympias, king of the Molossi instead of Arybbas, and so secured his own influence in that region. Arybbas was honourably received at Athens. Philip next threatened Ambracia and Leucas, which were colonies of Corinth, and promised to restore Naupactus, which was in the hands of the Achaeans, to the Aetolians. But Athens sent Demosthenes, Hegesippus, Polyeuctus and others to rouse the Corinthians to resistance, and also dispatched a force of citizens to Acarnania to help in the defence against Philip. Philip thereupon returned, captured Echinus and Nicaea on the Malian Gulf, and established a tetrarch in each division of Thessaly (343 B.C., or early in 342). In 342 Philistides was established, by Philip's influence, as tyrant at Oreus in Euboea (as Cleitarchus had been at Eretria in the preceding year), and the democratic leader Euphraeus committed suicide in prison.[1] The town of Chalcis, however, under Callias and Taurosthenes, remained friendly to Athens, and made a treaty of alliance with her.

About the same time a controversy, begun in the previous year, in regard to Halonnesus, was renewed. This island had belonged to Athens, but had been occupied by pirates. At some time not recorded (but probably since the Peace of 346) Philip had expelled the pirates and taken possession of the island. He now sent a letter, offering to *give* Halonnesus to Athens, but not to *give it back* (since this would concede their right to it); or else to submit the dispute to arbitration. He also offered to discuss a treaty for the settlement of private disputes between Athenians and Macedonians,

[1] See Third Philippic §§ 59 sqq.

and to concert measures with Athens for clearing the Aegean of pirates. He was willing to extend the advantages of the Peace to other Greek States, but not to agree that he and Athens should respectively possess 'what was their own', instead of 'what they held'; though he was ready to submit to arbitration in regard to Cardia and other disputed places. He again denied having made the promises attributed to him, and asked for the punishment of those who slandered him. Hegesippus replied in an extant speech ('On Halonnesus'), while Demosthenes insisted that no impartial arbitrator could possibly be found. Philip's terms in regard to Halonnesus were refused, but the Athenian claim to the island was not withdrawn.

Philip spent the greater part of 342 and 341 in Thrace, mainly in the valley of the Hebrus, where he endured very great hardships through the winter, and founded colonies of Macedonian soldiers, the chief of these being Philippopolis and Cabyle. He also entered into relations with the Getae, beyond the Haemus, and garrisoned Apollonia on the Euxine. These operations were all preparatory to his projected attack upon Byzantium. (Byzantium and Athens were at this time on unfriendly terms, owing to the part taken by the latter in the Social War.)

But the immediate subject of the present Speech was the state of affairs in the Chersonese in 342. The Chersonese (with the exception of Cardia) had been secured for Athens in 357, but had been threatened by Philip in 352,[1] when he made alliance with Cardia, and forced the neighbouring Thracian Prince Cersobleptes to submit. Soon after the Peace of Philocrates, Athens sent settlers to the Chersonese under Diopeithes. Cardia alone refused to receive them, and Diopeithes, with a mercenary force, prepared to compel the Cardians to admit them; while Philip sent troops to hold the town, and complained to Athens in threatening terms of the actions of Diopeithes, and more particularly of an inroad which Diopeithes had made upon Philip's territory

[1] See Introduction to First Philippic.

in Thrace. Diopeithes had been ill-supported with money and men by Athens, and had had recourse to piratical actions, in order to obtain supplies, thus arousing some indignation at Athens; but the prospect of the heavy expenditure which would be necessary, if an expedition were sent to his aid, was also unattractive. Demosthenes, however, proposed that Diopeithes should be vigorously supported, on the ground that Philip was really at war with Athens, and that this was not the time to interfere with the general who alone was pushing the Athenian cause. The speech was delivered early in the spring of 341. It is a masterpiece of oratory, at once statesmanlike and impassioned, and shows a complete command of every variety of tone. The latter part of it contains a strong denunciation of the Macedonian party in Athens, a defence of the orator's own career, and an urgent demand for the punishment of disloyalty. At the same time Demosthenes does not embody the policy which he advises in any formal motion. For this we have to wait for the Third Philippic.]

It was the duty, men of Athens, of every speaker not to allow either malice or favour to influence any speech which he might make, but simply to declare the policy which he considered to be the best, particularly when your deliberations were concerned with public affairs of great importance. But since there are some who are led on to address you, partly out of contentiousness, partly from causes which I need not discuss, it is for you, men of Athens—you, the People—to dismiss all other considerations, and both in the votes that you give and in the measures that you take to attend solely to what you believe to be for the good of the city. Now our present anxiety arises out of affairs in the Chersonese, and the campaign, now in its eleventh month, which Philip is conducting in Thrace. But most of the speeches which we have

heard have been about the acts and intentions of Diopeithes. For my part, I conceive that all charges made against any one who is amenable to the laws and can be punished by you when you will are matters which you are free to investigate, either immediately or after an interval, as you think fit; and there is no occasion for me or any one else to use strong
3 language about them. But all those advantages which an actual enemy of the city, with a large force in the Hellespont, is trying to snatch from you, and which, if we once fall behind-hand, we shall no longer be able to recover—these, surely, are matters upon which our interest demands that our plans be formed and our preparations made with the utmost dispatch; and that no clamour, no accusations about other matters, be allowed to drive us from this point.

4 Often as I am surprised at the assertions which are habitually made in your presence, nothing, men of Athens, has surprised me more than the remark which I heard only lately in the Council—that one who advises you ought, forsooth, to advise
5 you plainly either to go to war or to keep the peace. Very good.[1] If Philip is remaining inactive, if he is keeping nothing that is ours, in violation of the Peace, if he is not organizing all mankind against us, there is nothing more to be said—we have simply to observe the Peace; and I see that, for your part, you are quite ready to do so. But what if the oath that we swore, and the terms upon which we made the Peace,
6 stand inscribed for our eyes to see? What if it is proved that from the outset, before Diopeithes sailed from Athens with the settlers who are now accused of having brought about the war, Philip wrongfully seized many of our possessions—and here, unrepealed, are your resolutions charging him with

[1] ἔστω δή.

this—and that all along he has been uninterruptedly seizing the possessions of the other Hellenic and foreign peoples, and uniting their resources against us? What is *then* the meaning of the statement that we ought either to go to war or to keep the Peace? For we have no choice in the matter: 7 nothing remains open to us but the most righteous and most necessary of all acts—the act that they deliberately refuse to consider—I mean the act of retaliation against the aggressor: unless indeed, they intend to argue that, so long as Philip keeps away from Attica and the Peiraeus, he does the city no wrong and is not committing acts of war. But if *this* is their 8 criterion of right and wrong, if *this* is their definition of peace, then, although what they say is iniquitous, intolerable, and inconsistent with your security, as all must see, at the same time these very statements are actually contradictory of the charges which they are making against Diopeithes. Why, 9 I beg to ask, are we to give Philip full leave to act in whatever way he chooses, so long as he does not touch Attica, when Diopeithes is not to be allowed even to assist the Thracians, without being accused of initiating war? But even if this inconsistency is brought home to them, still, we are told, the conduct of the mercenaries in ravaging the Hellespontine country is outrageous, and Diopeithes has no right to drive the vessels to shore, and ought to be stopped. I grant it: 10 let it be done: I have nothing to say against it. Yet nevertheless, if their advice is genuinely based on considerations of right, and right alone, I consider that they are bound to prove that, as surely as they are seeking to break up the force on which *Athens* at present relies, by slandering its commander to you when he tries to provide funds to support it, so surely *Philip's* force will be disbanded if you accept their advice. If they fail to prove this, you must consider that they are simply setting the city once more upon the same course which has already resulted in the utter ruin 11 of her fortunes. For surely you know that nothing in the world has contributed so much to Philip's successes, as his being always first on the scene of action. With a standing force always about him, and knowing beforehand what he intends to do, he suddenly falls upon whomsoever he pleases: while we wait until we learn that something is happening, 12 and only then, in a turmoil, make our preparations. It follows, of course, that every position which he has attacked, he holds in undisturbed possession; while we are all behindhand; all our expenditure proves to have been so much useless waste; we have displayed our hostility and our desire to check him; but we are too late for action, and so we add disgrace to failure.

13 You must therefore not fail to recognize, men of Athens, that now, as before, all else that you hear consists of mere words and pretexts; and that the real aim of all that is being done is to secure that you may remain at home, that Athens may have no force outside the city, and that thus Philip may give effect to all his desires without let or hindrance. Consider, in the first place, what is actually occurring at 14 the present moment. He is at present passing the time in Thrace, with a great army under him; and, as we are told by those who are on the spot, he is sending for a large addition to it from Macedonia and Thessaly. Now if he waits for the Etesian winds, and then goes to Byzantium and besieges it, tell me first whether you think that the Byzantines will persist in their present infatuation, and will not 15 call upon you and entreat you to go to their aid? I do not

think so. Why, I believe that they would open their gates to men whom they distrust even more than they distrust you (if such exist), rather than surrender the city to Philip—supposing, that is, that he does not capture them first. And then, if we are unable to set sail from Athens, and if there are no forces there on the spot to help them, nothing can prevent their destruction. 'Of course,' you say, 'for the men are 16 possessed, and their infatuation passes all bounds.' Very true; and yet they must be preserved; for the interests of Athens require it. And besides, we cannot by any means be certain that he will not invade the Chersonese. Indeed, if we are to judge by the letter which he has sent to you, he there says that he *will* punish the settlers in the Chersonese. If then the army that is now formed there is in existence, it 17 will be able to help the Chersonese, and to injure some part of Philip's country. But when once it is dissolved, what shall we do if he marches against the Chersonese? 'We shall of course put Diopeithes on his trial.' And how will that improve our position? 'Well, we should go to the rescue from Athens ourselves.' What if the winds make it impossible? 'But, of course, he will not really get there.' And who can 18 guarantee that? Do you realize, men of Athens, or take into account, what the coming season of the year is, the season against which some think you ought to evacuate the Hellespont and hand it over to Philip? What if, when he leaves Thrace, he does not go near the Chersonese or Byzantium at all—for this, too, is a possibility which you must consider—but comes to Chalcis or Megara, just as he lately came to Oreus? Is it better to resist him here, and to allow the war to come into Attica, or to provide something to keep him busy there? The latter course is surely the better.

19 Realizing these things, therefore, as you all must, and taking due account of them, you must not, Heaven knows, look askance at the force which Diopeithes is trying to provide for Athens, or attempt to disband it. You must yourselves prepare another force to support it: you must help him freely with money, and give him in all other respects your 20 loyal co-operation. If Philip were asked to say whether he would wish these soldiers who are now with Diopeithes—describe them as you will, for I in no way dispute your description—to be prosperous and in high favour with the Athenians, and to be augmented in numbers by the co-operation of the city; or whether he would rather see them broken up and destroyed in consequence of calumnious charges against them; he would prefer, I imagine, the latter alternative. Can it then be, that there are men among us here who are trying to bring about the very thing that Philip would pray Heaven for? And if so, do you need to seek any further for the cause of the total ruin of the city's fortunes?

21 I wish, therefore, to examine without reserve the present crisis of our affairs, to inquire what we ourselves are now doing, and how we are dealing with it. We do not wish to contribute funds, nor to serve with the forces in person; we cannot keep our hands from the public revenues; we do not give the contributions of the allies to Diopeithes, nor do we 22 approve of such supplies as he raises for himself; but we look malignantly at him, we ask whence he gets them, what he intends to do, and every possible question of that kind: and yet we are still not willing to confine ourselves to our own affairs, in consequence of the attitude which we have adopted; we still praise with our lips those who uphold the dignity of the city, though in our acts we are fighting on the side of their

opponents. Now whenever any one rises to speak, you always put to him the question 'What are we to do?' I wish to put to *you* the question, 'What are we to *say*?' For if you will neither contribute, nor serve in person, nor leave the public funds alone, nor grant him the contributions, nor let him get what he can for himself, nor yet confine yourselves to your own affairs, I do not know what I can say. For when you give such licence to those who desire to make charges and accusations, that you listen to them even when they denounce him by anticipation for his alleged intentions—well, what *can* one say? 23

The possible effect of this is a matter which some of you require to understand, and I will speak without reserve; for indeed I could not speak otherwise. All the commanders who have ever yet sailed from Athens—if I am wrong, I consent to any penalty that you please—take money from the Chians, from the Erythraeans, from any people from whom they can severally get it—I mean, any of the Asiatic settlers who are now in question. Those who have one or two ships take less, those who have a larger force take more. And those who give to them do not give either little or much for nothing; they are not so insane: in fact, with these sums they buy immunity from injury for the merchants who sail from their ports, freedom from piracy, the convoying of their vessels, and so on. They call the gifts 'benevolences', and that is the name given to the sums thus obtained. And in the present case, when Diopeithes is there with his army, it is obvious that all these peoples will give him money. From what other source do you imagine that a general can maintain his troops, when he has received nothing from you, and has no resources from which he can pay his men? Will 24 25 26

money drop from the sky? Of course not. He subsists upon
27 what he can collect or beg or borrow. The real effect, therefore, of the accusations made against him here, is simply to warn every one that they should refuse to give him anything, since he is to pay the penalty for his very intentions, not to speak of any action that he may have taken or any success that he may have achieved. That is the only meaning of the cry that 'he is preparing a blockade', or 'he is surrendering the Hellenes'. Do any of his critics care about the Hellenes who
28 live in Asia? Were it so, they would be more thoughtful for the rest of mankind than for their own country. And the proposal to send another general to the Hellespont amounts to no more than this. For if Diopeithes is acting outrageously and is driving the vessels to shore, then, gentlemen, one little wax-tablet is enough to put an end to it all: and what the laws command is that for these offences we should impeach the wrong-doers—not that we should keep a watch upon
29 our own forces at such expense and with so many ships. Such insanity really passes all bounds. No! Against the enemy whom we cannot arrest and render amenable to the laws, it is both right and necessary to maintain a force, to send war-ships, and to contribute war-funds: but against one of ourselves, a decree, an impeachment, a dispatch-boat will answer our purpose. These are the means which sensible men would use: the policy of the other side is the policy
30 of men whose spitefulness is ruining your fortunes. And that there should be some such men, bad though it is, is not the worst. No! for you who sit there are already in such a frame of mind, that if any one comes forward and says that Diopeithes is the cause of all the mischief, or Chares, or Aristophon, or any Athenian citizen that he happens to

name, you at once agree, and clamorously declare that he is right; but if any one comes forward and tells you the 31 truth, and says, 'Men of Athens, this is nonsense. It is Philip that is the cause of all this mischief and trouble; for if he were quiet, the city would have nothing to disturb her,' you cannot, indeed, deny the truth of his words, but you seem, I think, to be annoyed, as though you were losing something. And the cause of these things is this—and 32 I beseech you, in Heaven's name, to let me speak unreservedly, when I am speaking for your true good—that some of your politicians have contrived that you should be terrifying and severe in your assemblies, but easy-going and contemptible in your preparations for war. And accordingly, if any one names as the culprit some one whom you know you can arrest in your own midst, you agree and you wish to act; but if one is named whom you must first master by force of arms, if you are to punish him at all, you are at a loss, I fancy, what to do, and you are vexed when this is brought home to you. For your politicians, men of Athens, should have 33 treated you in exactly the opposite way to this; they should train you to be kind and sympathetic in your assemblies; for there it is with the members of your own body and your own allies that your case is argued: but your terrors and your severity should be displayed in your preparations for war, where the struggle is with your enemies and your rivals. As it is, by their popular speeches, and by courting your 34 favour to excess, they have brought you into such a condition that, while in your assemblies you give yourselves airs and enjoy their flattery, listening to nothing but what is meant to please you, in the world of facts and events you are in the last extremity of peril. Imagine, in

God's name, what would happen, if the Hellenes were to call you to account for the opportunities which, in your indolence, you have now let pass, and were to put to you the 35 question, 'Is it true, men of Athens, that you send envoys to us on every possible occasion, to tell us of Philip's designs against ourselves and all the Hellenes, and of the duty of keeping guard against the man, and to warn us in every way?' We should have to confess that it was true. We do act thus. 'Then,' they would proceed, 'is it true, you most contemptible of all men, that though the man has been 36 away for ten months, and has been cut off from every possibility of returning home, by illness and by winter and by wars, you have neither liberated Euboea nor recovered any of your own possessions? Is it true that you have remained at home, unoccupied and healthy—if such a word can be used of men who behave thus—and have seen him set up two tyrants in Euboea, one to serve as a fortress directly menacing 37 Attica, the other to watch Sciathus; and that you have not even rid yourselves of these dangers—granted that you did not want to do anything more—but have let them be? Obviously you have retired in his favour, and have made it evident that if he dies ten times over, you will not make any move the more. Why trouble us then with your embassies and your accusations?' If they speak thus to us, what will be our answer? What shall we say, Athenians? I do not see what we can say.

38 Now there are some who imagine that they confute a speaker, as soon as they have asked him the question, 'What then are we to do?' I will first give them this answer—the most just and true of all—'Do not do what you are doing 39 now.' But at the same time I will give them a minute and

detailed reply; and then let them show that their willingness to act upon it is not less than their eagerness to interrogate. First, men of Athens, you must thoroughly make up your minds to the fact that Philip is at war with Athens, and has broken the Peace—you must cease to lay the blame at one another's doors—and that he is evilly-disposed and hostile to the whole city, down to the very ground on which it is built; nay, I will go further—hostile to every single man 40 in the city, even to those who are most sure that they are winning his favour. (If you think otherwise, consider the case of Euthycrates and Lasthenes of Olynthus, who fancied that they were on the most friendly terms with him, but, after they had betrayed their city, suffered the most utter ruin of all.) But his hostilities and intrigues are aimed at nothing so much as at our constitution, whose overthrow is the very first object in the world to him. And in a sense 41 it is natural that he should aim at this. For he knows very well that even if he becomes master of all the rest of the world, he can retain nothing securely, so long as you are a democracy; and that if he chances to stumble anywhere, as may often happen to a man, all the elements which are now forced into union with him will come and take refuge with you. For 42 though you are not yourselves naturally adapted for aggrandizement or the usurpation of empire, you have the art of preventing any other from seizing power and of taking it from him when he has it; and in every respect you are ready to give trouble to those who are ambitious of dominion, and to lead all men forth into liberty. And so he would not have Freedom, from her home in Athens, watching for every opportunity he may offer—far from it—and there is nothing unsound or careless in his reasoning. The first essential 43 point, therefore, is this—that you conceive him to be the irreconcilable foe of your constitution and of democracy: for unless you are inwardly convinced of this, you will not be willing to take an active interest in the situation. Secondly, you must realize clearly that all the plans which he is now so busily contriving are in the nature of preparations against this country; and wherever any one resists him, he there 44 resists him on our behalf. For surely no one is so simple as to imagine that when Philip is covetous of the wretched hamlets of Thrace—one can give no other name to Drongilum, Cabyle, Masteira, and the places which he is now seizing—and when to get these places he is enduring heavy labours, 45 hard winters, and the extremity of danger;—no one can imagine, I say, that the harbours and the dockyards, and the ships of the Athenians, the produce of your silver-mines, and your huge revenue, have no attraction for him, or that he will leave you in possession of these, while he winters in the very pit of destruction for the sake of the millet and the spelt in the silos of Thrace. No, indeed! It is to get these into his power that he pursues both his operations in Thrace 46 and all his other designs. What then, as sensible men, must you do? Knowing and realizing your position, as you do, you must lay aside this excessive, this irremediable indolence: you must contribute funds, and require them from your allies; you must so provide and act, that this force which is now assembled may be held together; in order that, as Philip has the force in readiness that is to injure and enslave all the Hellenes, you may have in readiness that which shall 47 preserve and succour them. You cannot effect by isolated expeditions any of the things which must be effected. You *must* organize a force, and provide maintenance for it, and paymasters, and a staff of servants; and when you have taken such steps as will ensure the strictest possible watch being kept over the funds, you must hold these officials accountable for the money, and the general for the actual operations. If you act thus, and honestly make up your minds to take this course, you will either compel Philip to observe a righteous peace and remain in his own land—and no greater blessing could you obtain than that—or you will fight him on equal terms.

It may be thought that this policy demands heavy expenditure, and great exertions and trouble. That is true indeed; but let the objector take into account what the consequences to the city must be, if he is unwilling to assent to this policy, and he will find that the ready performance of duty brings its reward. If indeed some god is offering us his guarantee—for no human guarantee would be sufficient in so great a matter—that if you remain at peace and let everything slide, Philip will not in the end come and attack yourselves; then, although, before God and every Heavenly Power, it would be unworthy of you and of the position that the city holds, and of the deeds of our forefathers, to abandon all the rest of the Hellenes to slavery for the sake of our own ease—although, for my part, I would rather have died than have suggested such a thing—yet, if another proposes it and convinces you, let it be so: do not defend yourselves: let everything go. But if no one entertains such a belief, if we all know that the very opposite is true, and that the wider the mastery we allow him to gain, the more difficult and powerful a foe we shall have to deal with, what further subterfuge is open to us? Why do we delay? When shall we ever be willing, men of Athens, to do our duty? 'When

48 49 50 51

we are compelled,' you say. But the hour of compulsion, as the word is applied to free men, is not only here already, but has long passed; and we must surely pray that the compulsion which is put upon slaves may not come upon us. And what is the difference? It is this—that for a free man the greatest compelling force is his shame at the course which events are taking—I do not know what greater we can imagine; but the slave is compelled by blows and bodily tortures, which I pray may never fall to our lot; it is not fit to speak of them.

52 I would gladly tell you the whole story, and show how certain persons are working for your ruin by their policy. I pass over, however, every point but this. Whenever any question of our relations with Philip arises, at once some one stands up and talks of the blessings of peace, of the difficulty of maintaining a large force, and of designs on the part of certain persons to plunder our funds; with other tales of the same kind, which enable them to delay your action, and give Philip time 53 to do what he wishes unopposed. What is the result? For you the result is your leisure, and a respite from immediate action—advantages which I fear you will some day feel to have cost you dear; and for them it is the favour they win, and the wages for these services. But I am sure that there is no need to persuade you to keep the Peace—you sit here fully persuaded. It is the man who is committing acts of war that we need to persuade; for if he is persuaded, you are ready 54 enough. Nor is it the expenditure which is to ensure our preservation that ought to distress us, but the fate which is in prospect for us, if we are not willing to take this action: while the threatened 'plunder of our funds' is to be prevented by the proposal of some safeguard which will render them

secure, not by the abandonment of our interests. [55] And even so, men of Athens, I feel indignant at the very fact that some of you are so much pained at the prospect of the plunder of our funds, when you have it in your power both to protect them and to punish the culprits, and yet feel no pain when Philip is seizing all Hellas piecemeal for his plunder, and seizing it to strengthen himself against you. [56] What then is the reason, men of Athens, that though Philip's campaigns, his aggressions, his seizure of cities, are so unconcealed, none of my opponents has ever said that *he* was bringing about war? Why is it those who advise you not to allow it, not to make these sacrifices, that they accuse, and say that *they* will be the cause of the war? I will inform you. [57] It is because they wish to divert the anger which you are likely to show, if you suffer at all from the war, on to the heads of those who are giving you the best advice in your own interests. They want you to sit and try such persons, instead of resisting Philip; and they themselves are to be the prosecutors, instead of paying the penalty for their present actions. That is the meaning of their assertion that there are some here, forsooth, who want to bring about war. [58] That is the real point of these allegations of responsibility. But this I know beyond all doubt—that without waiting for any one in Athens to propose the declaration of war, Philip has not only taken many other possessions of ours, but has just now sent an expedition to Cardia. If, in spite of this, we wish to pretend that he is not making war on us, he would be the most senseless man living, were he to attempt to convince us of our error. [59] But what shall we say, when his attack is made directly upon ourselves? He of course will say that he is not at war with us—just as he was not at war with Oreus, when his soldiers were in the land ; nor with the Pheraeans, before that, when he was assaulting their walls ; nor with the Olynthians, first of all, until he and his army were actually within their territory. Or shall we still say that those who urge resistance are bringing about war ? If so, all that is left to us is slavery. If we may neither offer resistance, nor yet be suffered to remain at peace, no other compromise is possible.

60 And further, the issues at stake are not for you merely what they are for other states. What Philip desires is not your subjection, but your utter annihilation. For he knows full well that you will never consent to be his slaves, and that even if you were willing, you would not know the way, accustomed as you are to govern ; and he knows that you will be able to give him more trouble, if you get the oppor-

61 tunity, than all the rest of the world. The struggle, then, is a struggle for existence ; and as such you ought to think of it : and you should show your abhorrence of those who have sold themselves to Philip by beating them to death. For it is impossible, utterly impossible, to master your enemies outside the city, before you punish your enemies in the city itself.

62 Whence comes it, think you, that he is insulting us now (for his conduct seems to me to be nothing less than this), and that while he at least deceives all other peoples by doing them favours, he is using threats against you without more ado ? For instance, he enticed the Thessalians by large gifts into their present servitude ; and words cannot describe how greatly he deceived the Olynthians at first by the gift

63 of Poteidaea and much beside. At this moment he is alluring the Thebans, by delivering up Boeotia to them, and ridding them of a long and arduous campaign. Each of these peoples has first reaped some advantage, before falling into those

calamities which some of them have already suffered, as all the world knows, and some are destined to suffer whenever their time comes. But as for yourselves, to pass over all that you have been robbed of at an earlier period, what deception, what robbery have been practised upon you in the very act of making the Peace! Have not the Phocians, and Thermopylae, and the Thracian seaboard—Doriscus, Serrhium, Cersobleptes himself—been taken from you? Does not Philip at this moment occupy the city of the Cardians, and avow it openly? Why is it then, that he behaves as he does to all others, and so differently to you? Because yours is the one city in the world where men are permitted to speak on behalf of the enemy without fear; because here a man may take bribes, and still address you with impunity, even when you have been robbed of your own. In Olynthus it was only safe to take Philip's side when the people of Olynthus as a whole had shared Philip's favours, and was enjoying the possession of Poteidaea. In Thessaly it was only safe to take Philip's side when the Thessalian commons had shared Philip's favours; for he had expelled the tyrants for them, and restored to them their Amphictyonic position. In Thebes it was not safe, until he had restored Boeotia to Thebes and annihilated the Phocians. But at Athens—though Philip has not only robbed you of Amphipolis and the territory of the Cardians, but has turned Euboea into a fortress overlooking your country, and is now on his way to attack Byzantium—at Athens it *is* safe to speak in Philip's interest. Aye, and you know that, of such speakers, some who were poor are rapidly growing rich; and some who were without name or fame are becoming famous and distinguished, while you, on the other hand, are becoming inglorious

64

65

66

instead of famous, bankrupt instead of wealthy. For a city's wealth consists, I imagine, in allies, confidence, loyalty—
67 and of all these you are bankrupt. And because you are indifferent to these advantages, and let them drift away from you, he has become prosperous and powerful, and formidable to all, Hellenes and foreigners alike; while you are deserted and humbled, with a splendid profusion of commodities in your market, and a contemptible lack of all those things with which you should have been provided. But I observe that certain speakers do not follow the same principles in the advice which they give you, as they follow for themselves. *You*, they tell you, ought to remain quiet, even when you are wronged; but *they* cannot remain quiet in your presence, even when no one is wronging them.

68 But now some one or other comes forward and says, 'Ah, but you will not move a motion or take any risk. You are a poor-spirited coward.' Bold, offensive, shameless, I am not, and I trust I may never be; and yet I think I have more courage than very many of
69 your dashing statesmen. For one, men of Athens, who overlooks all that the city's interest demands—who prosecutes, confiscates, gives, accuses—does so not from any bravery, but because in the popular character of his speeches and public actions he has a guarantee of his personal safety, and therefore is bold without risk. But one who in acting for the best sets himself in many ways against your wishes—who never speaks to please, but always to advise what is best; one who chooses a policy in which more issues must be decided by chance than by calculation, and yet makes himself responsible to you for both—that is
70 the courageous man, and such is the citizen who is of value

to his country, rather than those who, to gain an ephemeral popularity, have ruined the supreme interests of the city. So far am I from envying these men, or thinking them worthy citizens of their country, that if any one were to ask me to say, what good *I* had really done to the city, although, men of Athens, I could tell how often I had been trierarch and choregus, how I had contributed funds, ransomed prisoners, and done other like acts of generosity, I would mention none of these things; I would say only that my policy is not 71 one of measures like theirs—that although, like others, I could make accusations and shower favours and confiscate property and do all that my opponents do, I have never to this day set myself to do any of these things; I have been influenced neither by gain nor by ambition; but I continue to give the advice which sets me below many others in your estimation, but which must make you greater, if you will listen to it; for so much, perhaps, I may say without offence. Nor, 72 I think, should I be acting fairly as a citizen, if I devised such political measures as would at once make me the first man in Athens, and you the last of all peoples. As the measures of a loyal politician develop, the greatness of his country should develop with them; and it is the thing which is best, not the thing which is easiest, that every speaker should advocate. Nature will find the way to the easiest course unaided. To the best, the words and the guidance of the loyal citizen must show the way.

I have heard it remarked before now, that though what 73 I *say* is always what is best, still I never contribute anything but words; whereas the city needs work of some practical kind. I will tell you without any concealment my own sentiments on this matter. There *is* no work that can be demanded of any of your public advisers, except that he should advise what is best; and I think I can easily show 74 you that this is so. No doubt you know how the great Timotheus delivered a speech to the effect that you ought to go to the rescue and save the Euboeans, when the Thebans were trying to reduce them to servitude; and how, in the course of his speech, he spoke somewhat in this strain:—'What?' said he, 'when you actually have the Thebans in the island, do you debate what you are to do with them, and how you are to act? Will you not cover the sea with warships, men of Athens? Will you not rise from your seats and go instantly to the Peiraeus and launch your vessels?' 75 So Timotheus spoke, and you acted as he bade you; and through his speech and your action the work was done But if he had given you the best possible advice (as in fact he did), and you had lapsed into indolence and paid no attention to it, would the city have achieved any of the results which followed on that occasion? Impossible! And so it is with all that I say to-day, and with all that this or that speaker may say. For the actions you must look to yourselves; from the speaker you must require that he give you the best counsel that he can.

76 I desire now to sum up my advice and to leave the platform. I say that we must contribute funds, and must keep together the force now in existence, correcting anything that may seem amiss in it, but not disbanding the whole force because of the possible criticisms against it. We must send envoys everywhere to instruct, to warn, and to act. Above all, we must punish those who take bribes in connexion with public affairs, and must everywhere display our abhorrence of them; in order that reasonable men, who offer their

honest services, may find their policy justified in their own eyes and in those of others. If you treat the situation thus, 77 and cease to ignore it altogether, there is a chance—a chance I say, even now—that it may improve. If, however, you sit idle, with an interest that stops short at applause and acclamation, and retires into the background when any action is required, I can imagine no oratory, which, without action on your part, will be able to save your country.

THE THIRD PHILIPPIC (Or. IX)

[*Introduction.* The Third Philippic seems to have been delivered in the late spring or early summer of 341 B.C., about two months after the Speech on the Chersonese, which apparently had little positive result, though it probably prevented the recall and prosecution of Diopeithes. The immediate occasion of the Third Philippic was a request from the forces in the Chersonese for supplies. The general situation is the same as at the date of the last speech, but the danger to Byzantium is more pressing. Demosthenes now takes the broad ground of Panhellenic policy, and formally proposes to send envoys throughout Greece, to unite all the Greek states against Philip, as well as to send immediate reinforcements and supplies to the Chersonese.

Many critics, ancient and modern, have regarded this as the greatest of all Demosthenes' political orations. The lessons of history (from the speaker's point of view) are repeated and enforced by the citation of instance after instance. The tone of the speech, while less varied than that of the last, is grave and intense. The passage (§§ 36 ff.) in which the orator contrasts the spirit of Athenian political life in the past with that of his own day is one of the most impressive in all his works, and the nobility of his appeal to the traditional ideals of Athenian policy has been universally recognized even by his most severe critics.

The speech is found in the MSS. in two forms, of which the shorter omits a number of passages[1] which the longer includes, though there are signs of an imperfect blending of the two versions in certain places. It seems probable that both versions are due to Demosthenes, and the speech

[1] These are printed in square brackets in the translation.

may have been more than once revised by him before publication or republication. In which form it was delivered there is not sufficient evidence to show.]

MANY speeches are made, men of Athens, at almost every 1 meeting of the Assembly, with reference to the aggressions which Philip has been committing, ever since he concluded the Peace, not only against yourselves but against all other peoples; and I am sure that all would agree, however little they may act on their belief, that our aim, both in speech and in action, should be to cause him to cease from his insolence and to pay the penalty for it. And yet I see that in fact the treacherous sacrifice of our interests has gone on, until what seems an ill-omened saying may, I fear, be really true—that if all who came forward desired to propose, and you desired to carry, the measures which would make your position as pitiful as it could possibly be, it could not (so I believe), be made worse than it is now. It may be that 2 there are many reasons for this, and that our affairs did not reach their present condition from any one or two causes. But if you examine the matter aright, you will find that the chief responsibility rests with those whose aim is to win your favour, not to propose what is best. Some of them, men of Athens, so long as they can maintain the conditions which bring them reputation and influence, take no thought for the future [and therefore think that you also should take none]; while others, by accusing and slandering those who are actively at work, are simply trying to make the city spend its energies in punishing the members of its own body, and so leave Philip free to say and do what he likes. Such political 3 methods as these, familiar to you as they are, are the real causes of the evil. And I beg you, men of Athens, if I tell you certain truths outspokenly, to let no resentment on your part fall upon me on this account. Consider the matter in this light. In every other sphere of life, you believe that the right of free speech ought to be so universally shared by all who are in the city, that you have extended it both to foreigners and to slaves; and one may see many a servant in Athens speaking his mind with greater liberty than is granted to citizens in some other states: but from the sphere of political 4 counsel you have utterly banished this liberty. The result is that in your meetings you give yourselves airs and enjoy their flattery, listening to nothing but what is meant to please you, while in the world of facts and events, you are in the last extremity of peril. If then you are still in this mood to-day, I do not know what I can say; but if you are willing to listen while I tell you, without flattery, what your interest requires, I am prepared to speak. For though our position is very bad indeed, and much has been sacrificed, it is still possible, even now, if you will do your 5 duty, to set all right once more. It is a strange thing, perhaps, that I am about to say, but it is true. The worst feature in the past is that in which lies our best hope for the future. And what is this? It is that you are in your present plight because you do not do any part of your duty, small or great; for of course, if you were doing all that you should do, and were still in this evil case, you could not even hope for any improvement. As it is, Philip has conquered your indolence and your indifference; but he has not conquered Athens. You have not been vanquished—you have never even stirred.

6 [Now if it was admitted by us all that Philip was at war with Athens, and was transgressing the Peace, a speaker would have to do nothing but to advise you as to the safest and

easiest method of resistance to him. But since there are some who are in so extraordinary a frame of mind that, though he is capturing cities, though many of your possessions are in his hands, and though he is committing aggressions against all men, they still tolerate certain speakers, who constantly assert at your meetings that it is some of *us* who are provoking the war, it is necessary to be on our guard and come to a right understanding on the matter. For there is a danger lest 7 any one who proposes or advises resistance should find himself accused of having brought about the war.]

[Well, I say this first of all, and lay it down as a principle, that if it is open to us to deliberate whether we should remain at peace or should go to war . . .]

Now if it is possible for the city to remain at peace—if the 8 decision rests with us (that I may make this my starting-point) —then, I say that we ought to do so, and I call upon any one who says that it is so to move his motion, and to act and not to defraud us. But if another with weapons in his hands and a large force about him holds out to you the *name* of peace, while his own acts are acts of war, what course remains open to us but that of resistance? though if you wish to profess peace in the same manner as he, I have no quarrel with you. But if any man's conception of peace is that it 9 is a state in which Philip can master all that intervenes till at last he comes to attack ourselves, such a conception, in the first place, is madness; and, in the second place, this peace that he speaks of is a peace which you are to observe towards Philip, while he does not observe it towards you: and this it is—this power to carry on war against you, without being met by any hostilities on your part—that Philip is purchasing with all the money that he is spending.

10 Indeed, if we intend to wait till the time comes when he admits that he is at war with us, we are surely the most innocent persons in the world. Why, even if he comes to Attica itself, to the very Peiraeus, he will never make such an admission, if we are to judge by his dealings with others.
11 For, to take one instance, he told the Olynthians, when he was five miles from the city, that there were only two alternatives—either they must cease to live in Olynthus, or he to live in Macedonia: but during the whole time before that, whenever any one accused him of any such sentiments, he was indignant and sent envoys to answer the charge. Again, he marched into the Phocians' country, as though visiting his allies: it was by Phocian envoys that he was escorted on the march; and most people in Athens contended strongly that his crossing the Pass would bring no good to
12 Thebes. Worse still, he has lately seized Pherae and still holds it, though he went to Thessaly as a friend and an ally. And, latest of all, he told those unhappy citizens of Oreus that he had sent his soldiers to visit them and to make kind inquiries; he had heard that they were sick, and suffering from faction, and it was right for an ally and a true friend
13 to be present at such a time. Now if, instead of giving them warning and using open force, he deliberately chose to deceive these men, who could have done him no harm, though they might have taken precautions against suffering any themselves, do you imagine that he will make a formal declaration of war upon you before he commences hostilities,
14 and that, so long as you are content to be deceived? Impossible! For so long as you, though you are the injured party, make no complaint against him, but accuse some of your own body, he would be the most fatuous man

on earth if *he* were to interrupt your strife and contentions with one another—to bid you turn upon himself, and so to cut away the ground from the arguments by which his hirelings put you off, when they tell you that *he* is not at war with Athens.

In God's name, is there a man in his senses who would 15 judge by words, and not by facts, whether another was at peace or at war with him? Of course there is not. Why, from the very first, when the Peace had only just been made, before those who are now in the Chersonese had been sent out, Philip was taking Serrhium and Doriscus, and expelling the soldiers who were in the castle of Serrhium and the Sacred Mountain, where they had been placed by your general. But what was he doing, in acting thus? For he had sworn 16 to a Peace. And let no one ask, 'What do these things amount to? What do they matter to Athens?' For whether these acts were trifles which could have no interest for you is another matter; but the principles of religion and justice, whether a man transgress them in small things or great, have always the same force. What? When he is sending mercenaries into the Chersonese, which the king and all the Hellenes have acknowledged to be yours; when he openly avows that he is going to the rescue, and states it in his letter, what is it that he is doing? He tells you, 17 indeed, that he is not making war upon you. But so far am I from admitting that one who acts in this manner is observing the Peace which he made with you, that I hold that in grasping at Megara, in setting up tyrants in Euboea, in advancing against Thrace at the present moment, in pursuing his machinations in the Peloponnese, and in carrying out his entire policy with the help of his army, he is violating the

Peace and is making war against you;—unless you mean to say that even to bring up engines to besiege you is no breach of the Peace, until they are actually planted against your walls. But you will not say this; for the man who is taking the steps and contriving the means which will lead to my capture is at war with me, even though he has not 18 yet thrown a missile or shot an arrow. Now what are the things which would imperil your safety, if anything should happen? The alienation of the Hellespont, the placing of Megara and Euboea in the power of the enemy, and the attraction of Peloponnesian sympathy to his cause. Can I then say that one who is erecting such engines of war as 19 these against the city is at peace with you? Far from it! For from the very day when he annihilated the Phocians—from that very day, I say, I date the beginning of his hostilities against you. And for your part, I think that you will be wise if you resist him at once; but that if you let him be, you will find that, when you wish to resist, resistance itself is impossible. Indeed, so widely do I differ, men of Athens, from all your other advisers, that I do not think there is any room for discussion to-day in regard to the Chersonese or Byzantium. 20 We *must* go to their defence, and take every care that they do not suffer [and we must send all that they need to the soldiers who are at present there]. But we *have* to take counsel for the good of all the Hellenes, in view of the grave peril in which they stand. And I wish to tell you on what grounds I am so alarmed at the situation, in order that if my reasoning is correct, you may share my conclusions, and exercise some forethought for yourselves at least, if you are actually unwilling to do so for the Hellenes as a whole; but that if you think that I am talking nonsense, and am out of my senses, you may both now and hereafter decline to attend to me as though I were a sane man.

The rise of Philip to greatness from such small and humble beginnings; the mistrustful and quarrelsome attitude of the Hellenes towards one another; the fact that his growth out of what he was into what he is was a far more extraordinary thing than would be his subjugation of all that remains, when he has already secured so much;—all this and all similar themes, upon which I might speak at length, I will pass over. But I see that all men, beginning with yourselves, have conceded to him the very thing which has been at issue in every Hellenic war during the whole of the past. And what is this? It is the right to act as he pleases—to mutilate and to strip the Hellenic peoples, one by one, to attack and to enslave their cities. For seventy-three years you were the leading people of Hellas, and the Spartans for thirty years save one; and in these last times, after the battle of Leuctra, the Thebans too acquired some power: yet neither to you nor to Thebes nor to Sparta was such a right ever conceded by the Hellenes, as the right to do whatever you pleased. Far from it! First of all it was your own behaviour—or rather that of the Athenians of that day—which some thought immoderate; and all, even those who had no grievance against Athens, felt bound to join the injured parties, and to make war upon you. Then, in their turn, the Spartans, when they had acquired an empire and succeeded to a supremacy like your own, attempted to go beyond all bounds and to disturb the established order to an unjustifiable extent; and once more, all, even those who had no grievance against them, had recourse to war. Why mention the others? For we ourselves and the Spartans,

21 22 23 24 25

though we could originally allege no injury done by the one people to the other, nevertheless felt bound to go to war on account of the wrongs which we saw the rest suffering. And yet all the offences of the Spartans in those thirty years of power, and of your ancestors in their seventy years, were less, men of Athens, than the wrongs inflicted upon the Greeks by Philip, in the thirteen years, not yet completed, during 26 which he has been to the fore. Less do I say? They are not a fraction of them. [A few words will easily prove this.] I say nothing of Olynthus, and Methone, and Apollonia, and thirty-two cities in the Thracian region, all annihilated by him with such savagery, that a visitor to the spot would find it difficult to tell that they had ever been inhabited. I remain silent in regard to the extirpation of the great Phocian race. But what is the condition of Thessaly? Has he not robbed their very cities of their governments, and set up tetrarchies, that they may be enslaved, not merely 27 by whole cities, but by whole tribes at a time? Are not the cities of Euboea even now ruled by tyrants, and that in an island that is neighbour to Thebes and Athens? Does he not write expressly in his letters, 'I am at peace with those who choose to obey me'? And what he thus writes he does not fail to act upon; for he is gone to invade the Hellespont; he previously went to attack Ambracia; the great city of Elis in the Peloponnese is his; he has recently intrigued against Megara; and neither Hellas nor the world beyond 28 it is large enough to contain the man's ambition. But though all of us, the Hellenes, see and hear these things, we send no representatives to one another to discuss the matter; we show no indignation; we are in so evil a mood, so deep have the lines been dug which sever city from city, that up to this very day we are unable to act as either our interest or our duty require. We cannot unite; we can form no 29 combination for mutual support or friendship; but we look on while the man grows greater, because every one has made up his mind (as it seems to me) to profit by the time during which his neighbour is being ruined, and no one cares or acts for the safety of the Hellenes. For we all know that Philip is like the recurrence or the attack of a fever or other illness, in his descent upon those who fancy themselves for the present well out of his reach. And further, you must 30 surely realize that all the wrongs that the Hellenes suffered from the Spartans or ourselves they at least suffered at the hands of true-born sons of Hellas; and (one might conceive) it was as though a lawful son, born to a great estate, managed his affairs in some wrong or improper way;—his conduct would in itself deserve blame and denunciation, but at least it could not be said that he was not one of the family, or was not the heir to the property. But had it been a slave 31 or a supposititious son that was thus ruining and spoiling an inheritance to which he had no title, why, good Heavens! how infinitely more scandalous and reprehensible all would have declared it to be. And yet they show no such feeling in regard to Philip, although not only is he no Hellene, not only has he no kinship with Hellenes, but he is not even a barbarian from a country that one could acknowledge with credit;—he is a pestilent Macedonian, from whose country it used not to be possible to buy even a slave of any value.

And in spite of this, is there any degree of insolence to 32 which he does not proceed? Not content with annihilating cities, does he not manage the Pythian games, the common meeting of the Hellenes, and send his slaves to preside over the competition in his absence? [Is he not master of Thermopylae, and of the passes which lead into Hellenic territory? Does he not hold that district with garrisons and mercenaries? Has he not taken the precedence in consulting the oracle, and thrust aside ourselves and the Thessalians and Dorians and the rest of the Amphictyons, though the right is not one which

33 is given even to all of the Hellenes?] Does he not write to the Thessalians to prescribe the constitution under which they are to live? Does he not send one body of mercenaries to Porthmus, to expel the popular party of Eretria, and another to Oreus, to set up Philistides as tyrant? And yet the Hellenes see these things and endure them, gazing (it seems to me) as they would gaze at a hailstorm—each people praying that it may not come their way, but no one trying to prevent it. Nor is it only his outrages upon Hellas that go unresisted.

34 No one resists even the aggressions which are committed against himself. Ambracia and Leucas belong to the Corinthians—he has attacked them: Naupactus to the Achaeans—he has sworn to hand it over to the Aetolians: Echinus to the Thebans—he has taken it from them, and is now march-

35 ing against their allies the Byzantines—is it not so? And of our own possessions, to pass by all the rest, is not Cardia, the greatest city in the Chersonese, in his hands? Thus are we treated; and we are all hesitating and torpid, with our eyes upon our neighbours, distrusting one another, rather than the man whose victims we all are. But if he treats us collectively in this outrageous fashion, what do you think he will do, when he has become master of each of us separately?

36 What then is the cause of these things? For as it was not without reason and just cause that the Hellenes in old days

were so prompt for freedom, so it is not without reason or cause that they are now so prompt to be slaves. There was a spirit, men of Athens, a spirit in the minds of the people in those days, which is absent to-day—the spirit which vanquished the wealth of Persia, which led Hellas in the path of freedom, and never gave way in face of battle by sea or by land; a spirit whose extinction to-day has brought universal ruin and turned Hellas upside down. What was this spirit? [It was nothing subtle nor clever.] It meant that men who **37** took money from those who aimed at dominion or at the ruin of Hellas were execrated by all; that it was then a very grave thing to be convicted of bribery; that the punishment for the guilty man was the heaviest that could be inflicted; that for him there could be no plea for mercy, nor hope of pardon. No orator, no general, would then sell the critical **38** opportunity whenever it arose—the opportunity so often offered to men by fortune, even when they are careless and their foes are on their guard. They did not barter away the harmony between people and people, nor their own mistrust of the tyrant and the foreigner, nor any of these high sentiments. Where are such sentiments now? They **39** have been sold in the market and are gone; and those have been imported in their stead, through which the nation lies ruined and plague-stricken—the envy of the man who has received his hire; the amusement which accompanies his avowal; [the pardon granted to those whose guilt is proved;] the hatred of one who censures the crime; and all the appurtenances of corruption. For as to ships, numerical **40** strength, unstinting abundance of funds and all other material of war, and all the things by which the strength of cities is estimated, every people can command these in greater plenty and on a larger scale by far than in old days. But all these resources are rendered unserviceable, ineffectual, unprofitable, by those who traffic in them.

41 That these things are so to-day, you doubtless see, and need no testimony of mine: and that in times gone by the opposite was true, I will prove to you, not by any words of my own, but by the record inscribed by your ancestors on a pillar of bronze, and placed on the Acropolis [not to be a lesson to themselves—they needed no such record to put them in a right mind—but to be a reminder and an example to you 42 of the zeal that you ought to display in such a cause]. What then is the record? 'Arthmius, son of Pythonax, of Zeleia, is an outlaw, and is the enemy of the Athenian people and their allies, he and his house.' Then follows the reason for which this step was taken—'because he brought the gold 43 from the Medes into the Peloponnese.' Such is the record. Consider, in Heaven's name, what must have been the mind of the Athenians of that day, when they did this, and their conception of their position. They set up a record, that because a man of Zeleia, Arthmius by name, a slave of the King of Persia (for Zeleia is in Asia), as part of his service to the king, had brought gold, not to Athens, but to the Peloponnese, he should be an enemy of Athens and her allies, he and his house, and that they should be outlaws. And 44 this outlawry is no such disfranchisement as we ordinarily mean by the word. For what would it matter to a man of Zeleia, that he might have no share in the public life of Athens? But there is a clause in the Law of Murder, dealing with those in connexion with whose death the law does not allow a prosecution for murder [but the slaying of them is to be a holy act]: 'And let him die an outlaw,' it runs. The meaning, accordingly, is this—that the slayer of such

a man is to be pure from all guilt. They thought, therefore, 45 that the safety of all the Hellenes was a matter which concerned themselves—apart from this belief, it could not have mattered to them whether any one bought or corrupted men in the Peloponnese; and whenever they detected such offenders, they carried their punishment and their vengeance so far as to pillory their names for ever. As the natural consequence, the Hellenes were a terror to the foreigner, not the foreigner to the Hellenes. It is not so now. Such is not your attitude in these or in other matters. But what is it? [You know it yourselves; for why should 46 I accuse you explicitly on every point? And that of the rest of the Hellenes is like your own, and no better; and so I say that the present situation demands our utmost earnestness and good counsel.] And what counsel? Do you bid me tell you, and will you not be angry if I do so?

[*He reads from the document.*]

Now there is an ingenuous argument, which is used by 47 those who would reassure the city, to the effect that, after all, Philip is not yet in the position once held by the Spartans, who ruled everywhere over sea and land, with the king for their ally, and nothing to withstand them; and that, none the less, Athens defended herself even against them, and was not swept away. Since that time the progress in every direction, one may say, has been great, and has made the world to-day very different from what it was then; but I believe that in no respect has there been greater progress or development than in the art of war. In the first place, 48 I am told that in those days the Spartans and all our other enemies would invade us for four or five months—during, that is, the actual summer—and would damage Attica with infantry and citizen-troops, and then return home again. And so old-fashioned were the men of that day—nay rather, such true citizens—that no one ever purchased any object from another for money, but their warfare was of a legitimate 49 and open kind. But now, as I am sure you see, most of our losses are the result of treachery, and no issue is decided by open conflict or battle; while you are told that it is not because he leads a column of heavy infantry that Philip can march wherever he chooses, but because he has attached to himself a force of light infantry, cavalry, archers, mercenaries, 50 and similar troops. And whenever, with such advantages, he falls upon a State which is disordered within, and in their distrust of one another no one goes out in defence of its territory, he brings up his engines and besieges them. I pass over the fact that summer and winter are alike to him—that there is no close season during which he suspends 51 operations. But if you all know these things and take due account of them, you surely must not let the war pass into Attica, nor be dashed from your seat through looking back to the simplicity of those old hostilities with Sparta. You must guard against him, at the greatest possible distance, both by political measures and by preparations; you must prevent his stirring from home, instead of grappling with him 52 at close quarters in a struggle to the death. For, men of Athens, we have many natural advantages for a war, if we are willing to do our duty. There is the character of his country, much of which we can harry and damage, and a thousand other things. But for a pitched battle he is in better training than we.

53 Nor have you only to recognize these facts, and to resist

him by actual operations of war. You must also by reasoned judgement and of set purpose come to execrate those who address you in his interest, remembering that it is impossible to master the enemies of the city, until you punish those who are serving them in the city itself. And this, before 54 God and every Heavenly Power—this you will not be able to do; for you have reached such a pitch of folly or distraction or—I know not what to call it; for often has the fear actually entered my mind, that some more than mortal power may be driving our fortunes to ruin—that to enjoy their abuse, or their malice, or their jests, or whatever your motive may chance to be, you call upon men to speak who are hirelings, and some of whom would not even deny it; and you laugh to hear their abuse of others. And terrible as 55 this is, there is yet worse to be told. For you have actually made political life safer for these men, than for those who uphold your own cause. And yet observe what calamities the willingness to listen to such men lays up in store. I will mention facts known to you all.

In Olynthus, among those who were engaged in public 56 affairs, there was one party who were on the side of Philip, and served his interests in everything; and another whose aim was their city's real good, and the preservation of their fellow citizens from bondage. Which were the destroyers of their country? which betrayed the cavalry, through whose betrayal Olynthus perished? Those whose sympathies were with Philip's cause; those who, while the city still existed brought such dishonest and slanderous charges against the speakers whose advice was for the best, that, in the case of Apollonides at least, the people of Olynthus was even induced to banish the accused.

57 Nor is this instance of the unmixed evil wrought by these practices in the case of the Olynthians an exceptional one, or without parallel elsewhere. For in Eretria, when Plutarchus and the mercenaries had been got rid of, and the people had control of the city and of Porthmus, one party wished to entrust the State to you, the other to entrust it to Philip. And through listening mainly, or rather entirely, to the latter, these poor luckless Eretrians were at last persuaded to banish the advocates of their own interests.
58 For, as you know, Philip, their ally, sent Hipponicus with a thousand mercenaries, stripped Porthmus of its walls, and set up three tyrants—Hipparchus, Automedon, and Cleitarchus; and since then he has already twice expelled them from the country when they wished to recover their position [sending on the first occasion the mercenaries commanded by Eurylochus, on the second, those under Parmenio].

59 And why go through the mass of the instances? Enough to mention how in Oreus Philip had, as his agents, Philistides, Menippus, Socrates, Thoas, and Agapaeus—the very men who are now in possession of the city—and every one knew the fact; while a certain Euphraeus, who once lived here in Athens, acted in the interests of freedom, to save his
60 country from bondage. To describe the insults and the contumely with which he met would require a long story; but a year before the capture of the town he laid an information of treason against Philistides and his party, having perceived the nature of their plans. A number of men joined forces, with Philip for their paymaster and director, and haled Euphraeus off to prison as a disturber of the peace.
61 Seeing this, the democratic party in Oreus, instead of coming to the rescue of Euphraeus, and beating the other

party to death, displayed no anger at all against them, and agreed with a malicious pleasure that Euphraeus deserved his fate. After this the conspirators worked with all the freedom they desired for the capture of the city, and made arrangements for the execution of the scheme; while any of the democratic party, who perceived what was going on, maintained a panic-stricken silence, remembering the fate of Euphraeus. So wretched was their condition, that though this dreadful calamity was confronting them, no one dared open his lips, until all was ready and the enemy was advancing up to the walls. Then the one party set about the defence, the other about the betrayal of the city. And when the city 62 had been captured in this base and shameful manner, the successful party governed despotically: and of those who had been their own protectors, and had been ready to treat Euphraeus with all possible harshness, they expelled some and murdered others; while the good Euphraeus killed himself, thus testifying to the righteousness and purity of his motives in opposing Philip on behalf of his countrymen.

Now for what reason, you may be wondering, were the 63 peoples of Olynthus and Eretria and Oreus more agreeably disposed towards Philip's advocates than towards their own? The reason was the same as it is with you—that those who speak for your true good can never, even if they would, speak to win popularity with you; they are constrained to inquire how the State may be saved: while their opponents, in the very act of seeking popularity, are co-operating with Philip. The one party said, 'You must pay taxes;' the 64 other, 'There is no need to do so.' The one said, 'Go to war, and do not trust him;' the other, 'Remain at peace,'—until they were in the toils. And—not to mention each separately

—I believe that the same thing was true of all. The one side said what would enable them to win favour; the other, what would secure the safety of their State. And at last the main body of the people accepted much that they proposed—not now from any such desire for gratification, nor from ignorance, but as a concession to circumstances,
65 thinking that their cause was now wholly lost. It is this fate, I solemnly assure you, that I dread for you, when the time comes that you make your reckoning, and realize that there is no longer anything that can be done. May you never find yourselves, men of Athens, in such a position! Yet in any case, it were better to die ten thousand deaths, than to do anything out of servility towards Philip [or to sacrifice any of those who speak for your good]. A noble recompense did the people in Oreus receive, for entrusting themselves to Philip's friends, and thrusting Euphraeus
66 aside! and a noble recompense the democracy of Eretria, for driving away your envoys, and surrendering to Cleitarchus! They are slaves, scourged and butchered! A noble clemency did he show to the Olynthians, who elected Lasthenes to command the cavalry, and banished Apollonides!
67 It is folly, and it is cowardice, to cherish hopes like these, to give way to evil counsels, to refuse to do anything that you should do, to listen to the advocates of the enemy's cause, and to fancy that you dwell in so great a city that, whatever
68 happens, you will not suffer any harm. Aye, and it is shameful to exclaim after the event, 'Why, who would have expected this? Of course, we ought to have done, or not to have done, such and such things!' The Olynthians could tell you of many things, to have foreseen which in time would have saved them from destruction. So too could the people

of Oreus, and the Phocians, and every other people that has been destroyed. But how does that help them now? So 69 long as the vessel is safe, be it great or small, so long must the sailor and the pilot and every man in his place exert himself and take care that no one may capsize it by design or by accident: but when the seas have overwhelmed it, all their efforts are in vain. So it is, men of Athens, with us. While 70 we are still safe, with our great city, our vast resources, our noble name, what are we to do? Perhaps some one sitting here has long been wishing to ask this question. Aye, and I will answer it, and will move my motion; and you shall carry it, if you wish. We ourselves, in the first place, must conduct the resistance and make preparation for it—with ships, that is, and money, and soldiers. For though all but ourselves give way and become slaves, we at least must contend for freedom. And when we have made all these 71 preparations ourselves, and let them be seen, then let us call upon the other states for aid, and send envoys to carry our message [in all directions—to the Peloponnese, to Rhodes, to Chios, to the king; for it is not unimportant for his interests either that Philip should be prevented from subjugating the world]; that so, if you persuade them, you may have partners to share the danger and the expense, in case of need; and if you do not, you may at least delay the march of events. For since the war is with a single 72 man, and not against the strength of a united state, even delay is not without its value, any more than were those embassies of protest which last year went round the Peloponnese, when I and Polyeuctus, that best of men, and Hegesippus and the other envoys went on our tour, and forced him to halt, so that he neither went to attack

73 Acarnania, nor set out for the Peloponnese. But I do not mean that we should call upon the other states, if we are not willing to take any of the necessary steps ourselves. It is folly to sacrifice what is our own, and then pretend to be anxious for the interests of others—to neglect the present, and alarm others in regard to the future. I do not propose this. I say that we must send money to the forces in the Chersonese, and do all that they ask of us; that we must make preparation ourselves, while we summon, convene, instruct, and warn the rest of the Hellenes. That is the
74 policy for a city with a reputation such as yours. But if you fancy that the people of Chalcis or of Megara will save Hellas, while you run away from the task, you are mistaken. They may well be content if they can each save themselves. The task is yours. It is the prerogative that your forefathers won, and through many a great peril bequeathed to you.
75 But if each of you is to sit and consult his inclinations, looking for some way by which he may escape any personal action, the first consequence will be that you will never find any one who will act; and the second, I fear, that the day will come when we shall be forced to do, at one and the same time, all the things we wish to avoid.

76 This then is my proposal, and this I move. If the proposal is carried out, I think that even now the state of our affairs may be remedied. But if any one has a better proposal to make, let him make it, and give us his advice. And I pray to all the gods that whatever be the decision that you are about to make, it may be for your good.

ON THE CROWN (Or. XVIII)

[*Introduction.* The advice given by Demosthenes in the Third Philippic (spoken before the middle of 341) was in the main followed. He himself was sent almost immediately to Byzantium, where he renewed the alliance between that city and Athens, and at the same time entered into relations with Abydos and the Thracian princes. Rhodes, and probably Chios and Cos, were also conciliated, and an embassy was sent to the King of Persia to ask for aid against Philip. The king appears to have sent assistance to Diopeithes, and it is also stated (not on the best authority) that he sent large sums of money to Demosthenes and Hypereides. Demosthenes further succeeded, in conjunction with Callias of Chalcis, in organizing a league against Philip, which included Corinth, Megara, Corcyra, and the Acarnanians, and which at least supplied a considerable number of men and some funds. The cities of Euboea, most of which had been in the hands of Philip's party, were also formed into a confederacy, in alliance with Athens, under the leadership of Chalcis; Philistides was expelled from Oreus, about July 341, by the allied forces under Cephisophon; and later in the summer, Phocion drove Cleitarchus from Eretria. On the motion of Aristonicus, the Athenians voted Demosthenes a golden crown, which was conferred on him in the theatre at the Great Dionysia in March 340. The arrest of Anaxinus of Oreus, and his condemnation as a spy, acting in Philip's interest, must have occurred about the same time. Not long afterwards Demosthenes succeeded in carrying out a complete reorganization of the trierarchic system, by which he made the burden of the expense vary strictly according to property, and secured a regular and efficient supply of ships, money, and men.

In the meantime (in 341 or 340) the island of Peparethus

was attacked by Philip's ships, in revenge for the seizure of the Macedonian garrison in Halonnesus by the Peparethians: and the Athenian admirals were ordered to retaliate. Philip himself had been pursuing his course in Thrace; and on the rejection of his request to Byzantium for an alliance, he laid siege (late in 340) to Perinthus (which lay on his way to Byzantium), sending part of his forces through the Chersonese. Aided by Byzantine and Persian soldiers, Perinthus held out, till at last Philip took off most of his forces and besieged Byzantium itself. He had shortly before this sent to Athens an express declaration of war, and received a similar declaration from her, the formal excuse for which was found in the recent seizure by his ships of some Athenian merchant-vessels. But with help from Athens, Chios, Rhodes, and Cos, the Byzantines maintained the defence. Philip's position became serious; but he managed by a ruse to get his ships away into the open sea, and even to do some damage to the Athenian settlers in the Chersonese. In the winter he withdrew from Byzantium, and in 339 made an incursion into Scythia; but, returning through the country of the Triballi, he sustained some loss, and was severely wounded. Later in the year a new Sacred War which had arisen gave him a convenient opportunity for the invasion of Greece.

At the meeting of the Amphictyonic Council in the autumn of 340,[1] Aeschines was one of the representatives of Athens. The Athenians had recently offended Thebes by re-gilding and dedicating in the restored temple at Delphi fifty shields, with an inscription stating that they were spoil 'taken from the Medes and the Thebans, when they fought against the Hellenes' (probably at Plataeae in 479). The Locrians of Amphissa intended (according to Aeschines' account) to propose that the Council should fine Athens fifty talents. Aeschines rose to state the case for Athens; but a delegate from Amphissa forbade all mention of the Athenians, and

[1] Some writers suppose that it was at the meeting in the spring of 339. The evidence is not conclusive, but appears to point to the date given here.

demanded their exclusion from the temple, on the ground of their alliance with the accursed Phocians. Aeschines retorted by charging the Amphisseans with cultivating and building upon the sacred plain of Cirrha—acts forbidden for all time in 586 B.C.—and roused the Council to such indignation that they gathered a body of men and destroyed the harbour and the unlawful buildings of Cirrha; but they were severely handled by the Amphisseans, and the Council now voted that the Amphictyonic states should send representatives, to discuss the question of war against Amphissa, to a meeting to be held at Thermopylae before the spring meeting of the Council. To this preliminary meeting, the Athenians (though inclined to view Aeschines' performance with favour), on the advice of Demosthenes, sent no representatives; nor did the Thebans (the allies of Amphissa). War was declared by the Amphictyons against Amphissa; but Cottyphus, the Thessalian, who had been appointed general, made little headway, and (at the spring or the autumn meeting of the Council) declared that the Amphictyonic states must either send men and money, or else make Philip their general. Philip was, of course, at once appointed; but instead of proceeding against Amphissa, marched to Elateia and fortified it. This caused the greatest alarm at Athens. Demosthenes was immediately dispatched to Thebes, where he succeeded, by what appear to have been liberal and judicious proposals, in making an alliance between Thebes and Athens, in spite of the attempts of Philip's envoys to counteract his influence. Euboea, Megara, Corinth, and other members of the league also sent help. Philip himself called upon his own friends in the Peloponnese for aid, and at last moved towards Amphissa. Demosthenes seems now to have succeeded in applying the festival-money to purposes of war, and with the aid of Lycurgus, who became Controller of the Festival Fund, to have amassed a large sum for the use of the State. At the Dionysia of 338 he was again crowned, on the proposal of Demomeles and Hypereides. The allies at first won some successes and refortified some of the Phocian towns, but afterwards unfortunately divided their forces, and so enabled Philip to defeat the two divisions separately, and to destroy Amphissa. Philip's proposals of peace found supporters both in Thebes and in Athens, but were counteracted by Demosthenes. Late in the summer of 338, the decisive battle was fought at Chaeroneia, and resulted in the total rout of the allies. Demosthenes himself was one of the fugitives. Philip placed a Macedonian garrison in Thebes, restored his exiled friends to power there, established a Council of Three Hundred, and (through them) put to death or banished his enemies. He also gave Orchomenus, Thespiae, and Plataeae their independence. After a moment of panic, the Athenians, led by Demosthenes, Lycurgus, and Hypereides, proceeded to take all possible measures for the defence of the city, while private munificence supplied the treasury. Demosthenes himself superintended the repair of the fortifications, and went on a mission to secure a supply of corn. But Philip, instead of marching upon Athens, sent a message by Demades, whom he had taken prisoner at Chaeroneia; and the Assembly, in reply, instructed Demades, Aeschines, and Phocion to ask Philip to release his Athenian prisoners. Philip released them without ransom, and sent Antipater and Alexander (with the ashes of the Athenian dead) to offer terms of peace. By the 'Peace of Demades', concluded while Demosthenes was still absent, the alliance between Athens and Philip was renewed; the independence of Athens was guaranteed; Oropus was taken from Thebes and restored to Athens; and she was permitted to retain Salamis, Samos, Delos, and probably Lemnos and Imbros. On the other hand, she lost all her possessions on the Hellespont and in the Chersonese, and promised to join the league which Philip intended to form for the invasion of Persia. Demosthenes was selected by the Assembly to deliver the funeral oration upon those who fell at Chaeroneia; and although the Macedonian party attacked him repeatedly in the law-courts, he was always acquitted. Philip paid a long visit to the Peloponnese, in the course of which he placed a Macedonian garrison in Corinth, ravaged Laconia, giving parts of it to his allies, the Argives and Arcadians, and announced his plans for the invasion of Persia at the head of the Greeks: he then returned to Macedonia.

In 337 Demosthenes was again Commissioner of Fortifications, as well as Controller of the Festival Fund—the most important office in the State. He not only performed his work most efficiently, but gave considerable sums for public purposes out of his private fortune; and early in 336 Ctesiphon proposed, and the Council resolved, that he should once more be crowned at the Dionysia. But before the proposal could be brought before the Assembly, Aeschines indicted Ctesiphon for its alleged illegality. The trial did not take place until late in the summer of 330. We do not know the reason for so long a delay, but probably the events of the intervening time were such as to render the state of public feeling unfavourable to Aeschines. In 336 Philip was assassinated, and was succeeded by Alexander. In 335 Alexander destroyed Thebes, which had revolted, and sold its inhabitants into slavery. He also demanded from Athens the surrender of Demosthenes and other anti-Macedonian politicians and generals, but was persuaded to be content with the banishment of Charidemus and Ephialtes, and the promise of the prosecution of Demosthenes for using subsidies from Persia to help Thebes—a prosecution which was allowed to drop. From 334 onwards Alexander was pursuing his conquests in the East, and we know practically nothing of the history of Athens until the trial of Ctesiphon came on in 330.

Aeschines alleged against Ctesiphon (1) that it was illegal to propose to crown any one who had not passed his examination before the Board of Auditors at the end of his term of office; and that Demosthenes, who had been Commissioner of Fortifications and Controller of the Festival Fund, was still in this position: (2) that it was illegal to proclaim the grant of a crown at the Dionysia, except in the case of crowns conferred by foreign states: (3) that it was illegal to insert untrue statements in the public records, and that the language in which Ctesiphon's decree described the political career of Demosthenes was untrue. On the first point Aeschines was almost certainly right: Demosthenes' defence is sophistical, and all that could really be said was that the rule had often been broken before. On the second point, certainty is impossible: the most probable view (though it also has its difficulties) is that there were two inconsistent laws, and that one of them permitted the proclamation in the theatre, if expressly voted by the people; but the alleged illegality had certainly been often committed. The third point, which raised the question of the value to Athens of Demosthenes' whole political life, was that upon which the case really turned; and it is to this that Demosthenes devotes the greater part of his speech, breaking up his reply into convenient stages by discussions (of a far less happy description) of the other counts of the indictment, and of the character and career of Aeschines. As in the Speech on the Embassy, certain facts are misrepresented, and there are passages which are in bad taste; but Demosthenes proves beyond doubt his unswerving loyalty to the high ideal of policy which he had formed for his country, and it is with good reason that parts of this speech have always been felt to reach a height of eloquence which has never been surpassed.

The jury acquitted Ctesiphon: and Aeschines, failing to obtain a fifth part of the votes, and thus incurring a heavy fine and the loss of some of the rights of a citizen, left Athens, and lived most of the remainder of his life at Rhodes.

The following is an analysis of the speech in outline:—

I. Introduction (§§ 1–8).
II. Defence against charges irrelevant to the indictment (§§ 9–52).
  (1) Introduction (§ 9).
  (2) Postponement of reply to charges against his private life (§§ 10, 11).
  (3) Reply to charges against his public life (§§ 12–52).

(*a*) Criticism of Aeschines' method of attack (§§ 12–16).
(*b*) Reply in reference to the Peace of Philocrates (§§ 17–52).

III. Defence against the indictment itself (§§ 53–125).
(1) Introduction (§§ 53–9).
(2) Defence of his policy B.C. 346–340 (§§ 60–109).
(3) The alleged illegality of crowning him before he had passed his audit (§§ 110–19).
(4) The alleged illegality of the proclamation in the theatre (§§ 120, 121).
(5) Conclusion, including criticism of Aeschines' method of attack (§§ 122–5).

IV. Aeschines' life and character (§§ 126–59).
(1) Introduction (§§ 126–8).
(2) Parentage and early life of Aeschines (§§ 129–31).
(3) Aeschines' connexion with Antiphon, Python, Anaxinus, and others (§§ 132–8).
(4) Aeschines' part in stirring up the war against Amphissa in 339 (§§ 139–59).

V. Demosthenes' own policy in 339 and 338 (§§ 160–226).
(1) Narrative and defence of the alliance with Thebes (§§ 160–95).
(2) Why did not Aeschines protest at the time? (§§ 196–8).
(3) Defence of his policy as true to the spirit of Athenian history (§§ 199–210).
(4) Narrative and defence, continued (§§ 211–22).
(5) Further criticism of Aeschines' method of attack (§§ 223–6).

VI. Replies to various arguments of Aeschines (§§ 227–96).
(1) Aeschines' comparison of the inquiry to the examination of a balance-sheet (§§ 227–31).
(2) A proper inquiry would show that Demosthenes had increased the resources of Athens (§§ 232–7).
(3) Reply to the charge of saddling Athens with an undue share of the expense of the war (§§ 238–43).
(4) Reply to the charge of responsibility for the defeat of Chaeroneia (§§ 244–7).
(5) Vindication of his policy after the battle of Chaeroneia (§§ 248–51).
(6) Reply to Aeschines' remarks about the harm done to Athens by Demosthenes' bad fortune (§§ 252–75).
(*a*) General remarks (§§ 252–5).
(*b*) The fortune of Demosthenes (§§ 257, 258).
(*c*) The fortune of Aeschines (§§ 259–64).
(*d*) Comparison of the two (§§ 265, 266).
(*e*) Demosthenes' use of his fortune for purposes of public and private munificence (§§ 267–9).
(*f*) Demosthenes not responsible for the misfortunes of Athens (§§ 270–5).

(7) Reply to Aeschines' warning against Demosthenes' cleverness (§§ 276–90).
(*a*) Comparison of the use made of their talents by the two orators (§§ 276–84).
(*b*) The choice of Demosthenes, not Aeschines, to deliver the Funeral Oration (§§ 285–90).
(8) Aeschines' feelings about the defeat of Chaeroneia (§§ 291–3).
(9) The part played by traitors in recent history (§§ 294–6).
VII. Epilogue (§§ 297–324).
(1) Demosthenes' incorruptibility (§§ 297, 298).
(2) Demosthenes' measures for the protection of Athens (§§ 299–305).
(3) Comparison of the services of the two orators to Athens (§§ 306–13).
(4) Reply to the comparison of Demosthenes with the men of old, by a final comparison of the two orators (§§ 314–23).
(5) Peroration (§ 324).]

1 I PRAY first, men of Athens, to every god and goddess, that the goodwill, which I ever feel towards this city and towards all of you, may in equal measure be vouchsafed to me by you at this present trial: and secondly—a prayer which especially touches yourselves, your consciences, and your reputation—that the gods may put it into your minds not to take counsel of my adversary in regard to the spirit in which you ought 2 to hear me (for that would surely be a cruel thing), but of the laws and of your oath; wherein besides all other precepts of justice, this also is written—that you shall listen to both sides with a like mind. And this means, not only that you should have formed no prejudice, and should accord equal goodwill to each, but also that you should give leave to every man who pleads before you to adopt that order, and make that defence, upon which he has resolved and fixed his choice.

3 I am in many respects at a disadvantage in the present controversy, as compared with Aeschines; and particularly, men of Athens, in two points of importance. The first is that I am not contending for the same stake as he. It is

not the same thing for me to lose your goodwill now, as it is for him to fail to win his case; since for me—but I would say nothing unpleasant at the opening of my address—I say only that Aeschines can well afford to risk this attack upon me. The second disadvantage lies in the natural and universal tendency of mankind to hear invective and denunciation with pleasure, and to be offended with those who praise themselves. And of the two courses in question, that 4 which contributes to men's pleasure has been given to Aeschines, and that which annoys (I may say) every one is left for me. If, to avoid giving such annoyance, I say nothing of all that I myself have done, it will be thought that I am unable to clear myself of the charges against me, or to show the grounds upon which I claim to deserve distinction. If, on the other hand, I proceed to speak of my past acts and my political life, I shall often be compelled to speak of myself. I will endeavour, then, to do this as modestly as possible; and for all that the necessities of the case compel me to say, the blame must in fairness be borne by the prosecutor, who initiated a trial of such a kind as this.

I think, men of Athens, that you would all admit that this 5 present trial equally concerns myself and Ctesiphon, and demands no less earnest attention from me than from him. For while it is a painful and a grievous thing for a man to be robbed of anything, particularly if it is at the hands of an enemy that this befalls him, it is especially so, when he is robbed of your goodwill and kindness, just in proportion as to win these is the greatest possible gain. And because 6 such is the issue at stake in the present trial, I request and entreat you all alike to give me, while I make my defence upon the charges that have been brought against me, a fair hearing, as you are commanded to do by the laws—those laws to which their original maker, your well-wisher and the People's friend, Solon, thought fit to give the sanction not of enactment only, but also of an oath on the part of those who 7 act as judges: not because he distrusted you (so at least it seems to me), but because he saw that a defendant cannot escape from the imputations and the slanders which fall with special force from the prosecutor, because he is the first to speak, unless each of you who sit in judgement, keeping his conscience pure in the sight of God, will receive the pleadings of the later speaker also with the same favour, and will thus, because his attention has been given equally and impartially to both sides, form his decision upon the case in its entirety.

8 And now, when I am about, as it seems, to render an account of my whole private life and public career, I would once more invoke the aid of the gods; and in the presence of you all I pray, first, that the goodwill which I ever feel towards this city and towards all of you, may in equal measure be vouchsafed to me by you at this trial; and secondly, that whatsoever judgement upon this present suit will conduce to your public reputation, and the purity of each man's conscience, that judgement they may put it into all your minds to give.

9 Now if Aeschines had confined his charges to the subject of the indictment, I too, in making my defence, would have dealt at once with the actual resolution of the Council. But since he has devoted no less a portion of his speech to the relation of other matters, and for the most part has spoken against me falsely, I think it is necessary, and at the same time just, that I should deal briefly, men of Athens, with

these, in order that none of you may be led by irrelevant arguments to listen less favourably to my pleas in answer to the indictment itself.

As for his slanderous vituperation of my private life, mark 10 how straightforward and how just is the reply that I make. If you know me as the man that he charged me with being (for my life has been spent nowhere but in your own midst), do not even suffer me to speak—no, not though my whole public career has been one of transcendent merit—but rise and condemn me without delay. But if, in your judgement and belief, I am a better man than Aeschines, and come of better men; if I and mine are no worse than any other respectable persons (to use no offensive expression); then do not trust him even in regard to other points, for it is plain that all that he said was equally fictitious; but once more accord to me to-day the goodwill which throughout the past you have so often displayed towards me in previous trials. Knave as you are, Aeschines, you were assuredly 11 more fool than knave, when you thought that I should dismiss all that I had to say with regard to my past acts and political life, and should turn to meet the abuse that fell from you. I shall not do so; I am not so brain-sick; but I will review the falsehoods and the calumnies which you uttered against my political career; and then, if the court desires it, I will afterwards refer to the ribald language that has been so incontinently used.

The offences charged against me are many; and for some of them the laws assign heavy and even the most extreme 12 penalties. But I will tell you what is the motive which animates the present suit. It gives play to the malice of a personal enemy, to his insolence, his abuse, his contumelies,

and every expression of his hostility: and yet, assuming that the charges and the imputations which have been made are true, it does not enable the State to exact a penalty that is adequate, or nearly adequate, to the offences.
13 For it is not right to seek to debar another from coming before the people and receiving a hearing, nor to do so in a spirit of malice and envy. Heaven knows, it is neither straightforward, nor citizen-like, nor just, men of Athens! If the crimes by which he saw me injuring the city were of such a magnitude as he just now so theatrically set forth, he should have had recourse to the punishments enjoined by the laws at the time of the crimes themselves. If he saw me so acting as to deserve impeachment, he should have impeached me, and so brought me to trial before you; if he saw me proposing illegal measures, he should have indicted me for their illegality. For surely, if he can prosecute Ctesiphon on my account, he would not have failed to indict me in person, had he thought that he could
14 convict me. And further, if he saw me committing any of those other crimes against you, which he just now slanderously enumerated, or any other crimes whatsoever, there are laws which deal with each, and punishments, and lawsuits and judgements involving penalties that are harsh and severe: to all of these he could have had recourse; and from the moment when it was seen that he had acted so, and had conducted his hostilities against me on that plan, his present accusation of me would have been in line with his past
15 conduct. But as it is, he has forsaken the straight path of justice; he has shrunk from all attempts to convict me at the time; and after all these years, with the imputations, the jests, the invectives, that he has accumulated, he appears

to play his part. So it is, that though his accusations are against me, it is Ctesiphon that he prosecutes; and though he sets his quarrel with me in the forefront of the whole suit, he has never faced me in person to settle the quarrel, and it is another whom we see him trying to deprive of his civil rights. Yet surely, besides everything else that may be 16 pleaded on behalf of Ctesiphon, this, I think, may surely be most reasonably urged—that we ought in justice to have brought our own quarrel to the test by ourselves, instead of avoiding all conflict with one another, and looking for a third party to whom we could do harm. Such iniquity really passes all bounds.

From this one may see the nature of all his charges alike, 17 uttered, as they have been, without justice or regard for truth. Yet I desire also to examine them severally, and more particularly the false statements which he made against me in regard to the Peace and the Embassy, when he ascribed to me the things which he himself had done in conjunction with Philocrates. And here it is necessary, men of Athens, and perhaps appropriate, that I should remind you of the state of affairs subsisting during that period, so that you may view each group of actions in the light of the circumstances of the time.

When the Phocian war had broken out (not through any 18 action of mine, for I had not yet entered public life), your own attitude, in the first place, was such, that you wished for the preservation of the Phocians, although you saw that their actions were unjustifiable; while you would have been delighted at anything that might happen to the Thebans, against whom you felt an indignation that was neither unreasonable nor unfair; for they had not used their good fortune at Leuctra with moderation. And, in the second place, the Peloponnese was all disunited : those who detested the Spartans were not strong enough to annihilate them, and those who had previously governed with the support of Sparta were no longer able to maintain their control over their cities ; but both these and all the other states were

19 in a condition of indeterminate strife and confusion. When Philip saw this (for it was not hard to see), he tried, by dispensing money to the traitors whom each state contained, to throw them all into collision and stir up one against another ; and thus, amid the blunders and perversity of others, he was making his own preparations, and growing great to the danger of all. And when it became clear to all that the then overbearing (but now unhappy) Thebans, distressed by the length of the war, would be forced to fly to you for aid, Philip, to prevent this—to prevent the formation of any union between the cities—made offers of peace to you, and

20 of assistance to them. Now what was it that helped him, and enabled him to find in you his almost willing dupes ? It was the baseness (if that is the right name to use), or the ignorance, or both, of the rest of the Hellenes, who, though you were engaged in a long and continuous war, and that on behalf of the interests of all, as has been proved by the event, never assisted you either with money or with men, or in any other way whatsoever. And in your just and proper indignation with them, you listened readily to Philip. It was for these reasons, therefore, and not through any action of mine, that the Peace which we then conceded was negotiated ; and any one who investigates the matter honestly will find that it is the crimes and the corrupt practices of these men, in the course of the negotiations, that are responsible for our

position to-day. It is in the interests of truth that I enter 21 into all these events with this exactitude and thoroughness; for however strong the appearance of criminality in these proceedings may be, it has, I imagine, nothing to do with me. The first man to suggest or mention the Peace was Aristodemus the actor; and the person who took the matter up and moved the motion, and sold his services for the purpose, along with Aeschines, was Philocrates of Hagnus—your partner, Aeschines, not mine, even if you split your sides with lying; while those who supported him, from whatever motive (for of that I say nothing at present), were Eubulus and Cephisophon. I had no part in the matter anywhere. And yet, although the facts are such as with 22 absolute truth I am representing them to be, he carried his effrontery so far as to dare to assert that I was not only responsible for the Peace, but had also prevented the city from acting in conjunction with a general assembly of the Hellenes in making it. What? and you—oh! how can one find a name that can be applied to you?—when you saw me (for you were there) preventing the city from taking this great step and forming so grand an alliance as you just now described, did you once raise a protest or come forward to give information and to set forth the crimes with which you now charge me? If I had covenanted with 23 Philip for money that I would prevent the coalition of the Hellenes, your only course was to refuse to keep silence—to cry aloud, to protest, to reveal the fact to your fellow countrymen. On no occasion did you do this: no such utterance of yours was ever heard by any one. In fact there was no embassy away at the time on a mission to any Hellenic state; the Hellenes had all long ago been tried and found wanting; and in all that he has said upon this matter there 24 is not a single sound word. And, apart from that, his falsehoods involve the greatest calumnies upon this city. For if you were at one and the same time convoking the Hellenes with a view to war, and sending ambassadors yourselves to Philip to discuss peace, it was a deed for a Eurybatus, not a task for a state or for honest men, that you were carrying out. But that is not the case; indeed it is not. For what could possibly have been your object in summoning them at that moment? Was it with a view to peace? But they all had peace already. Or with a view to war? But you were yourselves discussing peace. It is therefore evident that neither was it I that introduced or was responsible for the Peace in its original shape, nor is one of all the other falsehoods which he told of me shown to be true.

25 Again, consider the course of action which, when the city had concluded the Peace, each of us now chose to adopt. For from this you will know who it was that co-operated with Philip throughout, and who it was that acted in your interest and sought the good of the city. As for me, I proposed, as a member of the Council, that the ambassadors should sail as quickly as possible to any district in which they should ascertain Philip to be, and receive his oath from 26 him. But even when I had carried this resolution, they would not act upon it. What did this mean, men of Athens? I will inform you. Philip's interest required that the interval before he took the oath should be as long as possible; yours, that it should be as short as possible. And why? Because you broke off all your preparations for the war, not merely from the day when he took the oath, but from the day when you first hoped that Peace would be made; and for

his part, this was what he was all along working for; for he thought (and with truth) that whatever places he could snatch from Athens before he took the oath, would remain securely his, since no one would break the Peace for their sake. Foreseeing and calculating upon this, men of Athens, I proposed this decree—that we should sail to any district in which Philip might be, and receive his oath as soon as possible, in order that the oaths might be taken while the Thracians, your allies, were still in possession of those strongholds of which Aeschines just now spoke with contempt—Serrhium, Myrtenum, and Ergiske; and that Philip might not snatch from us the keys of the country and make himself master of Thrace, nor obtain an abundant supply of money and of soldiers, and so proceed without difficulty to the prosecution of his further designs. And now, instead of citing or reading this decree he slanders me on the ground that I thought fit, as a member of the Council, to introduce the envoys. But what should I have done? Was I to propose *not* to introduce those who had come for the express purpose of speaking with you? or to order the lessee of the theatre not to assign them seats? But they would have watched the play from the threepenny seats, if this decree had not been proposed. Should I have guarded the interests of the city in petty details, and sold them wholesale, as my opponents did? Surely not. (*To the clerk.*) Now take this decree, which the prosecutor passed over, though he knew it well, and read it. 27 28

[*The decree of Demosthenes is read.*] 29

Though I had carried this decree, and was seeking the good not of Philip, but of the city, these worthy ambassadors paid little heed to it, but sat idle in Macedonia for three 30 whole months, until Philip arrived from Thrace, after subduing the whole country; when they might, within ten days, or equally well within three or four, have reached the Hellespont, and saved the strongholds, by receiving his oath before he could seize them. For he would not have touched them when we were present; or else, if he had done so, we should have refused to administer the oath to him; and in that case he would have failed to obtain the Peace: he would not have had both the Peace and the strongholds as well.

31 Such was Philip's first act of fraud, during the time of the Embassy, and the first instance of venality on the part of these wicked men; and over this I confess that then and now and always I have been and am at war and at variance with them. Now observe, immediately after 32 this, a second and even greater piece of villainy. As soon as Philip had sworn to the Peace, after first gaining possession of Thrace because these men did not obey my decree, he obtained from them—again by purchase—the postponement of our departure from Macedonia, until all should be in readiness for his campaign against the Phocians; in order that, instead of our bringing home a report of his intentions and his preparations for the march, which would make you set out and sail round to Thermopylae with your war-ships as you did before, you might only hear our report of the facts when he was already on this side of Thermo-33 pylae, and you could do nothing. And Philip was beset with such fear and such a weight of anxiety, lest in spite of his occupation of these places, his object should slip from his grasp, if, before the Phocians were destroyed, you resolved to assist them, that he hired this despicable creature, not

now in company with his colleagues, but by himself alone, to make to you a statement and a report of such a character that owing to them all was lost. But I request and entreat 34 you, men of Athens, to remember throughout this whole trial, that, had Aeschines made no accusation that was not included in the indictment, I too would not have said a word that did not bear upon it; but since he has had recourse to all kinds of imputation and slander at once, I am compelled also to give a brief answer to each group of charges. What then were the statements uttered by him 35 that day, in consequence of which all was lost? 'You must not be perturbed,' he said, 'at Philip's having crossed to this side of Thermopylae; for you will get everything that you desire, if you remain quiet; and within two or three days you will hear that he has become the friend of those whose enemy he was, and the enemy of those whose friend he was, when he first came. For,' said he, 'it is not phrases that confirm friendships' (a finely sententious expression!) 'but identity of interest; and it is to the interest of Philip and of the Phocians and of yourselves alike, to be rid of the heartless and overbearing demeanour of the Thebans.' To 36 these statements some gave a ready ear, in consequence of the tacit ill-feeling towards the Thebans at the time. What then followed—and not after a long interval, but immediately? The Phocians were overthrown; their cities were razed to the ground; you, who had believed Aeschines and remained inactive, were soon afterwards bringing in your effects from the country; while Aeschines received his gold; and besides all this, the city reaped the ill-will of the Thebans and Thessalians, while their gratitude for what had been done went to Philip. To prove that this is so, (*to the clerk*) read me both 37 the decree of Callisthenes, and Philip's letter. (*To the jury.*) These two documents together will make all the facts plain. (*To the clerk.*) Read.

38 [*The decree of Callisthenes is read.*]

Were these the hopes, on the strength of which you made the Peace? Was this what this hireling promised you? 39 (*To the clerk.*) Now read the letter which Philip sent after this.

[*Philip's letter is read.*]

40 You hear how obviously, in this letter sent to you, Philip is addressing definite information to his own allies. 'I have done these things,' he tells them, 'against the will of the Athenians, and to their annoyance; and so, men of Thebes and Thessaly, if you are wise, you will regard them as enemies, and will trust me.' He does not write in those actual terms, but that is what he intends to indicate. By these means he so carried them away, that they did not foresee or realize any of the consequences, but allowed him to get everything into his own power: and that is why, poor 41 men, they have experienced their present calamities. But the man who helped him to create this confidence, who co-operated with him, who brought home that false report and deluded you, he it is who now bewails the sufferings of the Thebans and enlarges upon their piteousness—he, who is himself the cause both of these and of the misery in Phocis, and of all the other evils which the Hellenes have endured. Yes, it is evident that you are pained at what has come to pass, Aeschines, and that you are sorry for the Thebans, when you have property in Boeotia and are farming the land that was theirs; and that I rejoice at it—I, whose

surrender was immediately demanded by the author of the disaster! But I have digressed into subjects of which it 42 will perhaps be more convenient to speak presently. I will return to the proofs which show that it is the crimes of these men that are the cause of our condition to-day.

For when you had been deceived by Philip, through the agency of these men, who while serving as ambassadors had sold themselves and made a report in which there was not a word of truth—when the unhappy Phocians had been deceived and their cities annihilated—what followed? The 43 despicable Thessalians and the slow-witted Thebans regarded Philip as their friend, their benefactor, their saviour. Philip was their all-in-all. They would not even listen to the voice of any one who wished to express a different opinion. You yourselves, though you viewed what had been done with suspicion and vexation, nevertheless kept the Peace; for there was nothing else that you could have done. And the other Hellenes, who, like yourselves, had been deluded and disappointed of their hopes, also kept the Peace, and gladly; since in a sense they also were remotely aimed at by the war. For when Philip was going about and subduing the Illyrians 44 and Triballi and some of the Hellenes as well, and bringing many large forces into his own power, and when some of the members of the several States were taking advantage of the Peace to travel to Macedonia, and were being corrupted —Aeschines among them—at such a time all of those whom Philip had in view in thus making his preparations were really being attacked by him. Whether they failed to realize 45 it is another question, which does not concern me. For I was continually uttering warnings and protests, both in your midst and wherever I was sent. But the cities were stricken

with disease: those who were engaged in political and practical affairs were taking bribes and being corrupted by the hope of money; while the mass of private citizens either showed no foresight, or else were caught by the bait of ease and leisure from day to day; and all alike had fallen victims to some such delusive fancy, as that the danger would come upon every one but themselves, and that through the perils of others they would be able to secure
46 their own position as they pleased. And so, I suppose, it has come to pass that the masses have atoned for their great and ill-timed indifference by the loss of their freedom, while the leaders in affairs, who fancied that they were selling everything except themselves, have realized that they had sold themselves first of all. For instead of being called friends and guest-friends, as they were called at the time when they were taking their bribes, they now hear themselves called flatterers, and god-forsaken, and all the other names that
47 they deserve. For no one, men of Athens, spends his money out of a desire to benefit the traitor; nor, when once he has secured the object for which he bargains, does he employ the traitor to advise him with regard to other objects: if it were so, nothing could be happier than a traitor. But it is not so, of course. Far from it! When the aspirant after dominion has gained his object, he is also the master of those who have sold it to him: and because then he knows their villainy, he then hates and mistrusts them, and covers them
48 with insults. For observe—for even if the time of the events is past, the time for realizing truths like these is ever present to wise men. Lasthenes was called his 'friend'; but only until he had betrayed Olynthus. And Timolaus; but only until he had destroyed Thebes. And Eudicus and Simus

of Larissa; but only until they had put Thessaly in Philip's power. And now, persecuted as they are, and insulted, and subjected to every kind of misery, the whole inhabited world has become filled with such men. And what of Aristratus at Sicyon? what of Perillus at Megara? Are they not outcasts? From these instances one can see very clearly, that it is he who 49 best protects his own country and speaks most constantly against such men, that secures for traitors and hirelings like yourselves, Aeschines, the continuance of your opportunities for taking bribes. It is the majority of those who are here, those who resist your will, that you must thank for the fact that you live and draw your pay; for, left to yourselves, you would long ago have perished.

There is still much that I might say about the transactions 50 of that time, but I think that even what I have said is more than enough. The blame rests with Aeschines, who has drenched me with the stale dregs of his own villainy and crime, from which I was compelled to clear myself in the eyes of those who are too young to remember the events; though perhaps you who knew, even before I said a single word, of Aeschines' service as a hireling, may have felt some annoyance as you listened. He calls it, forsooth, 'friendship' 51 and 'guest-friendship'; and somewhere in his speech just now he used the expression, 'the man who casts in my teeth my guest-friendship with Alexander.' *I* cast in your teeth your guest-friendship with Alexander? How did you acquire it? How came you to be thought worthy of it? Never would I call you the guest-friend of Philip or the friend of Alexander—I am not so insane—unless you are to call harvesters and other hired servants the friends and guest-friends of those who have hired them. [But that is not the case, of course. Far from it!] Nay, I call you the hireling, formerly 52 of Philip, and now of Alexander, and so do all who are present. If you disbelieve me, ask them—or rather I will ask them for you. Men of Athens, do you think of Aeschines as the hireling or as the guest-friend of Alexander? You hear what they say.

53 I now wish, without more delay, to make my defence upon the indictment itself, and to go through my past acts, in order that Aeschines may hear (though he knows them well) the grounds on which I claim to have a right both to the gifts which the Council have proposed, and even to far greater than these. (*To the clerk.*) Now take the indictment and read it.

54, 55 [*The indictment is read.*]

56 These, men of Athens, are the points in the resolution which the prosecutor assails; and these very points will, I think, afford me my first means of proving to you that the defence which I am about to offer is an absolutely fair one. For I will take the points of the indictment in the very same order as the prosecutor: I will speak of each in succession, 57 and will knowingly pass over nothing. Any decision upon the statement that I 'consistently do and say what is best for the People, and am eager to do whatever good I can', and upon the proposal to vote me thanks for this, depends, I consider, upon my past political career: for it is by an investigation of my career that either the truth and the propriety, or else the falsehood, of these statements which 58 Ctesiphon has made about me will be discovered. Again, the proposal to crown me, without the addition of the clause 'when he has submitted to his examination', and the order to proclaim the award of the crown in the theatre, must, I imagine, stand or fall with my political

career; for the question is whether I deserve the crown and the proclamation before my fellow countrymen or not. At the same time I consider myself further bound to point out to you the laws under which the defendant's proposal could be made. In this honest and straightforward manner, men of Athens, I have determined to make my defence; and now I will proceed to speak of my past actions themselves. And let no one imagine that I am detaching 59 my argument from its connexion with the indictment, if I break into a discussion of international transactions. For it is the prosecutor who, by assailing the clause of the decree which states that I do and say what is best, and by indicting it as false, has rendered the discussion of my whole political career essentially germane to the indictment; and further, out of the many careers which public life offers, it was the department of international affairs that I chose; so that I have a right to derive my proofs also from that department.

I will pass over all that Philip snatched from us and 60 secured, in the days before I took part in public life as an orator. None of these losses, I imagine, has anything to do with me. But I will recall to you, and will render you an account of all that, from the day when I entered upon this career, he was *prevented* from taking, when I have made one remark. Philip, men of Athens, had a great advantage 61 in his favour. For in the midst of the Hellenic peoples—and not of some only, but of all alike—there had sprung up a crop of traitors—corrupt, god-forsaken men—more numerous than they have ever been within the memory of man. These he took to help and co-operate with him; and great as the mutual ill-will and dissensions of the Hellenes already were, he rendered them even worse, by deceiving some, making presents to others, and corrupting others in every way; and at a time when all had in reality but one interest—to prevent his becoming powerful—he divided 62 them into a number of factions. All the Hellenes then being in this condition, still ignorant of the growing and accumulating evil, you have to ask yourselves, men of Athens, what policy and action it was fitting for the city to choose, and to hold me responsible for this; for the person who assumed that responsibility in the State was 63 myself. Should she, Aeschines, have sacrificed her pride and her own dignity? Should she have joined the ranks of the Thessalians and Dolopes, and helped Philip to acquire the empire of Hellas, cancelling thereby the noble and righteous deeds of our forefathers? Or, if she should not have done this (for it would have been in very truth an atrocious thing), should she have looked on, while all that she saw would happen, if no one prevented it—all that she realized, it seems, 64 at a distance—was actually taking place? Nay, I should be glad to ask to-day the severest critic of my actions, which party he would have desired the city to join—the party which shares the responsibility for the misery and disgrace which has fallen upon the Hellenes (the party of the Thessalians and their supporters, one may call it), or the party which looked on while these calamities were taking place, in the hope of gaining some advantage for themselves—in which we should place the Arcadians and Messenians and 65 Argives. But even of these, many—nay, all—have in the end fared worse than we. For if Philip had departed immediately after his victory, and gone his way; if afterwards he had remained at peace, and had given no trouble whatever to any of his own allies or of the other Hellenes; then there would have been some ground for blaming and accusing those who had opposed his plans. But if he has stripped them all alike of their dignity, their paramountcy, and their independence—nay, even of their free constitutions, wherever he could do so—can it be denied that the policy which you adopted on my advice was the most glorious policy possible?

But I return to my former point. What was it fitting for 66 the city to do, Aeschines, when she saw Philip establishing for himself a despotic sway over the Hellenes? What language should have been used, what measures proposed, by the adviser of the people at Athens (for that it was at Athens makes the utmost difference), when I knew that from the very first, up to the day when I myself ascended the platform, my country had always contended for pre-eminence, honour, and glory, and in the cause of honour, and for the interests of all, had sacrificed more money and lives than any other Hellenic people had spent for their private ends: when 67 I saw that Philip himself, with whom our conflict lay, for the sake of empire and absolute power, had had his eye knocked out, his collar-bone broken, his hand and his leg maimed, and was ready to resign any part of his body that Fortune chose to take from him, provided that with what remained he might live in honour and glory? And surely no one would 68 dare to say that it was fitting that in one bred at Pella, a place then inglorious and insignificant, there should have grown up so lofty a spirit that he aspired after the empire of Hellas, and conceived such a project in his mind; but that in you, who are Athenians, and who day by day in all that you hear and see behold the memorials of the gallantry of your forefathers, such baseness should be found, that you would yield up your liberty to Philip by your own deliberate 69 offer and deed. No man would say this. One alternative remained, and that, one which you were bound to take—that of a righteous resistance to the whole course of action by which he was doing you injury. You acted thus from the first, quite rightly and properly; while I helped by my proposals and advice during the time of my political activity, and I do not deny it. But what ought I to have done? For the time has come to ask you this, Aeschines, and to dis- 70 miss everything else. Amphipolis, Pydna, Poteidaea, Halonnesus—all are blotted from my memory. As for Serrhium, Doriscus, the sack of Peparethus, and all the other injuries inflicted upon the city, I renounce all knowledge of their ever having happened—though you actually said that *I* involved my countrymen in hostility by talking of these things, when the decrees which deal with them were the work of Eubulus and Aristophon and Diopeithes, and not mine at all—so 71 glibly do you assert anything that suits your purpose! But of this too I say nothing at present. I only ask you whether Philip, who was appropriating Euboea, and establishing it as a stronghold to command Attica; who was making an attempt upon Megara, seizing Oreus, razing the walls of Porthmus, setting up Philistides as tyrant at Oreus and Cleitarchus at Eretria, bringing the Hellespont into his own power, besieging Byzantium, destroying some of the cities of Hellas, and restoring his exiled friends to others—whether he, I say, in acting thus, was guilty of wrong, violating the truce and breaking the Peace, or not? Was it fit that one of the Hellenes should arise to prevent it, or not? 72 If it was not fit—if it was fit that Hellas should become like the Mysian booty in the proverb before men's eyes, while the Athenians had life and being, then I have lost my labour in speaking upon this theme, and the city has lost its labour in obeying me: then let everything that has been done be counted for a crime and a blunder, and those my own! But if it was right that one should arise to prevent it, for whom could the task be more fitting than for the people of Athens? That then, was the aim of *my* policy; and when I saw Philip reducing all mankind to servitude, I opposed him, and without ceasing warned and exhorted you to make no surrender.

73 But the Peace, Aeschines, was in reality broken by Philip, when he seized the corn-ships, not by Athens. (*To the clerk.*) Bring the decrees themselves, and the letter of Philip, and read them in order. (*To the jury.*) For they will make it clear who is responsible, and for what.

74 [*A decree is read.*]

75 This decree then was proposed by Eubulus, not by me; and the next by Aristophon; he is followed first by Hegesippus, and he by Aristophon again, and then by Philocrates, then by Cephisophon, and then by all of them. But I proposed no decree upon this subject. (*To the clerk.*) Read.

[*Decrees are read.*]

76 As then I point to these decrees, so, Aeschines, do you point to a decree of any kind, proposed by me, which makes me responsible for the war. You cannot do so: for had you been able, there is nothing which you would sooner have produced. Indeed, even Philip himself makes no charge against me as regards the war, though he complains of others. (*To the clerk.*) Read Philip's letter itself.

77, 78 [*Philip's letter is read.*]

79 In this letter he has nowhere mentioned the name of Demosthenes, nor made any charge against me. Why is it then that, though he complains of others, he has not mentioned my own actions? Because, if he had written anything about me, he must have mentioned his own acts of wrong; for it was these acts upon which I kept my grip, and these which I opposed. First of all, when he was trying to steal into the Peloponnese, I proposed the embassy to the Peloponnese; then, when he was grasping at Euboea, the embassy to Euboea; then the expedition—not an embassy any more—to Oreus, and that to Eretria, when he had established 80 tyrants in those cities. After that I dispatched all the naval expeditions, in the course of which the Chersonese and Byzantium and all our allies were saved. In consequence of this, the noblest rewards at the hands of those who had benefited by your action became yours—votes of thanks, glory, honours, crowns, gratitude; while of the victims of his aggression, those who followed your advice at the time secured their own deliverance, and those who neglected it had the memory of your warnings constantly in their minds, and regarded you not merely as their well-wishers, but as men of wisdom and prophetic insight; for 81 all that you foretold has come to pass. And further, that Philistides would have given a large sum to retain Oreus, and Cleitarchus to retain Eretria, and Philip himself, to be able to count upon the use of these places against you, and to escape all exposure of his other proceedings and all investigation, by any one in any place, of his wrongful acts—all this is not unknown to any one, least of all to you, Aeschines.

For the envoys sent at that time by Cleitarchus and Philistides lodged at your house, when they came here, and you acted as their patron. Though the city rejected them, as enemies whose proposals were neither just nor expedient, to you they were friends. None of their attempts succeeded, slander me though you may, when you assert that I say nothing when I receive money, but cry out when I spend it. That, certainly, is not *your* way: for you cry out with money in your hands, and will never cease, unless those present cause you to do so by taking away your civil rights to-day. 82

Now on that occasion, gentlemen, you crowned me for my conduct. Aristonicus proposed a decree whose very syllables were identical with those of Ctesiphon's present proposal; the crown was proclaimed in the theatre; and this was already the second proclamation in my honour: and yet Aeschines, though he was there, neither opposed the decree, nor indicted the mover. (*To the clerk.*) Take this decree also and read it. 83

[*The decree of Aristonicus is read.*] 84

Now is any of you aware of any discredit that attached itself to the city owing to this decree? Did any mockery or ridicule ensue, such as Aeschines said must follow on the present occasion, if I were crowned? But surely when proceedings are recent and well known to all, then it is that, if they are satisfactory, they meet with gratitude, and if they are otherwise, with punishment. It appears, then, that on that occasion I met with gratitude, not with blame or punishment. 85

Thus the fact that, up to the time when these events took place, I acted throughout as was best for the city, has been 86 acknowledged by the victory of my advice and my proposals in your deliberations, by the successful execution of the measures which I proposed, and the award of crowns in consequence of them to the city and to myself and to all, and by your celebration of sacrifices to the gods, and processions, in thankfulness for these blessings.

87 When Philip had been expelled from Euboea—and while the arms which expelled him were yours, the statesmanship and the decrees (even though some of my opponents may split their sides) were mine—he proceeded to look for some other stronghold from which he could threaten the city. And seeing that we were more dependent than any other people upon imported corn, and wishing to get our corn-trade into his power, he advanced to Thrace. First, he requested the Byzantines, his own allies, to join him in the war against you; and when they refused and said (with truth) that they had not made their alliance with him for such a purpose, he erected a stockade against the city, brought up his engines, 88 and proceeded to besiege it. I will not ask again what you ought to have done when this was happening; it is manifest to all. But who was it that went to the rescue of the Byzantines, and saved them? Who was it that prevented the Hellespont from falling into other hands at that time? It was you, men of Athens—and when I say 'you', I mean this city. And who was it that spoke and moved resolutions and acted for the city, and gave himself up unsparingly to 89 the business of the State? It was I. But of the immense benefit thus conferred upon all, you no longer need words of mine to tell you, since you have had actual experience of it. For the war which then ensued, apart from the glorious reputation that it brought you, kept you supplied

with the necessaries of life in greater plenty and at lower prices than the present Peace, which these worthy men are guarding to their country's detriment, in their hopes of something yet to be realized. May those hopes be disappointed! May they share the fortune which you, who wish for the best, ask of the gods, rather than cause you to share that upon which their own choice is fixed! (*To the clerk.*) Read out to the jury the crowns awarded to the city in consequence of her action by the Byzantines and by the Perinthians.

[*The decree of the Byzantines is read.*] 90, 91

Read out also the crowns awarded by the peoples of the Chersonese. 92

[*The decree of the peoples of the Chersonese is read.*]

Thus the policy which I had adopted was not only successful in saving the Chersonese and Byzantium, in preventing the Hellespont from falling at that time into the power of Philip, and in bringing honours to the city in consequence, but it revealed to the whole world the noble gallantry of Athens and the baseness of Philip. For all saw that he, the ally of the Byzantines, was besieging them—what could be more shameful or revolting? and on the other hand, it was seen that you, who might fairly have urged many well-founded complaints against them for their inconsiderate conduct towards you at an earlier period, not only refused to remember your grudge and to abandon the victims of aggression, but actually delivered them; and in consequence of this, you won glory and goodwill on all hands. And further, though every one knows that you have crowned many public men before now, no one can name any but 93 94 myself—that is to say, any public counsellor and orator—for whose merits the city has received a crown.

95 In order to prove to you, also, that the slanders which he uttered against the Euboeans and Byzantines, as he recalled to you any ill-natured action that they had taken towards you in the past, are disingenuous calumnies, not only because they are false (for this, I think, you may all be assumed to know), but also because, however true they might be, it was still to your advantage to deal with the political situation as I have done, I desire to describe, and that briefly, one or two of the noble deeds which this city has done in your own time. For an individual and a State should strive always, in their respective spheres, to fashion their future conduct 96 after the highest examples that their past affords. Thus, men of Athens, at a time when the Spartans were masters of land and sea, and were retaining their hold, by means of governors and garrisons, upon the country all round Attica—Euboea, Tanagra, all Boeotia, Megara, Aegina, Ceos, and the other islands—and when Athens possessed neither ships nor walls, you marched forth to Haliartus, and again, not many days later, to Corinth, though the Athenians of that day might have borne a heavy grudge against both the Corinthians and the Thebans for the part they had played 97 in reference to the Deceleian War. But they bore no such grudge. Far from it! And neither of these actions, Aeschines, was taken by them to help benefactors; nor was the prospect before them free from danger. Yet they did not on that account sacrifice those who fled to them for help. For the sake of glory and honour they were willing to expose themselves to the danger; and it was a right and a noble spirit that inspired their counsels. For the life of all men

must end in death, though a man shut himself in a chamber and keep watch; but brave men must ever set themselves to do that which is noble, with their joyful hope for their buckler, and whatsoever God gives, must bear it gallantly. Thus did your forefathers, and thus did the elder among 98 yourselves: for, although the Spartans were no friends or benefactors of yours, but had done much grievous wrong to the city, yet, when the Thebans, after their victory at Leuctra, attempted to annihilate them, you prevented it, not terrified by the strength or the reputation which the Thebans then enjoyed, nor reckoning up what the men had done to you, for whom you were to face this peril. And 99 thus, as you know, you revealed to all the Hellenes, that whatever offences may be committed against you, though under all other circumstances you show your resentment of them, yet if any danger to life or freedom overtakes the transgressors, you will bear no grudge and make no reckoning. Nor was it in these instances only that you were thus disposed. For once more, when the Thebans were appropriating Euboea, you did not look on while it was done; you did not call to mind the wrong which had been done to you in the matter of Oropus by Themison and Theodorus: you helped even these; and it was then that the city for the first time had voluntary trierarchs, of whom I was one. But I will not speak of this yet. And although to save the 100 island was itself a noble thing to do, it was a yet nobler thing by far, that when their lives and their cities were absolutely in your power, you gave them back, as it was right to do, to the very men who had offended against you, and made no reckoning, when such trust had been placed in you, of the wrongs which you had suffered. I pass by the innumer-

able instances which I might still give—battles at sea, expeditions [by land, campaigns] both long ago and now in our day; in all of which the object of the city has been to defend
101 the freedom and safety of the other Hellenic peoples. And so, when in all these striking examples I had beheld the city ever ready to strive in defence of the interests of others, what was I likely to bid her do, what action was I likely to recommend to her, when the debate to some extent concerned her own interests? 'Why,' you would say, 'to remember her grudge against those who wanted deliverance, and to look for excuses for sacrificing everything!' And who would not have been justified in putting me to death, if I had attempted to bring shame upon the city's high traditions, though it were only by word? The deed itself you would never have done, I know full well; for had you desired to do it, what was there to hinder you? Were you not free so to act? Had you not these men here to propose it?

102 I wish now to return to the next in succession of my political acts; and here again you must ask yourselves, what was the best thing for the city? For, men of Athens, when I saw that your navy was breaking up, and that, while the rich were obtaining exemption on the strength of small payments, citizens of moderate or small means were losing all that they had; and further, that in consequence of these things the city was always missing her opportunities; I enacted a law in accordance with which I compelled the former—the rich—to do their duty fairly; I put an end to the injustice done to the poor, and (what was the greatest service of all to the
103 State) I caused our preparations to be made in time. When I was indicted for this, I appeared before you at the ensuing

trial, and was acquitted; the prosecutor failed to obtain the necessary fraction of the votes. But what sums do you think the leaders of the Taxation-Boards, or those who stood second or third, offered me, to induce me, if possible, not to enact the law, or at least to let it drop and lie under sworn notice of prosecution? They offered sums so large, men of Athens, that I should hesitate to mention them to you. It was a natural course for them to take. For under the 104 former laws it was possible for them to divide their obligation between sixteen persons, paying little or nothing themselves, and grinding down their poorer fellow citizens: while by my law each must pay down a sum calculated in proportion to his property; and a man came to be charged with two warships, who had previously been one of sixteen subscribers to a single one (for they used now to call themselves no longer captains of their ships, but subscribers). Thus there was nothing that they were not willing to give, if only the new plan could be brought to nothing, and they could escape being compelled to do their duty fairly. (*To the clerk.*) Now read me, first, the decree in accordance with which 105 I had to meet the indictment; and then the lists of those liable under the former law, and under my own, respectively. Read.

[*The decree is read.*]

Now produce that noble list. 106

[*A list is read.*]

Now produce, for comparison with this, the list under my own law.

[*A list is read.*]

Was this, think you, but a trifling assistance which I rendered 107 to the poor among you? Would the wealthy have spent but a trifling sum to avoid doing their duty fairly? I am proud not only of having refused all compromise upon the measure, not only of having been acquitted when I was indicted, but also of having enacted a law which was beneficial, and of having given proof of it in practice. For throughout the war the armaments were equipped under my law, and no trierarch ever laid the suppliants' branch before you in token of grievance, nor took sanctuary at Munychia; none was imprisoned by the Admiralty Board; no warship was abandoned at sea and lost to the State, or left behind here as unseaworthy. Under the former laws all these things 108 used to happen; and the reason was that the obligation rested upon the poor, and in consequence there were many cases of inability to discharge it. I transferred the duties of the trierarchy from the poor to the rich; and therefore every duty was properly fulfilled. Aye, and for this very reason I deserve to receive praise—that I always adopted such political measures as brought with them accessions of glory and honour and power to the city. No measure of mine is malicious, harsh, or unprincipled; none is degrading or unworthy of the city. The same spirit will be seen both 109 in my domestic and my international policy. For just as in home affairs I did not set the favour of the rich above the rights of the many, so in international affairs I did not embrace the gifts and the friendship of Philip, in preference to the common interests of all the Hellenes.

It still remains for me, I suppose, to speak about the pro-110 clamation, and about my examination. The statement that I acted for the best, and that I am loyal to you throughout and eager to do you good service, I have proved, I think, sufficiently, by what I have said. At the same time I am passing over the most important parts of my political life and actions; for I conceive that I ought first to render to you in their proper order my arguments in regard to the alleged illegality itself: which done, even if I say nothing about the rest of my political acts, I can still rely upon that personal knowledge of them which each of you possesses.

Of the arguments which the prosecutor jumbled together in utter confusion with reference to the laws accompanying 111 his indictment, I am quite certain that you could not follow the greater part, nor could I understand them myself; but I will simply address you straightforwardly upon the question of right. So far am I from claiming (as he just now slanderously declared) to be free from the liability to render an account, that I admit a life-long liability to account for every part of my administration and policy. But I do 112 not admit that I am liable for one single day—you hear me, Aeschines?—to account for what I have given to the People as a free-will offering out of my private estate; nor is any one else so liable, not even if he is one of the nine archons. What law is so replete with injustice and churlishness, that when a man has made a present out of his private property and done an act of generosity and munificence, it deprives him of the gratitude due to him, hales him before a court of disingenuous critics, and sets them to audit accounts of sums which he himself has given? There is no such law. If the prosecutor asserts that there is, let him produce it, and I will resign myself and say no more. But 113 the law does not exist, men of Athens; this is nothing but an informer's trick on the part of Aeschines, who, because I was Controller of the Festival Fund when I made this donation, says, 'Ctesiphon proposed a vote of thanks to him when he was still liable to account.' The vote of thanks was not for any of the things for which I was liable to account; it was for my voluntary gift, and your charge is a misrepresentation. 'Yes,' you say, 'but you were also a Commissioner of Fortifications.' I was, and thanks were rightly accorded me on the very ground that, instead of charging the sums which I spent, I made a present of them. A statement of account, it is true, calls for an audit and scrutineers; but a free gift deserves gratitude and thanks; and that is why the defendant proposed this motion in my favour.

114 That this principle is not merely laid down in the laws, but rooted in your national character, I shall have no difficulty in proving by many instances. Nausicles, to begin with, has often been crowned by you, while general, for sacrifices which he had made from his private funds. Again, when Diotimus gave the shields, and Charidemus afterwards, they were crowned. And again, Neoptolemus here, while still director of many public works, has received honours for his voluntary gifts. It would really be too bad, if any one who held any office must either be debarred thereby from making a present to the State, or else, instead of receiving due gratitude, must submit accounts of the sums given.

115 To prove the truth of my statements, (*to the clerk*) take and read the actual decrees which were passed in honour of these persons. Read.

116 [*Two decrees are read.*]

117 Each of these persons, Aeschines, was accountable as regards the office which he held, but not as regards the services for

which he was crowned. Nor am I, therefore; for I presume that I have the same rights as others with reference to the same matters. I made a voluntary gift. For this I receive thanks; for I am not liable to account for what I gave. I was holding office. True, and I have rendered an account of my official expenditure, but not of what I gave voluntarily. Ah! but I exercised my office iniquitously! What? and you were there, when the auditors brought me before them, and did not accuse me?

Now that the court may see that the prosecutor himself bears me witness that I was crowned for services of which I was not liable to render an account, (*to the clerk*) take and read the decree which was proposed in my honour, in its entirety. (*To the jury.*) The points which he has omitted to indict in the Council's resolution will show that the charges which he does make are deliberate misrepresentations. (*To the clerk.*) Read. **118**

[*The decree is read.*]

My donations then, were these, of which you have not made one the subject of indictment. It is the reward for these, which the Council states to be my due, that you attack. You admit that it was legal to accept the gifts offered, and you indict as illegal the return of gratitude for them. In Heaven's name, what must the perfect scoundrel, the really heaven-detested, malignant being be like? Must he not be a man like this? **119**

But as regards the proclamation in the theatre, I pass by the fact that ten thousand persons have been thus proclaimed on ten thousand different occasions, and that my own name has often been so proclaimed before. But, in Heaven's name, **120**

Aeschines, are you so perverse and stupid, that you cannot grasp the fact that the recipient of the crown feels the same pride wherever the crown is proclaimed, and that it is for the benefit of those who confer it that the proclamation is made in the theatre? For those who hear are stimulated to do good service to the State, and commend those who return gratitude for such service even more than they commend the recipient of the crown. That is why the city has enacted this law. (*To the clerk.*) Take the law itself and read it.

[*The law is read.*]

121 Do you hear, Aeschines, the plain words of the law? 'Except such as the People or the Council shall resolve so to proclaim. But let these be proclaimed.' Why, wretched man, do you lay this dishonest charge? Why do you invent false arguments? Why do you not take hellebore to cure you? What? Are you not ashamed to bring a case founded upon envy, not upon any crime—to alter some of the laws, and to leave out parts of others, when they ought surely, in justice, to be read entire to those who have sworn to give 122 their votes in accordance with the laws? And then, while you act in this way, you enumerate the qualities which should be found in a friend of the People, as if you had contracted for a statue, and discovered on receiving it that it had not the features required by the contract; or as if a friend of the People was known by a definition, and not by his works and his political measures! And you shout out expressions, proper and improper, like a reveller on a cart —expressions which apply to you and your house, not to me. I will add 123 this also, men of Athens. The difference between abuse and accusation is, I imagine, that an accusation is founded upon

crimes, for which the penalties are assigned by law; abuse, upon such slanders as their own character leads enemies to utter about one another. And I conceive that our forefathers built these courts of law, not that we might assemble you here and revile one another with improper expressions suggested by our adversary's private life, but that we might convict any one who happens to have committed some crime against the State. Aeschines knew this as well as I; 124 and yet he chose to make a ribald attack instead of an accusation. At the same time, it is not fair that he should go off without getting as much as he gives, even in this respect; and when I have asked him one question, I will at once proceed to the attack. Are we to call you, Aeschines, the enemy of the State, or of myself? Of myself, of course. What? And when you might have exacted the penalty from me, on behalf of your fellow countrymen, according to the laws—at public examinations, by indictment, by all other forms of trial—did you always omit to do so? And yet to-day, 125 when I am unassailable upon every ground—on the ground of law, of lapse of time, of the statutable limit, of the many previous trials which I have undergone upon every charge, without having once been convicted of any crime against you to this day—and when the city must necessarily share to a greater or smaller degree in the glory of acts which were really acts of the people, have you confronted me upon such an issue as this? Take care lest, while you profess to be *my* enemy, you prove to be the enemy of your fellow countrymen!

Since then I have shown you all what is the vote which 126 religion and justice demand of you, I am now obliged, it would seem, by the slanders which he has uttered (though

I am no lover of abuse) to reply to his many falsehoods by saying just what is absolutely necessary about himself, and showing who he is, and whence he is sprung, that he so lightly begins to use bad language, pulling to pieces certain expressions of mine, when he has himself used expressions which

127 any respectable man would have shrunk from uttering; for if the accuser were Aeacus or Rhadamanthus or Minos, instead of a scandal-monger, an old hand in the market-place, a pestilent clerk, I do not believe that he would have spoken thus, or produced such a stock of ponderous phrases, crying aloud, as if he were acting a tragedy, 'O Earth and Sun and Virtue,' and the like; or again, invoking 'Wit and Culture, by which things noble and base are discerned apart'—for, of course, you heard him speaking

128 in this way. Scum of the earth! What have you or yours to do with virtue? How should *you* discern what is noble and what is not? Where and how did you get your qualification to do so? What right have *you* to mention culture anywhere? A man of genuine culture would not only never have asserted such a thing of himself, but would have blushed to hear another do so: and those who, like you, fall far short of it, but are tactless enough to claim it, succeed only in causing distress to their hearers, when they speak—not in seeming to be what they profess.

129 But though I am not at a loss to know what to say about you and yours, I am at a loss to know what to mention first. Shall I tell first how your father Tromes was a slave in the house of Elpias, who kept an elementary school near the temple of Theseus, and how he wore shackles and a wooden halter? Or how your mother, by celebrating her daylight nuptials in her hut near the shrine of the Hero of the Lancet,

was enabled to rear you, her beautiful statue, the prince of third-rate actors? But these things are known to all without my telling them. Shall I tell how Phormio, the ship's piper, the slave of Dion of Phrearrii, raised her up out of this noble profession? But, before God and every Heavenly Power, I shudder lest in using expressions which are fitly applied to you, I may be thought to have chosen a subject upon which it ill befits myself to speak. So I will pass this by, 130 and will begin with the acts of his own life; for they were not like any chance actions, but such as the people curses. For only lately—lately, do I say? only yesterday or the day before—did he become at once an Athenian and an orator, and by the addition of two syllables converted his father from Tromes into Atrometus, and gave his mother the imposing name of Glaucothea, when every one knows that she used to be called Empusa —a name which was obviously given her because there was nothing that she would not do or have done to her; for how else should she have acquired it? Yet, 131 in spite of this, you are of so ungrateful and villainous a nature, that though, thanks to your countrymen, you have risen from slavery to freedom, and from poverty to wealth, far from feeling gratitude to them, you devote your political activity to working against them as a hireling. I will pass over every case in which there is any room for the contention that he has spoken in the interests of the city, and will remind you of the acts which he was manifestly proved to have done for the good of her enemies.

Which of you has not heard of Antiphon, who was struck 132 off the list of citizens, and came into the city in pursuance of a promise to Philip that he would burn the dockyards? I found him concealed in the Peiraeus, and brought him before the Assembly; but the malignant Aeschines shouted at the top of his voice, that it was atrocious of me, in a democratic country, to insult a citizen who had met with misfortune, and to go to men's houses without a decree;

133 and he obtained his release. And unless the Council of Areopagus had taken notice of the matter, and, seeing the inopportuneness of the ignorance which you had shown, had made a further search for the man, and arrested him, and brought him before you again, a man of that character would have been snatched out of your hands, and would have evaded punishment, and been sent out of the country by this pompous orator. As it was, you tortured and executed him—and so ought you also to have treated

134 Aeschines. The Council of Areopagus knew the part which he had played in this affair; and for this reason, when, owing to the same ignorance which so often leads you to sacrifice the public interests, you elected him to advocate your claims in regard to the Temple of Delos, the Council (since you had appointed it to assist you and entrusted it with full authority to act in the matter) immediately rejected Aeschines as a traitor, and committed the case to Hypereides. When the Council took this step, the members took their votes from the altar, and not one vote was given for this

135 abominable man. To prove that what I say is true, (*to the clerk*) call the witnesses who testify to it.

[*The witnesses are called.*]

136 Thus when the Council rejected him from the office of advocate, and committed the case to another, it declared at the same time that he was a traitor, who wished you ill.

Such was one of the public appearances of this fine fellow,

and such its character—so like the acts with which he charges me, is it not? Now recall a second. For when Philip sent Python of Byzantium, and with him envoys from all his allies, in the hope of putting the city to shame and showing her to be in the wrong, I would not give way before the torrent of insolent rhetoric which Python poured out upon you, but rose and contradicted him, and would not betray the city's rights, but proved the iniquity of Philip's actions so manifestly, that even his own allies rose up and admitted it. But Aeschines supported Python; he gave testimony in opposition to his country, and that testimony false.

Nor was this sufficient for him; for again after this he was detected going to meet Anaxinus the spy in the house of Thrason. But surely one who met the emissary of the enemy alone and conferred with him, must himself have been already a born spy and an enemy of his country. To prove the truth of what I say, (*to the clerk*) call the witnesses to these facts. 137

[*The witnesses are called.*]

There are still an infinite number of things which I might relate of him; but I pass them over. For the truth is something like this. I could still point to many instances in which he was found to be serving our enemies during that period, and showing his spite against me. But you do not store such things up in careful remembrance, to visit them with the indignation which they deserve; but, following a bad custom, you have given great freedom to any one who wishes to trip up the proposer of any advantageous measure by dishonest charges—bartering, as you do, the advantage of the State for the pleasure and gratification which 138 you derive from invective; and so it is always easier and safer to be a hireling in the service of the enemy, than a statesman who has chosen to defend your cause.

139 To co-operate with Philip before we were openly at war with him was—I call Earth and Heaven to witness—atrocious enough. How could it be otherwise—against his own country? Nevertheless, concede him this, if you will, concede him this. But when the corn-ships had been openly plundered, and the Chersonese was being ravaged, and the man was on the march against Attica; when the position of affairs was no longer in doubt, and war had begun; what action did this malignant mouther of verses ever do for your good? He can point to none. There is not a single decree, small or great, with reference to the interests of the city, standing in the name of Aeschines. If he asserts that there is, let him produce it in the time allotted to me. But no such decree exists. In that case, however, only two alternatives are possible: either he had no fault to find at the time with my policy, and therefore made no proposal contrary to it; or else he was seeking the advantage of the enemy, and therefore refrained from bringing forward any better policy than mine.

140 Did he then abstain from speaking, as he abstained from proposing any motion, when any mischief was to be done? On the contrary, no one else had a chance of speaking. But though, apparently, the city could endure everything else, and he could do everything else unobserved, there was one final deed which was the culmination of all that he had done before. Upon this he expended all that multitude of words, as he went through the decrees relating to the Amphisseans, in the hope of distorting the truth. But the

truth cannot be distorted. It is impossible. Never will you wash away the stain of your actions there! You will not say enough for that!

I call upon all the gods and goddesses who protect this land of Attica, in the presence of you all, men of Athens; and upon Apollo of Pytho, the paternal deity of this city, and I pray to them all, that if I should speak the truth to you—if I spoke it at that very time without delay, in the presence of the people, when first I saw this abominable man setting his hand to this business (for I knew it, I knew it at once),—that then they may give me good fortune and life: but if, to gratify my hatred or any private quarrel, I am now bringing a false accusation against this man, then they may take from me the fruition of every blessing. 141

Why have I uttered this imprecation with such vehemence and earnestness? Because, although I have documents, lying in the public archives, by which I will prove the facts clearly; although I know that you remember what was done; I have still the fear that he may be thought too insignificant a man to have done all the evil which he has wrought—as indeed happened before, when he caused the ruin of the unhappy Phocians by the false report which he brought home. For the war at Amphissa, which was the cause of Philip's coming to Elateia, and of one being chosen commander of the Amphictyons, who overthrew the fortunes of the Hellenes—*he* it is who helped to get it up; he, in his sole person, is to blame for disasters to which no equal can be found. I protested at the time, and cried out, before the Assembly, 'You are bringing war into Attica, Aeschines—an Amphictyonic War.' But a packed group of his supporters refused to let me speak, while the rest were amazed, and imagined that I was bringing 142 143 a baseless charge against him, out of personal animosity. 144 But what the true nature of these proceedings was, men of Athens—why this plan was contrived, and how it was executed—you must hear from me to-day, since you were prevented from doing so at the time. You will behold a business cunningly organized; you will advance greatly in your knowledge of public affairs; and you will see what cleverness there was in Philip.

145 Philip had no prospect of seeing the end of the war with you, or ridding himself of it, unless he could make the Thebans and Thessalians enemies of Athens. For although the war was being wretchedly and inefficiently conducted by your generals, he was nevertheless suffering infinite damage from the war itself and from the freebooters. The exportation of the produce of his country and the importation of what 146 he needed were both impossible. Moreover, he was not at that time superior to you at sea, nor could he reach Attica, if the Thessalians would not follow him, or the Thebans give him a passage through their country; and although he was overcoming in the field the generals whom you sent out, such as they were (for of this I say nothing), he found himself suffering from the geographical conditions themselves, and from the nature of the resources which 147 either side possessed. Now if he tried to encourage either the Thessalians or the Thebans to march against you in order to further his own quarrel, no one, he thought, would pay any attention to him; but if he adopted their own common grounds of action and were chosen commander, he hoped to find it easier to deceive or to persuade them, as the case might be. What then does he do? He attempts (and observe with what skill) to stir up an Amphictyonic

War, and a disturbance in connexion with the meeting of the Council. For he thought that they would at once find 148 that they needed his help, to deal with these. Now if one of his own or his allies' representatives on the Council brought the matter forward, he thought that both the Thebans and the Thessalians would regard the proceeding with suspicion, and that all would be on their guard: but if it was an Athenian, sent by you, his adversaries, that did so, he would easily escape detection—as, in fact, happened. How then did he manage this? He hired Aeschines. No 149 one, I suppose, either realized beforehand what was going on or guarded against it—that is how such affairs are usually conducted here; Aeschines was nominated a delegate to the Council; three or four people held up their hands for him, and he was declared elected. But when, bearing with him the prestige of this city, he reached the Amphictyons, he dismissed and closed his eyes to all other considerations, and proceeded to perform the task for which he had been hired. He composed and recited a story, in attractive language, of the way in which the Cirrhaean territory had come to be dedicated; and with 150 this he persuaded the members of the Council, who were unused to rhetoric and did not foresee what was about to happen, that they should resolve to make the circuit of the territory, which the Amphisseans said they were cultivating because it was their own, while he alleged that it was part of the consecrated land. The Locrians were not bringing any suit against us, or taking any such action as (in order to justify himself) he now falsely alleges. You may know this from the following consideration. It was clearly impossible for the Locrians to bring a suit against Athens to an actual issue, without summoning us. Who then served the summons upon us?

Before what authority was it served? Tell us who knows: point to him. You cannot do so. It was a hollow and a false 151 pretext of which you thus made a wrongful use. While the Amphictyons were making the circuit of the territory in accordance with Aeschines' suggestion, the Locrians fell upon them and came near to shooting them all down with their spears; some of the members of the Council they even carried off with them. And now that complaints and hostilities had been stirred up against the Amphisseans, in consequence of these proceedings, the command was first held by Cottyphus, and his force was drawn from the Amphictyonic Powers alone. But since some did not come, and those who came did nothing, the men who had been suborned for the purpose—villains of long standing, chosen from the Thessalians and from the traitors in other States—took steps with a view to entrusting the affair to Philip, as commander, at the 152 next meeting of the Council. They had adopted arguments of a persuasive kind. Either, they said, the Amphictyons must themselves contribute funds, maintain mercenaries, and fine those who refused to do so; or they must elect Philip. To make a long story short, the result was that Philip was appointed. And immediately afterwards, having collected a force and crossed the Pass, ostensibly on his way to the territory of Cirrha, he bids a long farewell to the Cirrhaeans 153 and Locrians, and seizes Elateia. Now if the Thebans had not changed their policy at once, upon seeing this, and joined us, the trouble would have descended upon the city in full force, like a torrent in winter. As it was, the Thebans checked him for the moment; chiefly, men of Athens, through the goodwill of some Heavenly Power towards us; but secondarily, so far as it lay in one man's power, through me also. (*To the clerk.*) Now give me the decrees in question, and the dates of each proceeding; (*to the jury*) that you may know what trouble this abominable creature stirred up, unpunished. (*To the clerk.*) Read me the decrees. 154

[*The decrees of the Amphictyons are read.*]

(*To the clerk.*) Now read the dates of these proceedings. 155 (*To the jury.*) They are the dates at which Aeschines was delegate to the Council. (*To the clerk.*) Read.

[*The dates are read.*]

Now give me the letter which Philip sent to his allies 156 in the Peloponnese, when the Thebans failed to obey his summons. For from this, too, you may clearly see that he concealed the real reason for his action—the fact that he was taking measures against Hellas and the Thebans and yourselves—and pretended to represent the common cause and the will of the Amphictyons. And the man who provided him with all these occasions and pretexts was Aeschines. (*To the clerk.*) Read.

[*Philip's letter is read.*] 157

You see that he avoids the mention of his own reasons for 158 action, and takes refuge in those provided by the Amphictyons. Who was it that helped him to prepare such a case? Who put such pretexts at his disposal? Who is most to blame for the disasters that have taken place? Is it not Aeschines? And so, men of Athens, you must not go about saying that Hellas has suffered such things as these at the hands of one man. I call Earth and Heaven to witness, that it was at the hands, not of one man, but of many villains in each State. And of these Aeschines is one; and, had I to speak the truth 159 without any reserve, I should not hesitate to describe him as the incarnate curse of all alike—men, regions or cities—that have been ruined since then. For he who supplied the seed is responsible for the crop. I wonder that you did not turn away your eyes at the very sight of him: but a cloud of darkness seems to hang between you and the truth.

160 I find that in dealing with the measures taken by Aeschines for the injury of his country, I have reached the time when I must speak of my own statesmanship in opposition to these measures; and it is fair that you should listen to this, for many reasons, but above all because it will be a shameful thing, if, when I have faced the actual realities of hard work for you, you will not even suffer the story of them to be told.

161 For when I saw the Thebans, and (I may almost say) yourselves as well, being led by the corrupt partisans of Philip in either State to overlook, without taking a single precaution against it, the thing which was really dangerous to both peoples and needed their utmost watchfulness—the unhindered growth of Philip's power; while, on the contrary, you were quite ready to entertain ill-feeling and to quarrel with one another; I kept unceasing watch to prevent this. Nor did I rely only on my own judgement in thinking that this was what your

162 interest required. I knew that Aristophon, and afterwards Eubulus, always wished to bring about this friendly union, and that, often as they opposed one another in other matters, they always agreed in this. Cunning fox! While they lived, you hung about them and flattered them; yet now that they are dead, you do not see that you are attacking them. For your censure of my policy in regard to Thebes is far more a denunciation of them than of me, since they were before me

163 in approving of that alliance. But I return to my previous

point—that it was when Aeschines had brought about the war at Amphissa, and the others, his accomplices, had effectually helped him to create the ill-feeling against the Thebans, that Philip marched against us. For it was to render this possible that their attempt to throw the two cities into collision was made; and had we not roused ourselves a little before it was too late, we should never have been able to regain the lost ground; to such a length had these men carried matters. What the relations between the two peoples already were, you will know when you have heard these decrees and replies. (*To the clerk.*) Take these and read them.

[*The decrees are read.*] 164, 165

(*To the clerk.*) Now read the replies. 166

[*The replies are read.*] 167

Having established such relations between the cities, 168 through the agency of these men, and being elated by these decrees and replies, Philip came with his army and seized Elateia, thinking that under no circumstances whatever should we and the Thebans join in unison after this. And though the commotion which followed in the city is known to you all, let me relate to you briefly just the bare facts.

It was evening, and one had come to the Prytanes with 169 the news that Elateia had been taken. Upon this they rose up from supper without delay; some of them drove the occupants out of the booths in the market-place and set fire to the wicker-work; others sent for the generals and summoned the trumpeter; and the city was full of commotion. On the morrow, at break of day, the Prytanes summoned the Council to the Council-Chamber, while you made your way to the Assembly; and before the Council had transacted its business and passed its draft-resolution, 170 the whole people was seated on the hill-side. And now, when the Council had arrived, and the Prytanes had reported the intelligence which they had received, and had brought forward the messenger, and he had made his statement, the herald proceeded to ask, 'Who wishes to speak?' But no one came forward; and though the herald repeated the question many times, still no one rose, though all the generals were present, and all the orators, and the voice of their country was calling for some one to speak for her deliverance. For the voice of the herald, uttered in accordance with the laws, is rightly to be regarded as the common voice of our country. 171 And yet, if it was for those to come forward who wished for the deliverance of the city, all of you and all the other Athenians would have risen, and proceeded to the platform, for I am certain that you all wished for her deliverance. If it was for the wealthiest, the Three Hundred would have risen; and if it was for those who had both these qualifications—loyalty to the city and wealth—then those would have risen, who subsequently made those large donations; 172 for it was loyalty and wealth that led them so to do. But that crisis and that day called, it seems, not merely for a man of loyalty and wealth, but for one who had also followed the course of events closely from the first, and had come to a true conclusion as to the motive and the aim with which Philip was acting as he was. For no one who was unacquainted with these, and had not scrutinized them from an early period, was any the more likely, for all his loyalty and wealth, to know what should be done, or to be able to advise you. 173 The man who was needed was found that day in me. I came forward and addressed you in words which I ask you to listen to with attention, for two reasons—first, because I would have you realize that I was the only orator or politician who did not desert his post as a loyal citizen in the hour of danger, but was found there, speaking and proposing what your need required, in the midst of the terror; and secondly, because by the expenditure of a small amount of time, you will be far better qualified for the future in the whole art of political administration. My words then were these: 174 'Those who are unduly disturbed by the idea that Philip can count upon the support of Thebes do not, I think, understand the present situation. For I am quite sure that, if this were so, we should have heard of his being, not at Elateia, but on our own borders. At the same time, I understand quite well, that he has come to prepare the way for himself at Thebes. Listen,' I said, 'while I tell you the 175 true state of affairs. Philip already has at his disposal all the Thebans whom he could win over either by bribery or by deception; and those who have resisted him from the first and are opposing him now, he has no chance of winning. What then is his design and object in seizing Elateia? He wishes, by making a display of force in their neighbourhood and bringing up his army, to encourage and embolden his own friends, and to strike terror into his enemies, that so they may either concede out of terror what they now refuse, or may be compelled. Now,' I said, 'if we make 176 up our minds at the present moment to remember any ill-natured action which the Thebans may have done us, and to distrust them on the assumption that they are on the side of our enemies, we shall be doing, in the first place, just what Philip would pray for: and further, I am afraid

that his present opponents may then welcome him, that all may philippize with one consent, and that he and they may march to Attica together. If, however, you follow my advice, and give your minds to the problem before us, instead of to contentious criticism of anything that I may say, I believe that I shall be able to win your approval for my proposals, and to dispel the danger which threatens the city.
177 What then must you do? You must first moderate your present alarm, and then change your attitude, and be alarmed, all of you, for the Thebans. They are far more within the reach of disaster than we: it is they whom the danger threatens first. Secondly, those who are of military age, with the cavalry, must march to Eleusis, and let every one see that you yourselves are in arms; in order that those who sympathize with you in Thebes may be enabled to speak in defence of the right, with the same freedom that their opponents enjoy, when they see that, just as those who are trying to sell their country to Philip have a force ready to help them at Elateia, so those who would struggle for freedom have you ready at hand to help them, and to go
178 to their aid, if any one attacks them. Next I bid you elect ten envoys, and give them full authority, with the generals, to decide the time of their own journey to Thebes, and to order the march of the troops. But when the envoys arrive in Thebes, how do I advise that they should handle the matter? I ask your special attention to this. They must require nothing of the Thebans—to do so at such a moment would be shameful; but they must undertake that we will go to their aid, if they bid us do so, on the ground that they are in extreme peril, and that we foresee the future better than they; in order that, if they accept our offer and take our

advice, we may have secured our object, and our action may wear an aspect worthy of this city; or, if after all we are unsuccessful, the Thebans may have themselves to blame for any mistakes which they now make, while we shall have done nothing disgraceful or ignoble.' When I had spoken 179 these words, and others in the same strain, I left the platform. All joined in commending these proposals; no one said a word in opposition; and I did not speak thus, and then fail to move a motion; nor move a motion, and then fail to serve as envoy; nor serve as envoy, and then fail to persuade the Thebans. I carried the matter through in person from beginning to end, and gave myself up unreservedly to meet the dangers which encompassed the city. (*To the clerk.*) Bring me the resolution which was then passed.

But now, Aeschines, how would you have me describe 180 your part, and how mine, that day? Shall I call myself, as you would call me by way of abuse and disparagement, *Battalus*? and you, no ordinary hero even, but a real stage-hero, *Cresphontes* or *Creon*, or—the character which you cruelly murdered at Collytus —*Oenomaus*? Then I, Battalus of Paeania, proved myself of more value to my country in that crisis than Oenomaus of Cothocidae. In fact you were of no service on any occasion, while I played the part which became a good citizen throughout. (*To the clerk.*) Read this decree.

[*The decree of Demosthenes is read.*] 181–7

This was the first step towards our new relations with 188 Thebes, and the beginning of a settlement. Up to this time the cities had been inveigled into mutual hostility, hatred, and mistrust by these men. But this decree caused the peril that encompassed the city to pass away like a cloud. It was for an honest citizen, if he had any better plan than mine, to make it public at the time, instead of attacking me now. 189 The true counsellor and the dishonest accuser, unlike as they are in everything, differ most of all in this: the one declares his opinion before the event, and freely surrenders himself as responsible, to those who follow his advice, to Fortune, to circumstances, to any one. The other is silent when he ought to speak, and then carps at anything 190 untoward that may happen. That crisis, as I have said, was the opportunity for a man who cared for his country, the opportunity for honest speaking. But so much further than I need will I go, that if any one can *now* point to any better course—or any course at all except that which I chose —I admit my guilt. If any one has discovered any course to-day, which would have been for our advantage, had we followed it at the time, I admit that it ought not to have escaped me. But if there neither is nor was such a possibility; if even now, even to-day, no one can mention any such course, what was the counsellor of the people to do? Had he not to choose the best of the plans which suggested themselves 191 and were feasible? This I did. For the herald asked the question, Aeschines, 'Who wishes to speak?' not 'Who wishes to bring accusations about the past?' nor 'Who wishes to guarantee the future?' And while you sat speechless in the Assembly throughout that period, I came forward and spoke. Since, however, you did not do so then, at least inform us now, and tell us what words, which should have been upon my lips, were left unspoken, what precious opportunity, offered to the city, was left unused, by me? What alliance was there, what course of action, to which I ought, by preference, to have guided my countrymen?

But with all mankind the past is always dismissed from 192 consideration, and no one under any circumstances proposes to deliberate about it. It is the future or the present that make their call upon a statesman's duty. Now at that time the danger was partly in the future, and partly already present; and instead of cavilling disingenuously at the results, consider the principle of my policy under such circumstances. For in everything the final issue falls out as Heaven wills; but the principle which he follows itself reveals the mind of the statesman. Do not, therefore, count it a crime on my 193 part, that Philip proved victorious in the battle. The issue of that event lay with God, not with me. But show me that I did not adopt every expedient that was possible, so far as human reason could calculate; that I did not carry out my plan honestly and diligently, with exertions greater than my strength could bear; or that the policy which I initiated was not honourable, and worthy of Athens, and indeed necessary: and then denounce me, but not before. But if the thunderbolt 194 [or the storm] which fell has proved too mighty, not only for us, but for all the other Hellenes, what are we to do? It is as though a ship-owner, who had done all that he could to ensure safety, and had equipped the ship with all that he thought would enable her to escape destruction, and had then met with a tempest in which the tackling had been strained or even broken to pieces, were to be held responsible for the wreck of the vessel. 'Why,' he would say, 'I was not steering the ship'—just as I was not the general—'I had no power over Fortune: she had power over everything.' But consider and observe this point. If it was fated 195 that we should fare as we did, even when we had the Thebans to help us in the struggle, what must we have expected, if we had not had even them for our allies, but they had joined Philip?——and this was the object for which Philip employed every tone that he could command. And if, when the battle took place, as it did, three days' march from Attica, the city was encompassed by such peril and terror, what should we have had to expect, if this same disaster had occurred anywhere within the borders of our own country? Do you realize that, as it was, a single day, and a second, and a third gave us the power to rally, to collect our forces, to take breath, to do much that made for the deliverance of the city: but that had it been otherwise—it is not well, however, to speak of things which we have not had to experience, thanks to the goodwill of one of the gods, and to the protection which the city obtained for herself in this alliance, which you denounce.

196 The whole of this long argument, gentlemen of the jury, is addressed to yourselves and to the circle of listeners outside the bar; for to this despicable man it would have been enough to address a short, plain sentence. If to you alone, Aeschines, the future was clear, before it came, you should have given warning, when the city was deliberating upon the subject; but if you had no such foreknowledge, you have the same ignorance to answer for as others. Why then should you make these charges against me, any more than I against you?

197 For I have been a better citizen than you with regard to this very matter of which I am speaking—I am not as yet talking of anything else—just in so far as I gave myself up to the policy which all thought expedient, neither shrinking from nor regarding any personal risk; while you

neither offered any better proposals than mine (for then they would not have followed mine), nor yet made yourself useful in advancing mine in any way. What the most worthless of men, the bitterest enemy of the city, would do, you are found to have done, when all was over ; and at the same time as the irreconcilable enemies of the city, Aristratus in Naxos, and Aristoleos in Thasos, are bringing the friends of Athens to trial, Aeschines, in Athens itself, is accusing Demosthenes. But surely one who treasured up the misfortunes 198 of the Hellenes, that he might win glory from them for himself, deserved to perish rather than to stand as the accuser of another ; and one who has profited by the very same crisis as the enemies of the city cannot possibly be loyal to his country. You prove it, moreover, by the life you live, the actions you do, the measures you take—and the measures, too, that you do not take. Is anything being done which seems advantageous to the city ? Aeschines is speechless. Has any obstruction, any untoward event occurred ? There you find Aeschines, like a rupture or a sprain, which wakes into life, so soon as any trouble overtakes the body.

But since he bears so hardly upon the results, I desire to 199 say what may even be a paradox ; and let no one, in the name of Heaven, be amazed at the length to which I go, but give a kindly consideration to what I say. Even if what was to come was plain to all beforehand ; even if all foreknew it ; even if you, Aeschines, had been crying with a loud voice in warning and protestation—you who uttered not so much as a sound ; even then, I say, it was not right for the city to abandon her course, if she had any regard for her fame, or for our forefathers, or for the ages to come. As it is, she is 200 thought, no doubt, to have failed to secure her object—

as happens to all alike, whenever God wills it: but then, by abandoning in favour of Philip her claim to take the lead of others, she must have incurred the blame of having betrayed them all. Had she surrendered without a struggle those claims in defence of which our forefathers faced every imaginable peril, who would not have cast scorn upon you, Aeschines—upon you, I say; not, I trust, upon Athens nor
201 upon me? In God's name, with what faces should we have looked upon those who came to visit the city, if events had come round to the same conclusion as they now have—if Philip had been chosen as commander and lord of all, and we had stood apart, while others carried on the struggle to prevent these things; and that, although the city had never yet in time past preferred an inglorious security to the
202 hazardous vindication of a noble cause? What Hellene, what foreigner, does not know, that the Thebans, and the Spartans, who were powerful still earlier, and the Persian king would all gratefully and gladly have allowed Athens to take what she liked and keep all that was her own, if she would do the bidding of another, and let another take
203 the first place in Hellas? But this was not, it appears, the tradition of the Athenians; it was not tolerable; it was not in their nature. From the beginning of time no one had ever yet succeeded in persuading the city to throw in her lot with those who were strong, but unrighteous in their dealings, and to enjoy the security of servitude. Throughout all time she has maintained her perilous struggle for pre-
204 eminence, honour, and glory. And this policy you look upon as so lofty, so proper to your own national character, that, of your forefathers also, it is those who have acted thus that you praise most highly. And naturally. For who would not

admire the courage of those men, who did not fear to leave their land and their city, and to embark upon their ships, that they might not do the bidding of another; who chose for their general Themistocles (who had counselled them thus), and stoned Cyrsilus to death, when he gave his voice for submission to a master's orders—and not him alone, for your wives stoned his wife also to death. For the Athenians 205 of that day did not look for an orator or a general who would enable them to live in happy servitude; they cared not to live at all, unless they might live in freedom. For every one of them felt that he had come into being, not for his father and his mother alone, but also for his country. And wherein lies the difference? He who thinks he was born for his parents alone awaits the death which destiny assigns him in the course of nature: but he who thinks he was born for his country also will be willing to die, that he may not see her in bondage, and will look upon the outrages and the indignities that he must needs bear in a city that is in bondage as more to be dreaded than death.

Now were I attempting to argue that *I* had induced you 206 to show a spirit worthy of your forefathers, there is not a man who might not rebuke me with good reason. But in fact, I am declaring that such principles as these are your own; I am showing that *before* my time the city displayed this spirit, though I claim that I, too, have had some share, as your servant, in carrying out your policy in detail. But in 207 denouncing the policy as a whole, in bidding you be harsh with me, as one who has brought terrors and dangers upon the city, the prosecutor, in his eagerness to deprive me of my distinction at the present moment, is trying to rob you of praises that will last throughout all time. For if you condemn the defendant on the ground that my policy was not for the best, men will think that your own judgement has been wrong, and that it was not through the unkindness of fortune 208 that you suffered what befell you. But it cannot, it cannot be that you were wrong, men of Athens, when you took upon you the struggle for freedom and deliverance. No! by those who at Marathon bore the brunt of the peril—our forefathers. No! by those who at Plataeae drew up their battle-line, by those who at Salamis, by those who off Artemisium fought the fight at sea, by the many who lie in the sepulchres where the People laid them, brave men, all alike deemed worthy by their country, Aeschines, of the same honour and the same obsequies—not the successful or the victorious alone! And she acted justly. For all these have done that which it was the duty of brave men to do; but their fortune has 209 been that which Heaven assigned to each. Accursed, poring pedant! if you, in your anxiety to deprive me of the honour and the kindness shown to me by my countrymen, recounted trophies and battles and deeds of long ago—and of which of them did this present trial demand the mention?—what spirit was I to take upon me, when I mounted the platform, I who came forward to advise the city how she should maintain her pre-eminence? Tell me, third-rate actor! The spirit of one who would propose things unworthy of 210 this people? I should indeed have deserved to die! For you too, men of Athens, ought not to judge private suits and public in the same spirit. The business transactions of everyday life must be viewed in the light of the special law and practice associated with each; but the public policy of statesmen must be judged by the principles that your forefathers set before them. And if you believe that you should act worthily of them, then, whenever you come into court to try a public suit, each of you must imagine that with his staff and his ticket there is entrusted to him also the spirit of his country.

But I have entered upon the subject of your forefathers' achievements, and have passed over certain decrees and transactions. I desire, therefore, to return to the point from which I digressed. 211

When we came to Thebes, we found envoys there from Philip, and from the Thessalians and his other allies—our friends in terror, his full of confidence. And to show you that I am not saying this now to suit my own purpose, read the letter which we, your envoys, dispatched without delay. The prosecutor, however, has exercised the art of misrepresentation to so extravagant a degree, that he attributes to circumstances, not to me, any satisfactory result that was achieved; but for everything that fell out otherwise, he lays the blame upon me and the fortune that attends me. In his eyes, apparently, I, the counsellor and orator, have no share in the credit for what was accomplished as the result of oratory and debate; while I must bear the blame alone for the misfortunes which we suffered in arms, and as a result of generalship. What more brutal, more damnable misrepresentation can be conceived? (*To the clerk.*) Read the letter. 212

[*The letter is read.*]

When they had convened the Assembly, they gave audience to the other side first, on the ground that they occupied the position of allies; and these came forward and delivered harangues full of the praises of Philip and of accusations against yourselves, recalling everything that you had ever done 213 in opposition to the Thebans. The sum of it all was that they required the Thebans to show their gratitude for the benefits which they had received from Philip, and to exact the penalty for the injuries they had received from you, in whichever way they preferred—either by letting them march through their country against you, or by joining them in the invasion of Attica; and they showed (as they thought) that the result of the course which they advised would be that the herds and slaves and other valuables of Attica would find their way into Boeotia; while the result of what (as they alleged) you were about to propose would be that those of Boeotia

214 would be plundered in consequence of the war. They said much more, but all tending to the same effect. As for our reply, I would give my whole life to tell it you in detail; but I fear lest, now that those times have gone by, you may feel as if a very deluge had overwhelmed all, and may regard anything that is said on the subject as vanity and vexation. But hear at least what we persuaded them to do, and their answer to us. (*To the clerk.*) Take this and read it.

[*The answer of the Thebans is read.*]

215 After this they invited and summoned you; you marched; you went to their aid; and (to pass over the events which intervened) they received you in so friendly a spirit that while their infantry and cavalry were encamped outside the walls, they welcomed your troops into their houses, within the city, among their children and wives, and all that was most precious to them. Three eulogies did the Thebans pronounce upon you before the world that day, and those of the most honourable kind—the first upon your courage, the second upon your righteousness, the third upon your self-control.

For when they chose to side with you in the struggle, rather than against you, they judged that your courage was greater, and your requests more righteous, than Philip's; and when they placed in your power what they and all men guard most jealously, their children and wives, they showed their confidence in your self-control. In all these points, men of Athens, 216 your conduct proved that their judgement had been correct. For the force came into the city; but no one made a single complaint—not even an unfounded complaint—against you; so virtuously did you conduct yourselves. And twice you fought by their side, in the earliest battles—the battle by the river and the winter-battle—and showed yourselves, not only irreproachable, but even admirable, in your discipline, your equipment, and your enthusiasm. These things called forth expressions of thanks to you from other states, and sacrifices and processions to the gods from yourselves. And I should 217 like to ask Aeschines whether, when all this was happening, and the city was full of pride and joy and thanksgiving, he joined in the sacrifices and the rejoicing of the multitude, or whether he sat at home grieving and groaning and angry at the good fortune of his country. If he was present, and was seen in his place with the rest, surely his present action is atrocious—nay, even impious—when he asks you, who have taken an oath by the gods, to vote to-day that those very things were not excellent, of whose excellence he himself on that day made the gods his witnesses. If he was not present, then surely he deserves to die many times, for grieving at the sight of the things which brought rejoicing to others. (*To the clerk.*) Now read these decrees also.

[*The decrees ordering sacrifices are read.*]

218 Thus we were occupied at that time with sacrifices, while the Thebans were reflecting how they had been saved by our help; and those who, in consequence of my opponents' proceedings, had expected that they would themselves stand in need of help, found themselves, after all, helping others, in consequence of the action they took upon my advice. But what the tone of Philip's utterance was, and how greatly he was confounded by what had happened, you can learn from his letter, which he sent to the Peloponnese. (*To the clerk.*) Take these and read them: (*to the jury*) that you may know what was effected by my perseverance, by my travels, by the hardships I endured, by all those decrees of which Aeschines spoke so disparagingly just now.

219 You have had, as you know, many great and famous orators, men of Athens, before my time—Callistratus himself, Aristophon, Cephalus, Thrasybulus, and a vast number of others. Yet not one of these ever gave himself up entirely to the State for any purpose: the mover of a decree would not serve as ambassador, the ambassador would not move the decree. Each left himself, at one and the same time, some respite from work, and somewhere to lay the blame,
220 in case of accidents. 'Well,' some one may say, 'did *you* so excel them in force and boldness, as to do everything yourself?' I do not say that. But so strong was my conviction of the seriousness of the danger that had overtaken the city, that I felt that I ought not to give my personal safety any place whatever in my thoughts; it was enough for a man to do his duty and to leave nothing
221 undone. And I was convinced with regard to myself—

foolishly perhaps, but still convinced—that no mover would make a better proposal, no agent would execute it better, no ambassador would be more eager or more honest in his mission, than I. For these reasons, I assigned every one of these offices to myself. (*To the clerk.*) Read Philip's letters.

[*Philip's letters are read.*]

To this condition, Aeschines, was Philip reduced by my statesmanship. This was the tone of his utterances, though before this he used to threaten the city with many a bold word. For this I was deservedly crowned by those here assembled, and though you were present, you offered no opposition; while Diondas, who indicted the proposer, did not obtain the necessary fraction of the votes. (*To the clerk.*) Read me these decrees, (*to the jury*) which escaped condemnation, and which Aeschines did not even indict. 222

[*The decrees are read.*]

These decrees, men of Athens, contain the very same syllables, the very same words, as those which Aristonicus previously employed in his proposal, and which Ctesiphon, the defendant, has employed now; and Aeschines neither prosecuted the proposer of them himself, nor supported the person who indicted him. Yet surely, if the charges which he is bringing against me to-day are true, he would have had better reason then for prosecuting Demomeles (the proposer of the decree) and Hypereides, than he has for prosecuting Ctesiphon. And why? Because Ctesiphon can refer you to them—to the decision of the courts, to the fact that Aeschines himself did not accuse them, though they had moved exactly what he has moved now, to the prohibition by law of further 223 224

prosecution in such cases, and to many other facts: whereas then the case would have been tried on its merits, before the defendant had got the advantage of any such precedent.
225 But of course it was impossible then for Aeschines to act as he has acted now—to select out of many periods of time long past, and many decrees, matters which no one either knew or thought would be mentioned to-day; to misrepresent them, to change the dates, to put false reasons for the actions taken in place of the true, and so
226 appear to have a case. At the time this was impossible. Every word spoken then must have been spoken with the truth in view, at no distance of time from the events, while you still remembered all the facts and had them practically at your fingers' ends. For that reason he evaded all investigation at the time; and he has come before you now, in the belief (I fancy) that you will make this a contest of oratory, instead of an inquiry into our political careers, and that it is upon our eloquence, not upon the interests of the city, that you will decide.

227 Yes, and he ingeniously suggests that you ought to disregard the opinion which you had of each of us when you left your homes and came into court; and that just as, when you draw up an account in the belief that some one has a balance, you nevertheless give way when you find that the counters all disappear and leave nothing over, so now you should give your adhesion to the conclusion which emerges from the argument. Now observe how inherently rotten everything that springs
228 from dishonesty seems to be. By his very use of this ingenious illustration he has confessed that to-day, at all events, our respective characters are well established—that I am known to speak for my country's good, and he to speak for Philip.

For unless that were your present conception of each of us, he would not have sought to change your view. And further, 229 I shall easily show you that it is not fair of him to ask you to alter this opinion—not by the use of counters—that is not how a political reckoning is made—but by briefly recalling each point to you, and treating you who hear me both as auditors of my account and witnesses to the facts. For that policy of mine which he denounces caused the Thebans, instead of joining Philip, as all expected them to do, in the invasion of our country, to range themselves by our side and stay his progress. It caused the war to take place not in Attica, but 230 on the confines of Boeotia, eighty miles from the city. Instead of our being harried and plundered by freebooters from Euboea, it gave peace to Attica from the side of the sea throughout the war. Instead of Philip's taking Byzantium and becoming master of the Hellespont, it caused the Byzantines to join us in the war against him. Can such achieve- 231 ments, think you, be reckoned up like counters? Are we to cancel them out, rather than provide that they shall be remembered for all time? I need not now add that it fell to others to taste the barbarity which is to be seen in every case in which Philip got any one finally into his power; while you reaped (and quite rightly) the fruits of the generosity which he feigned while he was bringing within his grasp all that remained. But I pass this over.

Nay, I will not even hesitate to say, that one who wished 232 to review an orator's career straightforwardly and without misrepresentation, would not have included in his charges such matters as you just now spoke of—making up illustrations, and mimicking words and gestures. Of course the fortune which befell the Hellenes—surely you see this?—

was entirely due to my using this word instead of that, or waving my hand in one direction rather than the other!

233 He would have inquired, by reference to the actual facts, what resources and what forces the city had at her command when I entered political life; what I subsequently collected for her when I took control; and what was the condition of our adversaries. Then if I had diminished our forces, he would have proved that the fault lay at my door; but if I had greatly increased them, he would have abstained from deliberate misrepresentation. But since you have avoided such an inquiry, I will undertake it; and do you, gentlemen, observe whether my argument is just.

234 The military resources of the city included the islanders—and not all, but only the weakest. For neither Chios nor Rhodes nor Corcyra was with us. Their contribution in money came to 45 talents, and these had been collected in advance. Infantry and cavalry, besides our own, we had none. But the circumstance which was most alarming to us and most favourable to our enemies was that these men had contrived that all our neighbours should be more inclined to enmity than to friendship—the Megareans, the Thebans,

235 and the Euboeans. Such was the position of the city at the time; and what I say admits of no contradiction. Now consider the position of Philip, with whom our conflict lay. In the first place, he held absolute sway over his followers—and this for purposes of war is the greatest of all advantages. Next, his followers had their weapons in their hands always. Then he was well off for money, and did whatever he resolved to do, without giving warning of it by decrees, or debating about it in public, or being put on trial by dishonest accusers, or defending himself against indictments for illegality, or

being bound to render an account to any one. He was himself absolute master, commander, and lord of all. But 236 I who was set to oppose him—for this inquiry too it is just to make—what had I under my control? Nothing! For, to begin with, the very right to address you—the only right I had—you extended to Philip's hirelings in the same measure as to me; and as often as they defeated me—and this frequently happened, whatever the reason on each occasion—so often you went away leaving a resolution recorded in favour of the enemy. But in spite of 237 all these disadvantages, I won for you the alliance of the Euboeans, Achaeans, Corinthians, Thebans, Megareans, Leucadians, and Corcyreans, from whom were collected—apart from their citizen-troops—15,000 mercenaries and 2,000 cavalry. And I instituted a money-contribution, on as 238 large a scale as I could. But if you refer, Aeschines, to what was fair as between ourselves and the Thebans or the Byzantines or the Euboeans—if at this time you talk to us of equal shares—you must be ignorant, in the first place, of the fact that in former days also, out of those ships of war, three hundred in all, which fought for the Hellenes, Athens provided two hundred, and did not think herself unfairly used, or let herself be seen arraigning those who had counselled her action, or taking offence at the arrangement. It would have been shameful. No! men saw her rendering thanks to Heaven, because when a common peril beset the Hellenes, she had provided double as much as all the rest to secure the deliverance of all. Moreover, it is but a hollow benefit that you 239 are conferring upon your countrymen by your dishonest charges against me. Why do you tell them *now*, what course they ought to have taken? Why did you not propose such a course at the time (for you were in Athens, and were present) if it was possible in the midst of those critical times, when we had to accept, not what we chose, but what circumstances allowed; since there was one at hand, bidding against us, and ready to welcome those whom we rejected, and to pay them into the bargain.

240 But if I am accused to-day, for what I have actually done, what if at the time I had haggled over these details, and the other states had gone off and joined Philip, and he had become master at once of Euboea and Thebes and Byzantium? What do you think these impious men would then 241 have done? What would they have said? Would they not have declared that the states had been surrendered? that they had been driven away, when they wished to be on your side? 'See,' they would have said (would they not?), 'he has obtained through the Byzantines the command of the Hellespont and the control of the corn trade of Hellas; and through the Thebans a trying border war has been brought into Attica; and owing to the pirates who sail from Euboea, the sea has become unnavigable,' and much 242 more in addition. A villainous thing, men of Athens, is the dishonest accuser always—villainous, and in every way malignant and fault-finding! Aye, and this miserable creature is a fox by nature, that has never done anything honest or gentlemanly—a very tragical ape, a clodhopping Oeno-243 maus, a counterfeit orator! Where is the profit to your country from your cleverness? Do you instruct us now about things that are past? It is as though a doctor, when he was paying his visits to the sick, were to give them no advice or instructions to enable them to become free from their illness, but, when one of his patients died and the customary offerings

were being paid him, were to explain, as he followed to the tomb, 'if this man had done such and such things, he would not have died.' Crazy fool! Do you tell us this *now*?

Nor again will you find that the defeat—if you exult at it, when you ought to groan, accursed man!—was determined by anything that was within my control. Consider the question thus. In no place to which I was sent by you as ambassador, did I ever come away defeated by the ambassadors of Philip—not from Thessaly nor from Ambracia, not from the Illyrians nor from the Thracian princes, not from Byzantium nor from any other place, nor yet, on the last occasion, from Thebes. But every place in which his ambassadors were defeated in argument, he proceeded to attack and subdue by force of arms. Do you then require those places at *my* hands? Are you not ashamed to jeer at a man as a coward, and in the same breath to require him to prove superior, by his own unaided efforts, to the army of Philip—and that with no weapons to use but words? For what else was at my disposal? I could not control the spirit of each soldier, or the fortune of the combatants, or the generalship displayed, of which, in your perversity, you demand an account from me. No; but every investigation that can be made as regards those duties for which an orator should be held responsible, I bid you make. I crave no mercy. And what are those duties? To discern events in their beginnings, to foresee what is coming, and to forewarn others. These things I have done. Again, it is his duty to reduce to the smallest possible compass, wherever he finds them, the slowness, the hesitation, the ignorance, the contentiousness, which are the errors inseparably connected

244

245

246

with the constitution of all city-states; while, on the other hand, he must stimulate men to unity, friendship, and eagerness to perform their duty. All these things I have done, and no one can discover any dereliction of duty on my part

247 at any time. If one were to ask any person whatever, by what means Philip had accomplished the majority of his successes, every one would reply that it was by means of his army, and by giving presents and corrupting those in charge of affairs. Now I had no control or command of the forces: neither, then, does the responsibility for anything that was done in that sphere concern me. And further, in the matter of being or not being corrupted by bribes, I have defeated Philip. For just as the bidder has conquered one who accepts his money, if he effects his purchase, so one who refuses to accept it [and is not corrupted] has conquered the bidder. In all, therefore, in which I am concerned, the city has suffered no defeat.

248 The justification, then, with which I furnished the defendant for such a motion as he proposed with regard to me, consisted (along with many other points) of the facts which I have described, and others like them. I will now proceed to that justification which all of you supplied. For immediately after the battle, the People, who knew and had seen all that I did, and now stood in the very midst of the peril and terror, at a moment when it would not have been surprising if the majority had shown some harshness towards me—the People, I say, in the first place carried my proposals for ensuring the safety of the city; and all the measures undertaken for its protection—the disposition of the garrisons, the entrenchments, the funds for the fortifications—were all provided for by decrees which I proposed. And, in the

second place, when the People chose a corn-commissioner, out of all Athens they elected me. Subsequently all those 249 who were interested in injuring me combined, and assailed me with indictments, prosecutions after audit, impeachments, and all such proceedings—not in their own names at first, but through the agency of men behind whom, they thought, they would best be screened against recognition. For you doubtless know and remember that during the early part of that period I was brought to trial every day; and neither the desperation of Sosicles, nor the dishonest misrepresentations of Philocrates, nor the frenzy of Diondas and Melantus, nor any other expedient, was left untried by them against me. And in all these trials, thanks to the gods above all, but secondarily to you and the rest of the Athenians, I was acquitted—and justly; for such a decision is in accordance both with truth and with the credit of jurors who have taken their oath, and given a verdict in conformity with it. So 250 whenever I was impeached, and you absolved me and did not give the prosecutor the necessary fraction of the votes, you were voting that my policy was the best. Whenever I was acquitted upon an indictment, it was a proof that my motion and proposals were according to law. Whenever you set your seal to my accounts at an audit, you confessed in addition that I had acted throughout with uprightness and integrity. And this being so, what epithet was it fitting or just that Ctesiphon should apply to my actions? Was it not that which he saw applied by the People, and by juries on their oath, and ratified by Truth in the judgement of all men?

'Yes,' he replies, 'but Cephalus' boast was a noble 251 one—that he had never been indicted at all.' True, and a happy thing also it was for him. But why should one who has often been tried, but has never been convicted of crime, deserve to incur criticism any the more on that account? Yet in truth, men of Athens, so far as Aeschines is concerned, I too can make this noble boast that Cephalus made. For he has never yet preferred or prosecuted any indictment against me; so that by you at least, Aeschines, I am admitted to be no worse a citizen than Cephalus.

252 His want of feeling and his malignity may be seen in many ways, and not least in the remarks which he made about fortune. For my part, I think that, as a rule, when one human being reproaches another with his fortune, he is a fool. For when he who thinks himself most prosperous and fancies his fortune most excellent, does not know whether it will remain so until the evening, how can it be right to speak of one's fortune, or to taunt another with his? But since Aeschines adopts a tone of lofty superiority upon this as upon many other subjects, observe, men of Athens, how much more truthful and more becoming in a human being my own 253 remarks upon Aeschines' fortune will be. I believe that the fortune of this city is good; and I see that the God of Dodona also declares this to you through his oracle. But I think that the prevailing fortune of mankind as a whole to-day is grievous and terrible. For what man, Hellene or foreigner, has not tasted abundance of evil at this present 254 time? Now the fact that we chose the noblest course, and that we are actually better off than those Hellenes who expected to live in prosperity if they sacrificed us, I ascribe to the good fortune of the city. But in so far as we failed, in so far as everything did not fall out in accordance with our wishes, I consider that the city has received the share

which was due to us of the fortune of mankind in general. But my personal fortune, and that of every individual 255 among us, ought, I think, in fairness to be examined with reference to our personal circumstances. That is my judgement with regard to fortune, and I believe (as I think you also do) that my judgement is correct and just. But Aeschines asserts that my personal fortune has more influence than the fortune of the city as a community—the insignificant and evil more than the good and important! How can this be?

If, however, you determine at all costs to scrutinize my 256 fortune, Aeschines, then compare it with your own; and if you find that mine is better than yours, then cease to revile it. Examine it, then, from the very beginning. And, in Heaven's name, let no one condemn me for any want of good taste. For I neither regard one who speaks insultingly of poverty, nor one who prides himself on having been brought up in affluence, as a man of sense. But the slanders and misrepresentations of this unfeeling man oblige me to enter upon a discussion of this sort; and I will conduct it with as much moderation as the facts allow.

I then, Aeschines, had the advantage as a boy of attending 257 the schools which became my position, and of possessing as much as one who is to do nothing ignoble owing to poverty must possess. When I passed out of boyhood, my life corresponded with my upbringing—I provided choruses and equipped warships; I paid the war-tax; I neglected none of the paths to distinction in public or private life, but gave my services both to my country and my friends; and when I thought fit to enter public life, the measures which I decided to adopt were of such a character that I have been crowned many times both by my country and by many other Hellenic peoples, while not even you, my enemies, attempt to say that my choice was not at least an honourable 258 one. Such is the fortune which has accompanied my life, and though I might say much more about it, I refrain from doing so, in my anxiety not to annoy any one by the expression of my pride. And you—the lofty personage, the despiser of others—what has been your fortune when compared with this?—the fortune, thanks to which you were brought up as a boy in the depths of indigence, in close attendance upon the school along with your father, pounding up the ink, sponging down the forms, sweeping the attendants' room, occupying the position of a menial, 259 not of a free-born boy! Then, when you became a man, you used to read out the books to your mother at her initiations, and help her in the rest of the hocus-pocus, by night dressing the initiated in fawnskins, drenching them from the bowl, purifying them and wiping them down with the clay and the bran, and (when they were purified) bidding them stand up and say, 'The ill is done, the good begun,' priding yourself upon raising the shout of joy more loudly than any one had ever done before—and I can believe it, for, when his voice is so loud, you dare not imagine that 260 his shout is anything but superlatively fine. But by day you used to lead those noble companies through the streets, men crowned with fennel and white poplar, throttling the puff-adders and waving them over your head, crying out 'Euoe, Saboe,' and dancing to the tune of 'Hyes Attes, Attes Hyes'—addressed by the old hags as leader, captain, ivy-bearer, fan-bearer, and so on; and as the reward of your services getting sops and twists and barley-bannocks! Who would not congratulate himself with good reason on such things, and bless his own fortune? But when you were enrolled 261 among your fellow parishioners, by whatever means (for of that I say nothing)—when, I say, you *were* enrolled, you at once selected the noblest of occupations, that of a clerk and servant to petty magistrates. And when at length you escaped from 262 this condition also, after yourself doing all that you impute to others, you in no way—Heaven knows!—disgraced your previous record by the life which you subsequently lived; for you hired yourself out to the actors Simylus and Socrates—the Roarers, they were nicknamed—and played as a third-rate actor, collecting figs and bunches of grapes and olives, like a fruiterer gathering from other peoples' farms, and getting more out of this than out of the dramatic competitions in which you were competing for your lives; for there was war without truce or herald between yourselves and the spectators; and the many wounds you received from them make it natural for you to jeer at the cowardice of those who have had no such experiences. But I will pass over all that might 263 be accounted for by your poverty, and proceed to my charges against your character itself. For you chose a line of political action (when at length it occurred to you to take up politics too), in pursuance of which, when your country's fortune was good, you lived the life of a hare, in fear and trembling, always expecting a thrashing for the crimes which lay on your conscience; whereas all have seen your boldness amid the misfortunes of others. But 264 when a man plucks up courage at the death of a thousand of his fellow citizens, what does he deserve to suffer at the hands of the living? I have much more to say about him, but I will leave it unsaid. It is not for me, I think, to mention lightly all the infamy and disgrace which I could prove to be connected with him, but only so much as it is not discreditable to myself to speak of.

265 And now review the history of your life and of mine, side by side—good temperedly, Aeschines, not unkindly: and then ask these gentlemen which fortune, of the two, each of them would choose. You taught letters; I attended school. You conducted initiations; I was initiated. You were a clerk; I a member of the Assembly: you, a third-rate actor, I a spectator of the play. You used to be driven from the stage, while I hissed. Your political life has all been lived for the good of our enemies, mine for the good of my 266 country. To pass over all besides, even on this very day, I am being examined with regard to my qualification for a crown —it is already admitted that I am clear of all crimes; while you have already the reputation of a dishonest informer, and for you the issue at stake is whether you are to continue such practices, or to be stopped once for all, through failing to obtain a fifth part of the votes. A good fortune indeed—can you not see?—is that which has accompanied your life, that you should denounce mine!

267 And now let me read to you the evidence of the public burdens which I have undertaken; and side by side with them, do you, Aeschines, read the speeches which you used to murder—

'I leave the abysm of death and gates of gloom,'

and

'Know that I am not fain ill-news to bring';

and 'evil in evil wise', may you be brought to perdition, by the gods above all, and then by all those here present, villainous citizen, villainous third-rate actor that you are. (*To the clerk.*) Read the evidence.

[*The evidence is read.*]

Such was I in my relation to the State. And as to my 268 private life, unless you all know that I was open-hearted and generous and at the disposal of all who had need of me, I am silent; I prefer to tell you nothing, and to produce no evidence whatever, to show whether I ransomed some from the enemy, or helped others to give their daughters in marriage, or rendered any such services. For my principle may perhaps be 269 expressed thus. I think that one who has received a kindness ought to remember it all his life; but that the doer of the kindness should forget it once for all; if the former is to behave like a good man, the latter like one free from all meanness. To be always recalling and speaking of one's own benefactions is almost like upbraiding the recipients of them. I will do nothing of the kind, and will not be led into doing so. Whatever be the opinion that has been formed of me in these respects, with that I am content.

But I desire to be rid of personal topics, and to say a little 270 more to you about public affairs. For if, Aeschines, you can mention one of all those who dwell beneath the sun above us, Hellene or foreigner, who has not suffered under the absolute sway, first of Philip, and now of Alexander, so be it! I concede that it is my fortune or misfortune, whichever you are pleased to call it, that has been to blame for everything. But if many of those who have never once 271 even seen me or heard my voice have suffered much and terribly—and not individuals alone, but whole cities and nations—how much more just and truthful it is to regard the common fortune (as it seems to be) of all mankind, and a certain stubborn drift of events in the wrong direction, 272 as the cause of these sufferings. Such considerations, however, you discard. You impute the blame to me, whose political life has been lived among my own fellow countrymen—and that, though you know that your slander falls in part (if not entirely) upon all of them, and above all upon yourself. For if, when I took part in the discussion of public affairs, I had had absolute power, it would have been possible for all of you, the other orators, to lay the blame 273 on me. But if you were present at every meeting of the Assembly; if the city always brought forward questions of policy for public consideration; if at the time my policy appeared the best to every one, and above all to you (for it was certainly from no goodwill that you relinquished to me the hopes, the admiration, the honours, which all attached themselves to my policy at that time, but obviously because the truth was too strong for you, and you had nothing better to propose); then surely you are guilty of monstrous iniquity, in finding fault to-day with a policy, than which, at the time, 274 you could propose nothing better. Among all the rest of mankind, I observe that some such principles as the following have been, as it were, determined and ordained. If a man commits a deliberate crime, indignation and punishment are ordained against him. If he commits an involuntary mistake, instead of punishment, he is to receive pardon. If, without crime or mistake, one who has given himself up wholly to that which seems to be for the advantage of all has, in company with all, failed to achieve success, then it is just, not to reproach or 275 revile such a man, but to sympathize with him. Moreover, it will be seen that all these principles are not so ordained in the laws alone. Nature herself has laid them down in her unwritten law, and in the moral consciousness of mankind. Aeschines, then, has so far surpassed all mankind in brutality and in the art of misrepresentation, that he actually denounces me for things which he himself mentioned under the name of misfortunes.

276 In addition to everything else, as though he had himself always spoken straightforwardly and in loyalty, he bade you keep your eyes on me carefully, and make sure that I did not mislead or deceive you. He called me 'a clever speaker', 'a wizard', 'a sophist', and so on: just as if it followed that when a man had the first word and attributed his own qualities to another, the truth was really as he stated, and his hearers would not inquire further who he himself was, that said such things. But I am sure that you all know this man, and are aware that these qualities belong to him far more than to me. 277 And again, I am quite sure that my cleverness—yes, let the word pass; though I observe that the influence of a speaker depends for the most part on his audience; for in proportion to the welcome and the goodwill which you accord to each speaker is the credit which he obtains for wisdom;—I am sure, I say, that if I too possess any such skill, you will all find it constantly fighting on your behalf in affairs of State, never in opposition to you, never for private ends; while the skill of Aeschines, on the contrary, is employed, not only in upholding the cause of the enemy, but in attacking any one who has annoyed him or come into collision with him anywhere. He neither employs it uprightly, nor to promote the interests of the city. 278 For a good and honourable citizen ought not to require from a jury, who have come into court to represent the interests

of the community, that they shall give their sanction to his anger, or his enmity, or any other such passion; nor ought he to come before you to gratify such feelings. It were best that he had no such passions in his nature at all; but if they are really inevitable, then he should keep them tame and subdued. Under what circumstances, then, should a politician and an orator show passion? When any of the vital interests of his country are at stake; when it is with its enemies that the People has to deal: those are the circumstances. For then is the opportunity of a loyal and 279 gallant citizen. But that when he has never to this day demanded my punishment, either in the name of the city or in his own, for any public—nor, I will add, for any private—crime, he should have come here with a trumped-up charge against the grant of a crown and a vote of thanks, and should have spent so many words upon it—that is a sign of personal enmity and jealousy and meanness, not of any good quality. And that he should further have discarded every form of lawsuit against myself, and should have come here to-day to attack the defendant, is the very extremity of 280 baseness. It shows, I think, Aeschines, that your motive in undertaking this suit was your desire, not to exact vengeance for any crime, but to give a display of rhetoric and elocution. Yet it is not his language, Aeschines, that deserves our esteem in an orator, nor the pitch of his voice, but his choice of the aims which the people chooses, his hatred or love of those whom his country loves or hates. 281 He whose heart is so disposed will always speak with loyal intent; but he who serves those from whom the city foresees danger to herself, does not ride at the same anchor as the People, and therefore does not look for safety to the same quarter. But I do, mark you! For I have made the interests of my countrymen my own, and have counted nothing as reserved for my own private advantage. What? You 282 have not done so either? How can that be, when immediately after the battle you went your way as an ambassador to Philip, the author of the calamities which befell your country at that time; and that, despite the fact that until then you always denied this intimacy with him, as every one knows? But what is meant by a deceiver of the city? Is it not one who does not say what he thinks? Upon whom does the herald justly pronounce the curse? Is it not upon such a man as this? With what greater crime can one charge a man who is an orator, than that of saying one thing and thinking another? Such a man you have been found to be. 283 And after this do you open your mouth, or dare to look this audience in the face? Do you imagine that they do not know who you are? or that the slumber of forgetfulness has taken such hold upon them all, that they do not remember the speeches which you used to deliver during the war, when you declared with imprecations and oaths that you had nothing to do with Philip, and that I was bringing this accusation against you, when it was not true, to satisfy my personal enmity? But so soon as the news of the battle had come, 284 you thought no more of all this, but at once avowed and professed that you stood on a footing of friendship and guest-friendship with him; though these were nothing but your hireling-service under other names; for upon what honest or equal basis could Aeschines, the son of Glaucothea the tambourine-player, enjoy the guest-friendship, or the friendship, or the acquaintance of Philip? I cannot see. In fact, you had been hired by him to ruin the interests of these your countrymen. And yet, though your own treason has been so plainly detected—though you have been an informer against yourself after the event—you still revile me, and reproach me with crimes of which, you will find, any one is more guilty than I.

285 Many a great and noble enterprise, Aeschines, did this city undertake and succeed in, inspired by me; and she did not forget them. It is a proof of this, that when, immediately after the event, the People had to elect one who should pronounce the oration over the dead, and you were nominated, they did not elect you, for all your fine voice, nor Demades, who had just negotiated the Peace, nor Hegemon, nor any other member of your party: they elected me. And when you and Pythocles came forward in a brutal and shameless fashion, God knows! and made the same charges against me as you are making again to-day, and abused me, the People elected me even more decidedly. And the reason you know 286 well; but I will tell it you nevertheless. They knew for themselves both the loyalty and zeal which inspired my conduct of affairs, and the iniquity of yourself and your friends. For what you denied with oaths when our cause was prosperous, you admitted in the hour of the city's failure; and those, accordingly, who were only enabled by the misfortunes of their country to express their views without fear, they decided to have been enemies of their own for a long while, though 287 only then did they stand revealed. And further, they thought that one who was to pronounce an oration over the dead, and to adorn their valour, should not have come beneath the same roof, nor shared the same libation, as those who were arrayed against them; that he should not there join with those who with their own hands had slain them, in the

revel and the triumph-song over the calamities of the Hellenes, and then come home and receive honour—that he should not play the mourner over their fate with his voice, but should grieve for them in his heart. What they required they saw in themselves and in me, but not in you; and this was why they appointed me, and not any of you. Nor, 288 when the people acted thus, did the fathers and brothers of the slain, who were then publicly appointed to conduct the funeral, act otherwise. For since (in accordance with the ordinary custom) they had to hold the funeral-feast in the house of the nearest of kin, as it were, to the slain, they held it at my house, and with reason; for though by birth each was more nearly akin to his dead than I, yet none stood nearer to them all in common. For he who had their life and their success most at heart, had also, when they had suffered what I would they had not, the greatest share of sorrow for them all.

(*To the clerk.*) Read him the epitaph which the city 289 resolved to inscribe above them at the public cost; (*to Aeschines*) that even by these very lines, Aeschines, you may know that you are a man destitute of feeling, a dishonest accuser, an abominable wretch!

The Inscription.

These for their country, fighting side by side,
By deeds of arms dispelled the foemen's pride.
Their lives they saved not, bidding Death make clear—
Impartial Judge!—their courage or their fear.
For Greece they fought, lest, 'neath the yoke brought low,
In thraldom she th' oppressor's scorn should know.

Now in the bosom of their fatherland
After their toil they rest—'tis God's command.
'Tis God's alone from failure free to live;
Escape from Fate to no man doth He give.

290 Do you hear, Aeschines [in these very lines], ''Tis God's alone from failure free to live'? Not to the statesman has he ascribed the power to secure success for those who strive, but to the gods. Why then, accursed man, do you revile *me* for our failure, in words which I pray the gods to turn upon the heads of you and yours?

291 But, even after all the other lying accusations which he has brought against me, the thing which amazed me most of all, men of Athens, was that when he mentioned what had befallen the city, he did not think of it as a loyal and upright citizen would have thought. He shed no tears; he felt no emotion of sorrow in his heart: he lifted up his voice, he exulted, he strained his throat, evidently in the belief that he was accusing me, though in truth he was giving us an illustration, to his own discredit, of the utter difference between his feelings and those of others, at the painful events 292 which had taken place. But surely one who professes, as Aeschines professes now, to care for the laws and the constitution, ought to show, if nothing else, at least that he feels the same griefs and the same joys as the People, and has not, by his political profession, ranged himself on the side of their opponents. That you have done the latter is manifest to-day, when you pretend that the blame for everything is mine, and that it is through me that the city was plunged in trouble: though it was not through my statesmanship or my policy, 293 gentlemen, that you began to help the Hellenes: for were

you to grant me this—that it was through me that you had resisted the dominion which was being established over the Hellenes—you would have granted me a testimonial which all those that you have given to others together could not equal. But neither would I make such an assertion; for it would be unjust to you; nor, I am sure, would you concede its truth: and if Aeschines were acting honestly, he would not have been trying to deface and misrepresent the greatest of your glories, in order to satisfy his hatred towards me.

But why do I rebuke him for this, when he has made 294 other lying charges against me, which are more outrageous by far? For when a man charges me—I call Heaven and Earth to witness!—with philippizing, what will he not say? By Heracles and all the gods, if one had to inquire truthfully, setting aside all calumny and all expression of animosity, who are in reality the men upon whose heads all would naturally and justly lay the blame for what has taken place, you would find that it was those in each city who resemble Aeschines, not those who resemble me. For they, when 295 Philip's power was weak and quite insignificant—when we repeatedly warned and exhorted you and showed you what was best—they, to satisfy their own avarice, sacrificed the interests of the community, each group deceiving and corrupting their own fellow citizens, until they brought them into bondage. Thus the Thessalians were treated by Daochus, Cineas, and Thrasydaeus; the Arcadians by Cercidas, Hieronymus and Eucampidas; the Argives by Myrtis, Teledamus, and Mnaseas; the Eleans by Euxitheus, Cleotimus and Aristaechmus; the Messenians by the sons of the godforsaken Philiadas—Neon and Thrasylochus; the Sicymians by Aristratus and Epichares; the Corinthians by

Deinarchus and Demaretus; the Megareans by Ptoeodorus, Helixus and Perillus; the Thebans by Timolaus, Theogeiton, and Anemoetas; the Euboeans by Hipparchus and Sosi-
296 stratus. Daylight will fail me before the list of the traitors is complete. All these, men of Athens, are men who pursue the same designs in their own cities, as my opponents pursue among you—abominable men, flatterers, evil spirits, who have hacked the limbs each of his own fatherland, and like boon companions have pledged away their freedom, first to Philip and now to Alexander; men whose measure of happiness is their belly, and their lowest instincts; while as for freedom, and the refusal to acknowledge any man as lord—the standard and rule of good to the Hellenes of old—they have flung it to the ground.

297 Of this shameful and notorious conspiracy and wickedness—or rather (to speak with all earnestness, men of Athens), of this treason against the freedom of the Hellenes—Athens has been guiltless in the eyes of all men, in consequence of my statesmanship, as I have been guiltless in your eyes. And do you then ask me for what merits I count myself worthy to receive honour? I tell you that at a time when every politician in Hellas had been corrupted—beginning with yourself—
298 [firstly by Philip, and now by Alexander], no opportunity that offered, no generous language, no grand promises, no hopes, no fears, nor any other motive, tempted or induced me to betray one jot of what I believed to be the rights and interests of the city; nor, of all the counsel that I have given to my fellow countrymen, up to this day, has any ever been given (as it has by you) with the scales of the mind inclining to the side of gain, but all out of an upright, honest, uncorrupted soul. I have taken the lead in greater affairs

than any man of my own time, and my administration has been sound and honest throughout all. That is why I count 299 myself worthy of honour. But as for the fortifications and entrenchments, for which you ridiculed me, I judge them to be deserving, indeed, of gratitude and commendation—assuredly they are so—but I set them far below my own political services. Not with stones, nor with bricks, did I fortify this city. Not such are the works upon which I pride myself most. But would you inquire honestly wherein my fortifications consist? You will find them in munitions of war, in cities, in countries, in harbours, in ships, in horses, and in men ready to defend my fellow countrymen. These 300 are the defences I have set to protect Attica, so far as by human calculation it could be done; and with these I have fortified our whole territory—not the circuit of the Peiraeus or of the city alone. Nor in fact, did *I* prove inferior to Philip in calculations—far from it!—or in preparations for war; but the generals of the confederacy, and their forces, proved inferior to him in fortune. Where are the proofs of these things? They are clear and manifest. I bid you consider them.

What was the duty of a loyal citizen—one who was acting 301 with all forethought and zeal and uprightness for his country's good? Was it not to make Euboea the bulwark of Attica on the side of the sea, and Boeotia on that of the mainland, and on that of the regions towards the Peloponnese, our neighbours in that direction? Was it not to provide for the corn-trade, and to ensure that it should pass along a continuously friendly coast all the way to the Peiraeus? Was it not to preserve the places which were ours—Proconnesus, the Chersonese, Tenedos—by dispatching expeditions 302 to aid them, and proposing and moving resolutions accordingly; and to secure the friendship and alliance of the rest —Byzantium, Tenedos, Euboea? Was it not to take away the greatest of the resources which the enemy possessed, and to add what was lacking to those of the city? All this 303 has been accomplished by my decrees and by the measures which I have taken; and all these measures, men of Athens, will be found by any one who will examine them without jealousy, to have been correctly planned, and executed with entire honesty: the opportunity for each step was not, you will find, neglected or left unrecognized or thrown away by me, and nothing was left undone, which it was within the power and the reasoning capacity of a single man to effect. But if the might of some Divine Power, or the inferiority of our generals, or the wickedness of those who were betraying your cities, or all these things together, continuously injured our whole cause, until they effected its overthrow, how is 304 Demosthenes at fault? Had there been in each of the cities of Hellas one man, such as I was, as I stood at my own post in your midst—nay, if all Thessaly and all Arcadia had each had but one man animated by the same spirit as myself—not one Hellenic people, either beyond or on this side of Thermopylae, would have experienced the evils which they now suffer. 305 All would have been dwelling in liberty and independence, free from all fears, secure and prosperous, each in their own land, rendering thanks for all these great blessings to you and the rest of the Athenian people, through me. But that you may know that in my anxiety to avoid jealousy, I am using language which is far from adequate to the actual facts, (*to the clerk*) read me this; and take and recite the list of the expeditions sent out in accordance with my decrees.

[*The list of expeditions is read.*]

These measures, and others like them, Aeschines, were 306 the measures which it was the duty of a loyal and gallant citizen to take. If they were successful, it was certain that we should be indisputably the strongest power, and that with justice as well as in fact: and now that they have resulted otherwise, we are left with at least an honourable name. No man casts reproach either upon the city, or upon the choice which she made: they do but upbraid Fortune, who decided the issue thus. It was not, God knows, a citizen's duty to abandon 307 his country's interests, to sell his services to her opponents, and cherish the opportunities of the enemy instead of those of his country. Nor was it, on the one hand, to show his malice against the man who had faced the task of proposing and moving measures worthy of the city, and persisting in that intention; while, on the other hand, he remembered and kept his eyes fixed upon any private annoyance which another had caused him: nor was it to maintain a wicked and festering inactivity, as you so often do. Assuredly 308 there is an inactivity that is honest and brings good to the State—the inactivity which you, the majority of the citizens, observe in all sincerity. But that is not the inactivity of Aeschines. Far from it! He, on the contrary, retires just when he chooses, from public life (and he often chooses to do so), that he may watch for the moment when you will be sated with the continual speeches of the same adviser, or when fortune has thrown some obstacle in your path, or some other disagreeable event has happened (for in the life of man many things are possible); and then, when such an opportunity comes, suddenly, like a gale of wind, out

of his retirement he comes forth an orator, with his voice in training, and his phrases and his sentences collected; and these he strings together lucidly, without pausing for breath, though they bring with them no profit, no accession of anything good, but only calamity to one or another of his
309 fellow citizens, and shame to all alike. Surely, Aeschines, if all this practice and study sprang from an honest heart, resolved to pursue the interests of your country, the fruits of it should have been noble and honourable and profitable to all—alliances of cities, supplies of funds, opening of ports, enactment of beneficial laws, acts of opposition to our proved enemies.
310 It was for all such services that men looked in bygone days; and the past has offered, to any loyal and gallant citizen, abundant opportunities of displaying them: but nowhere in the ranks of such men will you ever be found to have stood—not first, nor second, nor third, nor fourth, nor fifth, nor sixth, nor in any position whatsoever; at least, not in any matters whereby your country stood to gain.
311 For what alliance has the city gained by negotiations of yours? What assistance, what fresh access of goodwill or fame? What diplomatic or administrative action of yours has brought new dignity to the city? What department of our home affairs, or our relations with Hellenic and foreign states, over which you have presided, has shown any improvement? Where are your ships? Where are your munitions of war? Where are your dockyards? Where are the walls that you have repaired? Where are your cavalry? Where in the world *is* your sphere of usefulness? What pecuniary assistance have you ever given, as a good and generous fellow
312 citizen, either to rich or poor? 'But, my good sir,' you say, 'if I have done none of these things, I have at least given

my loyalty and goodwill.' Where? When? Why, even at a time when all who ever opened their lips upon the platform contributed voluntarily to save the city, till, last of all, Aristonicus gave what he had collected to enable him to regain his civil rights—even then, most iniquitous of men! you never came forward or made any contribution whatever: and assuredly it was not from poverty, when you had inherited more than five talents out of the estate of your father-in-law Philo, and had received two talents subscribed by the leaders of the Naval Boards, for your damaging attack upon my Naval Law. But I will say no more about 313 this, lest by passing from subject to subject I should break away from the matter in hand. It is at least plain that your failure to contribute was not due to your poverty, but to your anxiety to do nothing in opposition to those whose interest is the guide of your whole public life. On what occasions, then, do your spirit and your brilliancy show themselves? When something must be done to injure your fellow countrymen—then your voice is most glorious, your memory most perfect; then you are a prince of actors, a Theocrines on the tragic stage!

Again, you have recalled the gallant men of old, and you 314 do well to do so. Yet it is not just, men of Athens, to take advantage of the good feeling which you may be relied upon to entertain towards the dead, in order to examine me before you by their standard, and compare me, who am still living amongst you, with them. Who in all the world does not know 315 that against the living there is always more or less of secret jealousy, while none, not even their enemies, hate the dead any more? And am I, in spite of this law of nature, to be judged and examined to-day by the standard of those who were before me? By no means! It would be neither just nor fair, Aeschines. But let me be compared with yourself, or with any of those who have adopted the same 316 policy as yourself, and are still alive. And consider this also. Which of these alternatives is the more honourable? Which is better for the city?—that the good services done by men of former times—tremendous, nay even beyond all description though they may be—should be made an excuse for exposing to ingratitude and contumely those that are rendered to the present generation? or that all who act in loyalty should have a share in the honours and the kindness 317 which our fellow citizens dispense? Aye, and (if I must say this after all) the policy and the principles which I have adopted will be found, if rightly viewed, to resemble and to have the same aims as those of the men who in that age received praise; while yours resemble those of the dishonest assailants of such persons in those days. For in their time also there were obviously persons who disparaged the living and praised the men of old, acting in the same malicious way 318 as yourself. Do you say then, that I am in no way like them? But are *you* like them, Aeschines? or your brother? or any other orator of the present day? For my part, I should say, 'None.' Nay, my good sir—to use no other epithet—compare the living with the living, their contemporaries, as men do in every other matter, whether they are comparing poets or choruses or competitors in the games. 319 Because Philammon was not so powerful as Glaucus of Carystus and some other athletes of former times, he did not leave Olympia uncrowned: but because he fought better than all who entered against him, he was crowned and proclaimed victor. Do you likewise examine me beside the orators of the day—beside yourself, beside any one in the world that you choose. I fear no man's rivalry. For, while 320 the city was still free to choose the best course, and all alike could compete with one another in loyalty to their country, I was found the best adviser of them all. It was by my laws, by my decrees, by my diplomacy, that all was effected. Not one of your party appeared anywhere, unless some insult was to be offered to your fellow countrymen. But when there happened, what I would had never happened—when it was not statesmen that were called to the front, but those who would do the bidding of a master, those who were anxious to earn wages by injuring their country, and to flatter a stranger—then, along with every member of your party, you were found at your post, the grand and resplendent owner of a stud; while I was weak, I confess, yet more loyal to my fellow countrymen than you. Two characteristics, men of 321 Athens, a citizen of a respectable character (for this is perhaps the least invidious phrase that I can apply to myself) must be able to show: when he enjoys authority, he must maintain to the end the policy whose aims are noble action and the pre-eminence of his country: and at all times and in every phase of fortune he must remain loyal. For this depends upon his own nature; while his power and his influence are determined by external causes. And in me, you will find, this loyalty has persisted unalloyed. For mark this. Not when 322 my surrender was demanded, not when I was called to account before the Amphictyons, not in face either of threats or of promises, not when these accursed men were hounded on against me like wild beasts, have I ever been false to my loyalty towards you. For from the very first, I chose the straight and honest path in public life: I chose to foster

the honour, the supremacy, the good name of my country,
323 to seek to enhance them, and to stand or fall with them. I do not walk through the market, cheerful and exultant over the success of strangers, holding out my hand and giving the good tidings to any whom I expect to report my conduct yonder, but shuddering, groaning, bowing myself to the earth, when I hear of the city's good fortune, as do these impious men, who make a mock of the city—not remembering that in so doing they are mocking themselves—while they direct their gaze abroad, and, whenever another has gained success through the failure of the Hellenes, belaud that state of things, and declare that we must see that it endures for all time.

324 Never, O all ye gods, may any of you consent to their desire! If it can be, may you implant even in these men a better mind and heart. But if they are verily beyond all cure, then bring them and them alone to utter and early destruction, by land and sea. And to us who remain, grant the speediest release from the fears that hang over us, and safety that naught can shake!

EVERYMAN'S LIBRARY: A Selected List

BIOGRAPHY

Brontë, Charlotte (1816–55). LIFE, 1857. By *Mrs Gaskell*. 318
Burns, Robert (1759–96). LIFE, 1828. By *J. G. Lockhart* (1794–1854). 156
Byron, Lord (1788–1824). LETTERS. Edited by *R. G. Howarth*, B.LITT. 931
Dickens, Charles (1812–70). LIFE, 1874. By *John Forster* (1812–76). 2 vols. 781–2
Hudson, William Henry (1841–1922). FAR AWAY AND LONG AGO, 1918. 956
Johnson, Samuel (1709–84). LIVES OF THE ENGLISH POETS, 1781. 2 vols. 770–1. BOSWELL'S LIFE OF JOHNSON, 1791. A new edition (1949). 1–2
Keats, John (1795–1821). LIFE AND LETTERS, 1848, by *Lord Houghton* (1809–85). 801
Lamb, Charles (1775–1834). LETTERS. New edition (1945) arranged from the Complete Annotated Edition of the Letters. 2 vols. 342–3
Pepys, Samuel (1633–1703). DIARY. Newly edited (1953), with modernized spelling. 3 vols. 53–5
Scott, Sir Walter (1771–1832). LOCKHART'S LIFE OF SCOTT. An abridgement from the seven-volume work by *J. G. Lockhart* himself. 39

CLASSICAL

Aristotle (384–322 B.C.). POLITICS, etc. Edited and translated by *John Warrington*. 605. METAPHYSICS. Edited and translated by *John Warrington*. 1000
Homer (? ninth century B.C.). ILIAD. New verse translation by *S. O. Andrew* and *Michael Oakley*. 453. ODYSSEY. The new verse translation (first published 1953) by *S. O. Andrew*. 454
Marcus Aurelius (121–80). MEDITATIONS. *A. S. L. Farquharson* Translation. 9
Plato (427–347 B.C.). THE REPUBLIC. Translated by *A. D. Lindsay*, C.B.E., LL.D. 64. SOCRATIC DISCOURSES OF PLATO AND XENOPHON. 457. THE LAWS. *A. E. Taylor* (1869–1945) Translation. 275

ESSAYS AND BELLES-LETTRES

Bacon, Francis, Lord Verulam (1561–1626). ESSAYS, 1597–1626. 10
Bagehot, Walter (1826–77). LITERARY STUDIES, 1879. 2 vols. 520–1
Belloc, Hilaire (1870–1953). STORIES, ESSAYS AND POEMS. 948
Chesterton, Gilbert Keith (1874–1936). STORIES, ESSAYS AND POEMS. 913
Coleridge, Samuel Taylor (1772–1834). BIOGRAPHIA LITERARIA, 1817. 11. SHAKESPEAREAN CRITICISM, 1849. Edited by *Prof. T. M. Raysor* (1960), 2 vols. 162, 183
De la Mare, Walter (1873–1956), STORIES, ESSAYS AND POEMS. 940
De Quincey, Thomas (1785–1859). CONFESSIONS OF AN ENGLISH OPIUM-EATER, 1822. Edited by *Prof. J. E. Jordan* (1960). 223. ENGLISH MAIL-COACH AND OTHER WRITINGS. 609
Hazlitt, William (1778–1830). LECTURES ON THE ENGLISH COMIC WRITERS, 1819; and MISCELLANEOUS ESSAYS. 411. LECTURES ON THE ENGLISH POETS, 1818, etc., 1825. 459. THE ROUND TABLE and CHARACTERS OF SHAKESPEAR'S PLAYS, 1817–18. 65. TABLE TALK, 1821–2. 321
Huxley, Aldous Leonard (*b*. 1894). STORIES, ESSAYS AND POEMS. 935
Johnson, Samuel (1709–84). THE RAMBLER. 994
Lawrence, David Herbert (1885–1930). STORIES, ESSAYS AND POEMS. 958
Locke, John (1632–1704). AN ESSAY CONCERNING HUMAN UNDERSTAND NG, 1690. 2 vols. 332, 984
Lynd, Robert (1879–1949). ESSAYS ON LIFE AND LITERATURE. 990
Macaulay, Thomas Babington, Lord (1800–59). CRITICAL AND HISTORICAL ESSAYS, 1843. 2 vols. 225–6. MISCELLANEOUS ESSAYS, 1823–59; LAYS OF ANCIENT ROME, 1842; and MISCELLANEOUS POEMS, 1812–47. 439
Milton, John (1608–74). PROSE WRITINGS. 795
Napoleon Buonaparte (1769–1821). LETTERS. Some 300 letters. 995
Newman, John Henry (1801–90). ON THE SCOPE AND NATURE OF UNIVERSITY EDUCATION; and CHRISTIANITY AND SCIENTIFIC INVESTIGATION, 1852. 723
Quiller-Couch, Sir Arthur (1863–1944). CAMBRIDGE LECTURES. 974
Sévigné, Marie de Rabutin-Chantal, Marquise de (1626–96). SELECTED LETTERS. 98
Steele, Sir Richard (1672–1729). THE TATLER, 1709–11. 993
Swinnerton, Frank (*b*. 1884). THE GEORGIAN LITERARY SCENE. Revised 1951. 943

FICTION

American Short Stories of the 19th Century. 840
Austen, Jane (1775–1817). EMMA, 1816. 24. MANSFIELD PARK, 1814. 23. PRIDE AND PREJUDICE, 1823. 22. SENSE AND SENSIBILITY, 1811. 21. NORTHANGER ABBEY, 1818; and PERSUASION, 1818. 25

Balzac, Honoré de (1799–1850). AT THE SIGN OF THE CAT AND RACKET, 1830; and OTHER STORIES. Translated by *Clara Bell*. 349. EUGÉNIE GRANDET, 1834. Translated by *Ellen Marriage*. 169. OLD GORIOT, 1835. Translated by *Ellen Marriage*. 170. THE WILD ASS'S SKIN, 1831. 26

Bennett, Arnold (1867–1931). THE OLD WIVES' TALE, 1908. 919

Borrow, George (1803–81). THE ROMANY RYE, 1857. Practically a sequel to *Lavengro*. 120

Brontë, Anne (1820–49). THE TENANT OF WILDFELL HALL and AGNES GREY. 685

Brontë, Charlotte (1816–55). For Mrs Gaskell's 'Life' *see* Biography. JANE EYRE, 1847. Introduction by *Margaret Lane*. 287. THE PROFESSOR, 1857. Introduction by *Margaret Lane*. 417. SHIRLEY, 1849. Introduction by *Margaret Lane*. 288. VILLETTE, 1853. Introduction by *Margaret Lane*. 351

Brontë, Emily (1818–48). WUTHERING HEIGHTS, 1848; and POEMS. Introduction by *Margaret Lane*. 243

Butler, Samuel (1835–1902). EREWHON, 1872 (revised 1901); and EREWHON REVISITED, 1901. 881. THE WAY OF ALL FLESH, 1903. 895

Collins, Wilkie (1824–89). THE MOONSTONE, 1868. 979. THE WOMAN IN WHITE, 1860. 464

Conrad, Joseph (1857–1924). LORD JIM, 1900. Typically set in the East Indies. 925. THE NIGGER OF THE 'NARCISSUS'; TYPHOON; and THE SHADOW LINE. 980. NOSTROMO, 1904. New edition of Conrad's greatest novel. 38

Defoe, Daniel (1661?–1731). THE FORTUNES AND MISFORTUNES OF MOLL FLANDERS, 1722. 837. JOURNAL OF THE PLAGUE YEAR, 1722. 289. LIFE, ADVENTURES OF THE FAMOUS CAPTAIN SINGLETON, 1720. 74. ROBINSON CRUSOE, 1719. Parts 1 and 2 complete. 59

Dickens, Charles (1812–70). WORKS. (*See also* Biography.)

Dostoyevsky, Fyodor (1821–81). THE BROTHERS KARAMAZOV, 1879–80. Translated by *Constance Garnett*. 2 vols. 802–3. CRIME AND PUNISHMENT, 1866. *Constance Garnett* Translation. 501. THE IDIOT, 1873. Translated by *Eva M. Martin*. 682. LETTERS FROM THE UNDERWORLD, 1864; and OTHER TALES. 654. POOR FOLK, 1845; and THE GAMBLER, 1867. 711. THE POSSESSED, 1871. Translated by *Constance Garnett*. 2 vols. 861–2

Dumas, Alexandre (1802–70). THE BLACK TULIP, 1850. The brothers De Witt in Holland, 1672–5. 174. COUNT OF MONTE CRISTO, 1844. 2 vols. Napoleon's later phase. 393–4. MARGUERITE DE VALOIS, 1845. The Eve of St Bartholomew. 326. THE THREE MUSKETEERS, 1844. The France of Cardinal Richelieu. 81

Eliot, George. ADAM BEDE, 1859. 27. MIDDLEMARCH, 1872. 2 vols. 854–5. THE MILL ON THE FLOSS, 1860. 325. ROMOLA, 1863. The Florence of Savonarola. 231. SILAS MARNER, THE WEAVER OF RAVELOE, 1861. 121

Fielding, Henry (1707–54). AMELIA, 1751. 2 vols. Amelia is drawn from Fielding's first wife. 852–3. JONATHAN WILD, 1743; and JOURNAL OF A VOYAGE TO LISBON, 1755. 877. JOSEPH ANDREWS, 1742. A skit on Richardson's *Pamela*. 467. TOM JONES, 1749. 2 vols. The first great English novel of humour. 355–6

Flaubert, Gustave (1821–80). MADAME BOVARY, 1857. Translated by *Eleanor Marx-Aveling*. 808. SALAMMBO, 1862. Translated by *J. C. Chartres*. 869. SENTIMENTAL EDUCATION, 1869. Translated by *Anthony Goldsmith*. 969

Forster, Edward Morgan (*b*. 1879). A PASSAGE TO INDIA, 1924. 972

Galsworthy, John (1867–1933). THE COUNTRY HOUSE. 917

Gaskell, Mrs Elizabeth (1810–65). CRANFORD, 1853. 83

Gogol, Nikolay (1809–52). DEAD SOULS, 1842. 726

Goldsmith, Oliver (1728–74). THE VICAR OF WAKEFIELD, 1766. 295

Gorky, Maxim (1868–1936). THROUGH RUSSIA. 741

Hugo, Victor Marie (1802–85). LES MISÉRABLES, 1862. 2 vols. 363–4. NOTRE DAME DE PARIS, 1831. 422. TOILERS OF THE SEA, 1866. 509

James, Henry (1843–1916). THE AMBASSADORS, 1903. 987. THE TURN OF THE SCREW, 1898; and THE ASPERN PAPERS, 1888. 912

Jerome, Jerome K. (1859–1927). THREE MEN IN A BOAT and THREE MEN ON THE BUMMEL. 118

Kingsley, Charles (1819–75). HEREWARD THE WAKE, 1866. 296. WESTWARD HO!, 1855. 20

Lytton, Edward Bulwer, Baron (1803–73). THE LAST DAYS OF POMPEII, 1834. 80

Maugham, W. Somerset (*b*. 1874). CAKES AND ALE, 1930. 932

Maupassant, Guy de (1850–93). SHORT STORIES. Translated by *Marjorie Laurie*. 907

Melville, Herman (1819–91). MOBY DICK, 1851. 179. TYPEE, 1846; and BILLY BUDD (*published* 1924). South Seas adventures. 180

Meredith, George (1828–1909). THE ORDEAL OF RICHARD FEVEREL, 1859. 916

Modern Short Stories. Selected by *John Hadfield*. Twenty stories. 954

Moore, George (1852–1933). ESTHER WATERS, 1894. 933

Priestley, J. B. (*b*. 1894). ANGEL PAVEMENT, 1931. A finely conceived London novel. 938

Russian Short Stories. Translated by *Rochelle S. Townsend*. 758

Scott, Sir Walter (1771–1832). WORKS.

Shelley, Mary Wollstonecraft (1797–1851). FRANKENSTEIN, 1818. 616

Smollett, Tobias (1721–71). THE EXPEDITION OF HUMPHRY CLINKER, 1771. 975. PEREGRINE PICKLE, 1751. 2 vols. 838–9. RODERICK RANDOM, 1742. 790

Stendhal (pseudonym of Henri Beyle, 1783–1842). SCARLET AND BLACK, 1831. Translated by *C. K. Scott Moncrieff*. 2 vols. 945–6

Stevenson, Robert Louis (1850–94). DR JEKYLL AND MR HYDE, 1886; THE MERRY MEN, 1887; WILL O' THE MILL, 1878; MARKHEIM, 1886; THRAWN JANET, 1881; OLALLA, 1885; THE TREASURE OF FRANCHARD. 767. THE MASTER OF BALLANTRAE, 1869; WEIR OF HERMISTON, 1896. 764. ST IVES, 1898. Completed by Sir Arthur Quiller-Couch. 904. TREASURE ISLAND, 1883; and KIDNAPPED, 1886. 763

Tales of Detection. Nineteen stories. 928

Thackeray, William Makepeace (1811–63). HENRY ESMOND, 1852. 73. THE NEWCOMES, 1853–5. 2 vols. 465–6. PENDENNIS, 1848–50. 2 vols. 425–6. VANITY FAIR, 1847–8. 298. THE VIRGINIANS, 1857–9. 2 vols. 507–8

Tolstoy, Count Leo (1828–1910). ANNA KARENINA, 1873–7. Translated by *Rochelle S. Townsend*. 2 vols. 612–13. MASTER AND MAN, 1895; and OTHER PARABLES AND TALES. 469. WAR AND PEACE, 1864–9. 3 vols. 525–7

Trollope, Anthony (1815–82). THE WARDEN, 1855. 182. BARCHESTER TOWERS, 1857. 30. DOCTOR THORNE, 1858. 360. FRAMLEY PARSONAGE, 1861. 181. THE SMALL HOUSE AT ALLINGTON, 1864, 361. THE LAST CHRONICLE OF BARSET, 1867. 2 vols. 391–2

Twain, Mark (pseudonym of Samuel Langhorne Clemens, 1835–1910). TOM SAWYER, 1876; and HUCKLEBERRY FINN, 1884. 976

Verne, Jules (1828–1905). FIVE WEEKS IN A BALLOON, 1862, translated by *Arthur Chambers*; and AROUND THE WORLD IN EIGHTY DAYS, translated by *P. Desages*. 779. TWENTY THOUSAND LEAGUES UNDER THE SEA, 1869. 319

Wells, Herbert George (1866–1946). ANN VERONICA, 1909. 977. THE WHEELS OF CHANCE, 1896; and THE TIME MACHINE, 1895. 915

Woolf, Virginia (1882–1941). TO THE LIGHTHOUSE, 1927. 949

HISTORY

Creasy, Sir Edward (1812–78). FIFTEEN DECISIVE BATTLES OF THE WORLD, 1852. 300

Gibbon, Edward (1737–94). THE DECLINE AND FALL OF THE ROMAN EMPIRE, 1776–88. Complete text. 6 vols. 434–6, 474–6

Macaulay, Thomas Babington, Baron (1800–59). THE HISTORY OF ENGLAND. 4 vols. 34–7

Voltaire, François Marie Arouet de (1694–1778). THE AGE OF LOUIS XIV, 1751. Translated by *Martyn P. Pollack*. 780

POETRY AND DRAMA

Anglo-Saxon Poetry. A.D. 650 to 1000. Translated by *Prof. R. K. Gordon*, M.A. 794

Ballads, A Book of British. 572

Beaumont, Francis (1584–1616), and **Fletcher, John** (1579–1625). SELECT PLAYS. 506

Blake, William (1757–1827). POEMS AND PROPHECIES. Edited by *Max Plowman*. 792

Browning, Robert (1812–89). POEMS AND PLAYS, 1833–64. 2 vols. 41–2. POEMS, 1871–90. 964

Century. A CENTURY OF HUMOROUS VERSE, 1850–1950. 813

Chaucer, Geoffrey (*c*. 1343–1400). CANTERBURY TALES. New standard text edited by *A. C. Cawley*, M.A., PH.D. 307. TROILUS AND CRISEYDE. 992

Cowper, William (1731–1800). POEMS. 872

Dryden, John (1631–1700). POEMS. Edited by *Bonamy Dobrée*, O.B.E., M.A. 910

Goethe, Johann Wolfgang von (1749–1832). FAUST. Both parts of the tragedy, in the re-edited translation of *Sir Theodore Martin*. 335

Goldsmith, Oliver (1728–74). POEMS AND PLAYS. Edited by *Austin Dobson*. 415

Ibsen, Henrik (1828–1906). A DOLL'S HOUSE, 1879; THE WILD DUCK, 1884; and THE LADY FROM THE SEA, 1888. Translated by *R. Farquharson Sharp* and *Eleanor Marx-Aveling*. 494. GHOSTS, 1881; THE WARRIORS AT HELGELAND, 1857; and AN ENEMY OF THE PEOPLE, 1882. Translated by *R. Farquharson Sharp*. 552. PEER GYNT, 1867. Translated by *R. Farquharson Sharp*. 747. THE PRETENDERS, 1864; PILLARS OF SOCIETY, 1877; and ROSMERSHOLM, 1887. Translated by *R. Farquharson Sharp*. 659. BRAND, a poetic drama. 1866. Translated by *F. E. Garrett*. 716

Ingoldsby Legends. Edited by *D. C. Browning*, M.A., B.LITT. 185

International Modern Plays. 989

Marlowe, Christopher (1564–93). PLAYS AND POEMS. New edition by *M. R. Ridley*, M.A. 383

Milton, John (1608–74). POEMS. New edition by *Prof. B. A. Wright*, M.A. 384

Molière, Jean Baptiste de (1622–73). COMEDIES. 2 vols. 830–1

Poems of our Time. An Anthology edited by *Richard Church*, C.B.E., *M. M. Bozman* and *Edith Sitwell*, D.LITT., D.B.E. Nearly 400 poems by about 130 poets. 981

Rossetti, Dante Gabriel (1828–82). POEMS AND TRANSLATIONS. 627

Shakespeare, William (1564–1616). A Complete Edition. Cambridge Text. Glossary. 3 vols. Comedies, 153; Histories, Poems and Sonnets, 154; Tragedies, 155

Spenser, Edmund (1552–99). THE FAERIE QUEENE. Glossary. 2 vols. 443–4. THE SHEPHERD'S CALENDAR, 1579; and OTHER POEMS. 879

Swinburne, Algernon Charles (1837–1909). POEMS AND PROSE. A selection, edited with an Intro. by *Richard Church.* 961
Synge, J. M. (1871–1909). PLAYS, POEMS AND PROSE. 968
Tchekhov, Anton (1860–1904). PLAYS AND STORIES. 941
Twenty-four One-Act Plays. 947
Webster, John (1580 ?–1625 ?), and **Ford, John** (1586–1639). SELECTED PLAYS. 899
Wilde, Oscar (1854–1900). PLAYS, PROSE WRITINGS AND POEMS. 858
Wordsworth, William (1770–1850). POEMS. Ed. *Philip Wayne,* M.A. 3 vols. 203, 311, 998

ROMANCE

Boccaccio, Giovanni (1313–75). DECAMERON, 1471. The unabridged *Rigg* Translation. 2 vols. 845–6
Cervantes Saavedra, Miguel de (1547–1616). DON QUIXOTE DE LA MANCHA. Translated by *P. A. Motteux.* 2 vols. 385–6
Chrétien de Troyes (fl. 12th cent.). ARTHURIAN ROMANCES. 698
Kalevala, or **The Land of Heroes.** Translated by *W. F. Kirby.* 2 vols. 259–60
Njal's Saga. THE STORY OF BURNT NJAL (written about 1280–90). Translated from the Icelandic by *Sir G. W. Dasent* (1861). 558
Rabelais, François (1494 ?–1553). THE HEROIC DEEDS OF GARGANTUA AND PANTAGRUEL, 1532–5. 2 vols. *Urquhart and Motteux's* unabridged Translation, 1653–94. 826–7

SCIENCE

Darwin, Charles (1809–82). THE ORIGIN OF SPECIES, 1859. Embodies Darwin's final additions. 811
Eddington, Arthur Stanley (1882–1944). THE NATURE OF THE PHYSICAL WORLD, 1928. 922
Marx, Karl (1818–83). CAPITAL, 1867. Translated by *Eden* and *Cedar Paul.* 2 vols. 848–9
Owen, Robert (1771–1858). A NEW VIEW OF SOCIETY, 1813; and OTHER WRITINGS. 799
Smith, Adam (1723–90). THE WEALTH OF NATIONS, 1766. 2 vols. 412–13
Wollstonecraft, Mary (1759–97), THE RIGHTS OF WOMAN, 1792; and **Mill, John Stuart** (1806–73), THE SUBJECTION OF WOMEN, 1869. 825

THEOLOGY AND PHILOSOPHY

Berkeley, George (1685–1753). A NEW THEORY OF VISION, 1709. 483
Browne, Sir Thomas (1605–82). RELIGIO MEDICI, 1642. 92
Bunyan, John (1628–88). GRACE ABOUNDING, 1666; and THE LIFE AND DEATH OF MR BADMAN, 1658. 815
Burton, Robert (1577–1640). THE ANATOMY OF MELANCHOLY. 1621. 3 vols. 886–8
Chinese Philosophy in Classical Times. Covering the period 1500 B.C.–A.D. 100. 973
Descartes, René (1596–1650). A DISCOURSE ON METHOD, 1637; MEDITATIONS ON THE FIRST PHILOSOPHY, 1641; and PRINCIPLES OF PHILOSOPHY, 1644. Translated by *Prof. J. Veitch.* 570
Hobbes, Thomas (1588–1679). LEVIATHAN, 1651. 691
Hooker, Richard (1554–1600). OF THE LAWS OF ECCLESIASTICAL POLITY, 1597. 2 vols. 201–2
Koran, The. *Rodwells* Translation, 1861. 380
Law, William (1686–1761). A SERIOUS CALL TO A DEVOUT AND HOLY LIFE, 1728. 91
Leibniz, Gottfried Wilhelm (1646–1716). PHILOSOPHICAL WRITINGS. Selected and translated by *Mary Morris.* 905
Locke, John (1632–1704). TWO TREATISES OF CIVIL GOVERNMENT, 1690. 751
Mill, John Stuart (1806–73). UTILITARIANISM, 1863; LIBERTY, 1859; and REPRESENTATIVE GOVERNMENT, 1861. 482
Paine, Thomas (1737–1809). RIGHTS OF MAN, 1792. 718
Saint Augustine (353–430). CONFESSIONS. *Dr Pusey's* Translation, 1838. 200. THE CITY OF GOD. Complete text. 2 vols. 982–3
Saint Francis (1182–1226). THE LITTLE FLOWERS; THE MIRROR OF PERFECTION (by Leo of Assisi); and THE LIFE OF ST FRANCIS (by St Bonaventura). 485
Spinoza, Benedictus de (1632–77). ETHICS, 1677, etc. Translated by *Andrew Boyle.* 481

TRAVEL AND TOPOGRAPHY

Borrow, George (1803–81). THE BIBLE IN SPAIN, 1842. 151. WILD WALES, 1862. 49
Boswell, James (1740–95). JOURNAL OF A TOUR TO THE HEBRIDES WITH SAMUEL JOHNSON, 1786. 387
Calderón de la Barca, Mme (1804–82). LIFE IN MEXICO, 1843. 664
Cobbett, William (1762–1835). RURAL RIDES, 1830. 2 vols. 638–9
Darwin, Charles (1809–82). THE VOYAGE OF THE 'BEAGLE', 1839. 104
Kinglake, Alexander (1809–91). EOTHEN, 1844. 337
Polo, Marco (1254–1324). TRAVELS. 306
Portuguese Voyages, 1498–1663. Edited by *Charles David Ley.* 986
Stow, John (1525 ?–1605). THE SURVEY OF LONDON. Elizabethan London. 589